DESTINED FOR GLORY

DESTINED FOR
GLORY

Dive Bombing, Midway, and
the Evolution of Carrier Airpower

Thomas Wildenberg

NAVAL INSTITUTE PRESS
ANNAPOLIS, MARYLAND

Library of Congress Cataloging-in-Publication Data
Wildenberg, Thomas, 1947–
    Destined for glory : dive bombing, Midway, and the evolution of
carrier airpower / Thomas Wildenberg.
        p.   cm.
    Includes bibliographical references and index.
    ISBN 1-55750-947-6 (alk. paper)
    1. Naval aviation—United States—History. 2. Aircraft carriers—
United States—History. 3. Bombing, Aerial—United States—
History. 4. Dive bombers—United States—History. I. Title.
VG93.44 1998
359.9'4'0973—dc21   98-23235

Printed in the United States of America on acid-free paper ♾
 05 04 03 02 01 00 99 98   9 8 7 6 5 4 3 2
First printing

Frontispiece: A pilot of the *Yorktown*'s Bombing Five practicing his
dive-bombing technique in the BT-1. *National Archives*

Carrier-based aircraft are essentially offensive weapons. . . . Once the enemy is located all other considerations are secondary to the delivery of heavy bombing and torpedo attacks.

The surest and quickest means of gaining control of the air is the destruction of enemy carriers. . . .

Tactical Orders and Doctrine for the U.S. Fleet, 1941

CONTENTS

ILLUSTRATIONS

TABLES

ON 4 JUNE 1942, three squadrons of U.S. Navy Dauntless dive bombers achieved a spectacular victory over the Imperial Japanese Navy. In less than ten minutes they successfully attacked and set fire to three-quarters of the carrier strike force sent to neutralize the strategically important island of Midway. The destruction of the Japanese carrier force threatening this important U.S. base (a fourth carrier was destroyed later the same day) marked the end of the Japanese advance in the Pacific. Remarkably, none of the other squadrons that attempted to engage the enemy during the battle—with one lone exception— scored a single hit on any Japanese ship, even though they constituted a force of almost one hundred planes![1] While many factors contributed to the navy's success at Midway—excellent leadership, code breaking, and just plain "Lady Luck"—few realize that the outcome was predetermined years earlier as the navy sought to integrate the aerial weapon into its war-fighting doctrine.

Although several excellent books have been written about the Battle of Midway—most notably those by Mitsuo Fuchida and Masatake Okumiya (*Midway: The Battle that Doomed Japan*), Gordon W. Prange (*Miracle at Midway*), and Edwin T. Layton (*And I Was There*)—none has focused on how the U.S. Navy came to develop the one aerial weapon—dive bombing—which proved to be the decisive instrument of victory. For it was dive bombing, and only dive bombing, that turned the tide of Japanese expansion in the Pacific.

Introduced and developed in the interwar years, dive bombing became the cornerstone in the navy's efforts to secure command of the air. Although the development of the dive bomber played an extremely important role in the advancement of naval aviation during the interwar period, it is only part of a much broader story that illustrates an important lesson for naval historians. For as David Rosenberg has so eloquently noted, "What comes before the battle is as important as the battle itself."[2] It will become evident from reading the text that the aerial successes of 1942 were unequivocally rooted in the tactics and equipment developed during the previous seventeen years.

Dive bombing did not emerge full grown, but followed an evolutionary process that was driven by a confluence of factors—technical, organizational, operational, political, and economic—that characterized the development of naval aviation during this period. One of the purposes of this book is to show how these variables influenced the doctrine of seaborne airpower and the development of carrier aircraft in the U.S. Navy between 1925 and 1942.

The reader may be tempted to ask, Why 1925? There are several reasons for choosing this date as the starting point for a study about carrier airpower in the U.S. Navy. For one thing, it marked the beginning of fleet air operations conducted by the *Langley*. Prior to that date she had been used on an experimental basis to test the handling techniques and procedures needed to launch and recover aircraft from a floating air base. Two other notable events took place in 1925: on 4 February Fighting Squadron Two, the first unit trained to operate as a unit from a carrier, joined the *Langley;* then, on 13 October, Capt. Joseph M. Reeves—a man destined to transform the use of aviation within the fleet—assumed command of the Aircraft Squadrons, Battle Fleet.

Any worthy study of a topic such as this would be incomplete without some discussion of the key decision makers and personalities who drove the development of naval aviation. While frequently overlooked, this aspect of history often provides great insight into the advancement of certain ideas which later prove crucial for military success. Lastly, though not of least importance, is the discussion of the technological advancement of the aircraft themselves, for they ultimately provided the means of delivering the diving attack which proved so devastating to the Japanese.

The subject of the development of carrier aviation is a complex one that includes the entire spectrum of naval activities. It would be impractical to cover every aspect of this material in a work of this size. Thus, I have chosen to concentrate on those topics, events, and personalities which best characterize the development of carrier airpower during the interwar period.

A word of advice for those readers not familiar with the standard designations used by the U.S. Navy during the interwar period to identify specific aircraft types. These are used throughout the text and are essential to follow the evolution of aircraft development during these years. Readers unacquainted with this nomenclature should refer to the description of the classification system provided in Appendix A.

A number of people contributed their time and knowledge to this project on a voluntary basis. I wish to thank the following for their comments, suggestions, and/or editorial help: Hal Andrews, Chuck Haberlein, Thomas Hone, Fred Milford, Norman Polmar, and Ed Miller. I would also like to thank those who assisted me at the various institutions I visited in the course of my research, including Rebecca Livingston and the staff at National Archives; Evelyn Cherpak, curator, Naval Historical Collection, Naval War College; Kathy Lloyd of the Operational Archives at the Naval Historical Center; and Ed Finney and Jack Green of the Photographic Section at the Naval Historical Center.

CHRONOLOGY: MILESTONES IN THE DEVELOPMENT OF PRE–WORLD WAR II CARRIER AIRPOWER IN THE U.S. NAVY

Date	Event
July 1919	General Board authorizes conversion of the *Jupiter* into the navy's first aircraft carrier.
July 1921	Congress mandates that naval aviators command aviation units.
February 1922	Washington Treaty establishing carrier tonnage signed.
March 1922	*Langley* (ex-*Jupiter*) commissioned.
October 1922	First takeoffs and landings on *Langley*.
November 1924	*Langley* joins the Battle Fleet.
February 1925	VF-2, first squadron trained to operate from a carrier, joins *Langley*.
March 1925	First use of an aircraft carrier (*Langley*) in a fleet problem.
October 1925	Capt. J. M. Reeves assumes command of Aircraft Squadrons, Battle Fleet.
June 1926	Congress approves the 1,000-plane aviation navy; aircraft carriers and tenders to be commanded by naval aviators only.
July–August 1926	First summer concentration of aircraft held at NAS, North Island, San Diego.
October 1926	Lt. Cdr. Frank Wagner demonstrates effectiveness of attacking in a vertical dive.
December 1926	Dive bombing included in gunnery exercises for the first time.
January 1927	Cdr. Eugene Wilson proposes the design of a light bomber capable of delivering a 500-lb. bomb in the "diving attack."
October 1927	VF-5S conducts dive-bombing experiments against a moving target.
December 1927	*Lexington*, first of the big carriers, commissioned.
March 1928	CO of VT-9 derides capabilities of Mark VII aerial torpedo.

May 1928	Planes flying off the *Langley* conduct a surprise attack on the installations of Pearl Harbor.
November 1928	Fleet exercises test the offensive and defensive capabilities of aircraft in the "destroyer attack phase of the main engagement."
January 1929	First fleet problem in which *Saratoga* and *Lexington* play a major role.
March–April 1930	Vulnerability of carrier to air attack demonstrated in Fleet Problems X and XI; first trials of carrier task force concept.
August 1930	General Board approves the development of the Mark XIII aerial torpedo.
January 1931	XT5M-1 becomes the first aircraft to drop a 1,000-lb. bomb (practice) in a vertical dive; use of bomb crutch inaugurated.
December 1931	Navy orders the first production fighter with retractable landing gear (Grumman FF-1).
June 1933	National Industrial Recovery Act passed, providing funds for *Enterprise* and *Yorktown*.
March 1934	Vinson-Trammell Act passed; proviso allows president to authorize 1,650 aircraft for the navy, *Hornet* and *Wasp* authorized.
March 1934	Advanced Battle Practice conducted off coast of California casts doubt about the value of torpedo planes.
June 1934	Bureau of Aeronautics issues contracts to develop the first monoplane carrier attack planes.
May 1936	Admiral Reeves demands better performance from fighters assigned to the fleet.
November 1937	TBD-1 Devastator enters service.
February 1938	Bureau of Aeronautics requests proposals for high-performance monoplane carrier fighter.
August 1938	Radio homing equipment (YE-ZB combination) successfully demonstrated.
February 1939	Fleet Problem XX, first to involve two carrier divisions.
November 1940	SBD-2 Dauntless dive bomber enters navy service.
December 1940	F3F-3 Wildcat enters service.
March 1941	First test of radar-directed fighter control.

DESTINED FOR GLORY

CHAPTER 1

A Thousand and One Questions

Wᴴᴇɴ Cᴀᴘᴛ. Jᴏsᴇᴘʜ Mᴀsᴏɴ Rᴇᴇᴠᴇs arrived on board the USS *Langley* in the second week of October 1925, no one on board could have foreseen that this white-bearded, fifty-three-year-old captain was destined to become the first air admiral to command the U.S. Fleet. Reeves, known as "Bull" since his football-playing days at the academy, was a hard-boiled, demanding officer who knew how to get the most out of the men in his command. A shrewd and innovative tactician, he was an officer "trained to the gun, but not wedded to it."[1]

As Reeves climbed the gangway that fateful morning, he was walking on familiar ground, for the *Langley* had been converted from the collier *Jupiter,* the ship that had been his first command.[2] In those days he had tested the navy's first electric drive; now, a dozen years later, he was on board the same ship once again, this time with the far more difficult task of developing the airplane as a naval weapon. In this new assignment Reeves would command the aircraft squadrons of the Battle Fleet, and the "Covered Wagon," as the *Langley* was euphemistically called, was to serve as his headquarters at sea.

How and why Reeves, the foremost battleship tactician of his day, came to be appointed commander, Aircraft Squadrons, Battle Fleet (ComAirBatFlt)

The *Langley* as she looked when Capt. Joseph M. Reeves boarded her in October 1925 to take command of Aircraft Squadrons, Battle Fleet. *Naval Historical Center*

remains shrouded in mystery.[3] Regrettably, he left no personal papers, and those documents which have survived make no mention of the reasons behind his selection. Charles Melhorn, in his classic study of the aircraft carrier, *Two-Block Fox*, claims that Reeves asked for aviation duty to test his theories on the use of airpower, but there is no evidence to support this contention.[4] Clearly Reeves's studies of battleship tactics had piqued his interest in the potential use of new weapons, such as the submarine and airplane, albeit he readily admitted that he did not know which would be more decisive in the next war.[5] Though Reeves had been exposed to the possibilities of airpower at the Naval War College and had personally experienced flight when he was naval attaché in Rome, there is no record of his having any special interest in aviation prior to his selection to command the Battle Fleet's nascent air force.

It seems logical to conclude that the incumbent chief of naval operations (CNO), Adm. Edward W. Eberle, played a key role in choosing Reeves for what was then considered a controversial assignment. Aviation was still in its infancy and many organizational issues remained to be solved, including the standing of the airmen whose special status was frequently resented by the nonflyers. Eberle was certainly aware of these problems, having just chaired a board of high-ranking officers that examined aviation's place within the navy.

He knew Reeves from personal experience, as the two had served together on board the *Oregon* during the Spanish American War, when Reeves, then an engineering officer, received a commendation and was advanced four numbers on the promotion list for his stellar performance in the ship's engine room during her record-making voyage around Cape Horn.

Obtaining aviation's acceptance within the fleet was not furthered by the full-scale brouhaha which broke out in the spring of 1925 between Rear Adm. William A. Moffett, the chief of the Bureau of Aeronautics, and Rear Adm. William R. Shoemaker, the chief of the Bureau of Navigation, which was responsible for personnel matters, over the issue of where aviation officers were to serve and who had cognizance over their assignments.[6] The fight to secure control over the navy's fledgling airmen only added fuel to what was fast becoming a de rigueur feud between naval aviators and their brethren in the "Gun Club."

Under these circumstances the officer selected to command the Battle Fleet's aviation forces would have to be carefully chosen. Reeves was then serving as head of the Tactics Department at the Naval War College, where he had developed a reputation as a forward-looking officer recognized within the naval community for his innovative ideas. It is quite probable that Eberle discussed the forthcoming appointment with Reeves when the latter visited Washington in the spring of 1925. Reeves, who "had been an engineer, a gun man, [and] a BuNav man," was the ideal choice for this politically sensitive post.[7] In any case, by June Reeves was slated to command the Aircraft Squadrons, Battle Fleet and was immediately directed to report to the Naval Air Station (NAS) at Pensacola in order to attend the aviation observer course about to commence.

By a law passed in July 1921, all aviation units within the U.S. Navy, except for aircraft carriers and tenders, had to be commanded by a naval aviator.[8] This created somewhat of a dilemma for the newly formed Bureau of Aeronautics, since none of the navy's pilots had enough seniority to qualify for any of the major aviation commands. The most senior of these young flyers, Cdr. John H. Towers, would not achieve the rank of captain for another ten years! To make up for the lack of ranking aviators in the navy, a special course for naval aviation observers was established at Pensacola in the early 1920s to train senior officers destined for aviation commands in the rudimentary elements of flight. These latecomers to aviation were soon termed "Johnny-Come-Latelys" (JCLs) by the younger pilots. Reeves joined this select group on 3 September 1925, when he was awarded the wings of a naval aviation observer and officially pronounced "ready for duty involving actual flying in aircraft, including airships, balloons, and airplanes."[9]

After graduating from the observers course, Reeves remained in Pensacola for another week taking notes and asking questions, as was characteristic of the zeal with which he attacked each new task. He then traveled to Washington for several days of discussions with Admiral Moffett and other officials at the Navy Department. At the end of September Reeves set out for Naval Air Station, San Diego with orders to proceed to the aircraft carrier *Langley* and there to assume command of Aircraft Squadrons, Battle Fleet.

He could not have taken over the most important aviation unit in the fleet at a more critical time for naval aviation. Only a few weeks earlier, Brig. Gen. William (Billy) Mitchell, the army's contentious airman, had charged the Navy Department with "incompetence . . . and criminal negligence" in the events surrounding the crash of the navy airship *Shenandoah*.[10] Whatever the merits of these accusations, there can be little doubt that the command Reeves inherited was a lackadaisical outfit. The leisurely, measured pace, the almost scientific detachment with which aviation experiments had been conducted on board the *Langley* since 1922, was soon replaced with a hard-driving emphasis on more operational considerations. Reeves, now entitled to be addressed as commodore, was to recast the *Langley* into a combat-conscious command by the same methods that he formerly used to produce record-breaking gun crews in the old battleships *San Francisco, Wisconsin,* and *New Hampshire.* The carrier would still function as a test platform, but the focus of activity would be shifted from the evaluation of aircraft to their tactical deployment.

Upon his arrival in San Diego, Reeves was surprised to learn that the *Langley* was operating only eight planes. It seemed to him an absurdly small figure, but he kept silent for the first few weeks he was on the job, doing little more than observing flight operations. Then one day in the early part of November 1925, he gathered the officers of his command in the auditorium of their North Island air base and delivered an epoch-making lecture that was, in effect, a statement of the principles on which the air force was to be developed.[11]

From what he had seen, declared Reeves as he addressed the assembled officers of his command, it was evident that the lack of coordinated aircraft tactics had shown that they had "no conception of either the capabilities or limitations of the air force." This blunt appraisal of his command was followed by a series of pointed questions put forth to the assembled airmen about the need to develop coordinated aerial tactics of use to the fleet. "What is the most efficient method of launching planes from the *Langley,* and of handling them after they have landed?" he asked. How should the fighters attack other aircraft? What formations should be used in aerial spotting? How should an aircraft torpedo attack be made? What is the maximum interval between the planes in a scouting screen?

After raising a score of such problems, Reeves startled his audience with a bold and unexpected declaration: "I do not know the answer to these questions and dozens like them any more than you do, but until we can answer them, we will be very little use to the fleet. That means that we must become a school before we can become an air force."[12] The "school" into which Reeves proceeded to turn the aircraft squadrons of the Battle Fleet would have startled even the most enthusiastic supporters of naval aviation. The lessons were learned on the flight deck of the *Langley* or in the cockpit of a plane; the textbook was a set of mimeographed sheets containing the issues that had to be resolved before the airplane could be considered an effective weapon for use by the fleet. The latter was called "A Thousand and One Questions" and contained a list of all the questions originally posed by Reeves, along with many others which had been added in the weeks following his rousing lecture. Gradually, by dint of ceaseless practice and experimentation, the answers to these and other questions relating to aircraft operations on board a carrier began to reveal themselves.

In preparation for the fleet exercises scheduled for January 1926, Reeves ordered six additional aircraft on board the *Langley,* increasing the number of planes to fourteen. This created a storm of protest from the air staff and pilots, who argued that it couldn't be done. Nevertheless, the order stood. On the first day out, the *Langley* turned into the wind, lowered her two hinged smokestacks so that they would not create air disturbances over the flush deck, and began to launch planes. Lt. Frank "Spig" Wead, one of the navy's celebrated racing pilots and the skipper of Fighting Squadron Two, led six fighters off the flight deck to intercept an imaginary bombing raid by enemy planes.[13] Wead's group was immediately followed by a second launch of equal strength, demonstrating the aircraft carrier's ability to get her planes quickly into the air to defend herself from aerial attack by enemy aircraft.

In the months ahead Reeves concentrated on increasing the operating

One of Reeves's first actions was to increase the *Langley*'s complement from eight to fourteen airplanes. *Naval Historical Center*

tempo and number of aircraft that could be effectively handled by the *Langley*. He worked the ship relentlessly when at sea, dividing his time between an office at North Field, San Diego and the carrier. Reeves frequently took charge of flight operations while standing on the ladder leading from the flight deck to the bridge. There, he would order the officer of the deck to turn into the wind and put on full speed, then using hand signals he would tell the deck crew to start the planes' engines. When the course and speed were correct, he would wave another signal to the air officer on the flight deck to let him know that it was okay to start launching aircraft.[14]

While at the Naval War College, Reeves had learned the importance of numbers in combat at sea. The principle of concentrated fire was a much discussed tenet of naval warfare during those years, and it is more than likely that Reeves studied the N-square Law at some point during his stay at Newport. Invented by the English engineer Frederick W. Lanchester as a means to define the relative power of opposing forces, the N-square Law states that the fighting value of a military force is proportional to the square of its numerical strength multiplied by the fighting value of its individual units. Reeves understood the importance of numerical superiority and thus the need to place as many aircraft as possible in the air. To increase the number of planes operating from the *Langley,* he ordered that more aircraft be taken on board.

By the spring of 1926 the Covered Wagon was routinely operating up to twenty aircraft from her crowded flight deck. The haphazard fashion in which planes had previously been handled was replaced with a well orchestrated routine. The real danger came when aircraft were landing: it was essential to get a recovered plane out of the way of the next plane waiting to land as quickly as possible. Before Reeves took command of the *Langley* it had been the custom to let each plane land in the arresting gear and then lower it to the hangar deck to clear the way for the next one. This was a time-consuming process which greatly slowed the landing interval until the aircraft handling crews began to push each plane into a parking area ahead of a newly installed midship barrier that shielded parked aircraft on the flight deck from any planes that might miss the arresting gear while landing.[15]

With the help of Commander Towers, then *Langley*'s executive officer, Reeves organized the flight deck crew into small groups of specialists. Each group was assigned responsibility for one aspect of the flight operations to be conducted on the *Langley*'s flight deck. Specific tasks, such as operating the arresting gear, releasing tail hooks, and fueling aircraft, were allocated each team, along with a set of colored shirts. The members of each team wore the same color, which served to sort out who was doing what on the bustling flight deck: blue for plane pushers, brown for crew chiefs, purple for fuelers, and so on. Most important were the yellow-shirted directors, for they were responsible for seeing that the planes were safely moved about the dangerous deck. Considered the elite of the crews, the yellow shirts orchestrated the complex, bustling activity on the flight deck using hand signals to overcome the roar of the engines as they directed the movement of aircraft along the deck. Once all the planes were aboard, they were moved aft, where they could be more easily fueled and rearmed. Launchings were speeded by the introduction of a flight control officer, who quickly sent planes racing down the deck with each dip of his checkered flag. The increased speeds of launch and recovery enhanced the carrier's ability to perform all of its missions and enabled the air group to prepare for whichever role (defensive, scouting, or attack) was required next.

Thus far Reeves had devoted his time and attention to developing tactics for the aircraft squadrons stationed only aboard the *Langley* and had little occasion to either study or drill the other squadrons under his command based on the battleships and cruisers. Aware that the fleet would normally be ordered to Puget Sound and knowing of the poor flying weather there, Reeves requested that his entire force be gathered in San Diego during this period. With approval in hand, he began to formulate a program for the study and practical development of aircraft tactics that would be employed at the first summer concentration period scheduled to run from 12 June to 11 September 1926.[16]

Reeves ordered all of the aircraft squadrons under his command to North Field in San Diego for an intensive session of qualifications, training, and development. Included were the planes and personnel from Fighting Squadrons One and Two, Observation Squadrons One, Two, and Four, Utility Squadron One, and Torpedo Bombing Squadron Two, along with those from Langley and the aircraft tender Aroostook.[17] The work during this period was twofold: part of it involved the service testing of certain materials, while the other consisted of the development of aerial tactics. The Langley usually put to sea early in the morning several days a week to conduct carrier qualifications for the pilots, returning to harbor late in the day. Reeves hoped to increase speeds of launch and recovery still further in order to enhance the carrier's ability to protect herself from enemy planes by quickly refueling and arming her fighters. The rapid turnaround of aircraft would also enhance the scouting and attack missions.[18]

Early in August, the Langley took on dozens of airplanes, tons of stores and hundreds of men in preparation for a cruise to Seattle, where she would rejoin the Battle Fleet. Two of the planes were brand new Curtiss Hawks, the fastest fighter then in the navy's inventory. Factory fresh, these F6C-2s were the first Hawks equipped for deck landings, having been fitted with arrester hooks and strengthened landing gear to test their suitability for carrier use.[19] In the words of Commander Towers, the ship was "a perfect mass of men and aeroplanes. It is almost impossible to walk about the decks, on account of the congestion."[20]

Air operations began on the seventh, with Reeves timing each takeoff and landing with a stopwatch. Launch intervals were beginning to average fifteen seconds, the landings ninety. The latter was still too long for Reeves's satisfaction but was a tremendous improvement over the three and a half minutes that had been required the year before. Two days later Fighting One set a record for one day's operation, completing 127 takeoffs and landings.[21]

Reeves was delighted with the Langley's performance. Months of practice

NAS, North Island, San Diego was home port for the *Langley* and the aircraft squadrons of the Battle Fleet. Shown here c. 1926. The planes are Curtiss TS-2 float planes from VF-1. *Naval Historical Center*

and experimentation had resulted in the formulation of new operating procedures and tactical doctrine. Scores of the "Thousand and One Questions" had been answered and countless other problems solved. But one problem remained: How can we bomb effectively?

While attending the observer course at Pensacola, Reeves had personally participated in bombing exercises that had introduced him to the naval bombsight—a device he judged "to be a marvel of uncertainty and inaccuracy," an opinion confirmed during subsequent bombing practices which revealed the mechanism's disturbing tendency to lose calibration just before the moment of bomb release.[22] From this training Reeves knew that high-altitude bombing could only be effective under ideal conditions over a defenseless target. The solution to the problem of accurate bombing in the face of an enemy's concerted defense remained to be solved.

CHAPTER 2

The Diving Attack

T HE AERIAL MANEUVER WHICH would later be coined "dive bombing" was born on 22 October 1926. On that date, Lt. Cdr. Frank D. Wagner led a flight of Curtiss F6C Hawks from Fighting Squadron Two (VF-2) in a simulated attack on the heavy ships of the Battle Fleet as they sortied from San Pedro.[1] Coming down in almost vertical dives from 12,000 feet, the squadron achieved complete surprise of the battleships then bound for San Diego and the Navy Day festivities scheduled there the following week. Although the fleet had been forewarned, the Hawks were not detected until they were almost on the deck. Their height of approach was so high, the dives so nearly vertical, and their speed so fast, that they had pulled out, leveled off, and were headed for a landing at Long Beach before the ship's crews could get to their battle stations. The surprise achieved by the squadron was so complete and the effectiveness of the approach so great that Adm. Charles F. Hughes, the commander-in-chief of the U.S. Fleet, and all on board the battleships unanimously agreed that such an attack would succeed over any defense.

The events leading to the development of this radical new aerial technique have been obscured by the passage of time and the confusion surrounding the precise meaning of the term "dive bombing": an expression

The Curtiss F6C-1 Hawk could survive a vertical dive in part due to the reinforced metal construction of the leading edges of its wings. *U.S. Naval Institute*

which has frequently been misused to describe light bombing or strafing, tactics which are really forms of what was then described in contemporary records as the "diving attack." The critical difference between the two aerial maneuvers was the angle of descent relative to the horizon. As Charles Melhorn has aptly pointed out, dive bombing as we know it originated when the descent changed from a steep glide to an almost vertical dive.[2] As loosely defined among navy pilots in World War II, the latter was severe enough to cause the pilot to literally "hang from his shoulder straps." From all indications, it seems logical to conclude that Wagner was the first to demonstrate the feasibility of attacking in the near-vertical mode, that is, in dives of 70 degrees or greater. Unlike the pilots of World War II, Wagner was restrained by his seat belt only, as the shoulder strap had yet to be introduced.

The exact details of how Wagner's achievement come about will probably never be known; an official account of the event was never recorded, and all the players are long gone. Nevertheless, it seems safe to assume that the delivery of the Hawks, which were highly regarded and extremely rugged planes, opened the door for Wagner's impressive display. The F6C was one of the first aircraft strong enough to survive the pullout required from such a radical maneuver. It had a water-cooled engine which was beautifully streamlined, and when you nosed over, as one experienced naval aviator later explained, "the bottom dropped out from under you."[3] The plane "was really a smooth diver," and you had to be very careful when pulling out to avoid blacking out.

In the summer of 1926, Wagner, who had been flying for the navy since 1921, was detailed to command VF-2, then operating in support of the Battle Fleet on the West Coast. Arriving in San Diego at the beginning of July, Wagner discovered that he was just in time to participate in the first summer concentration period for aircraft inaugurated that year by Captain Reeves. Reeves ordered all squadrons in his command to North Island for six weeks of concentrated training, study, and practice as a cohesive unit. This was the first time that all aircraft assigned to the Battle Fleet would be assembled in one place in what was to become an annual ritual for the squadrons assigned to the Battle Fleet while Reeves was in command. In all, more than one hundred aircraft participated in the various activities conducted at North Island that summer.

Exactly what exercises were conducted by VF-2 during those months is not known. It seems probable, though, that the squadron engaged in all forms of maneuvers, including practice of the "diving attack," a relatively new tactic that had been perfected by then Maj. (later Lt. Gen.) Ross E. Rowell of Marine Observation Squadron One (VO-1M), who was also stationed at North Field during this time.

Major Rowell learned this technique from the army while attending the Advanced Flying School at Kelly Field. Though an army installation, it provided advanced training in land planes for both naval and marine aviators in the early 1920s. At the time of Rowell's arrival there in May 1923, it was also the home of the U.S. Army Air Corps' Third Attack Group. Although equipped with World War I–vintage DH-4s, this highly trained group of experienced pilots had developed a method of low-altitude attack which Rowell later characterized as dive bombing. In all likelihood, though, the planes never exceeded a 45-degree dive, for, even as he put it, "no one would believe that the wing structure of that type of plane could withstand the strains of dive bombing." To Rowell's knowledge, "no one ever lost a wing," but then the army pilots made sure that their dives weren't excessive. The army had fitted the DH-4s with the new A-3 bomb rack, which could hold up to five small

A DH-4B, similar to this one, was used by Maj. Ross E. Rowell, USMC, to perfect the diving attack in the early 1920s. *Naval Historical Center*

bombs under each wing, and installed a release handle in the pilot's cockpit of this two-seater. There were no bombsights; instead, the pilot would use some point on top of the engine as an aiming device. Each pilot, depending on the height of his eye above the seat, selected a particular part of the engine for use in determining the correct line of sight, entered a shallow dive from about 1,500 feet, lined up on the target as best as he could, then dropped his bombs before pulling out at around 600 feet. Rowell was so impressed with the accuracy of this approach to bombing that he later claimed to have immediately visualized its certainty of "naval employment where accuracy against small moving targets is paramount." Undoubtedly this proved to be the case, though it is unlikely that Rowell recognized the significance of this development at this time.[4]

After completing the course at Kelly Field, Rowell was transferred to the army's First Pursuit Group at Selfridge Field, which was then composed almost entirely of veteran pursuit pilots who had flown in Europe during the First World War. From Lt. (later Brig. Gen.) George P. Tourtellot, Rowell learned the details of the army's experiences off the Virginia Capes in 1921

Marines attaching bombs to the under-wing racks of a DH-4. *Naval Historical Center*

made famous by Billy Mitchell's sinking of the former German battleship *Ostfriesland*. Tourtellot had bombed the *Ostfriesland* using the same method which Rowell had seen employed by the attack group at Kelly Field. This was done before the 2,000-lb. death blow later delivered by the army's heavy bombers. Tourtellot had attacked the ship with Cooper 25-lb. bombs to determine if it was practicable to use fragmentation or gas bombs against exposed personnel on the decks of warships. The bombing run had been made in a British SE-5 fighter to which a single fuselage-mounted bomb rack had been attached. Though he hit the ship, Tourtellot was of the opinion that this form of attack would be too vulnerable to antiaircraft fire to be used successfully in combat. Perhaps this is why it was never pursued vigorously by the U.S. Army Air Corps.[5]

Tourtellot told Rowell that he had learned the technique from the British while flying with them during the First World War. At times, he explained, they would temporarily gain air superiority over the Germans, sweeping the skies of enemy planes. When this happened the air patrols conducted over German lines would come up empty handed. In order to avoid wasting fuel in a fruitless search for the enemy, some British commander decided that it would be a good idea to attach one or two light bombs to the fighter planes, which could then be dropped on suitable targets in enemy territory. The British soon discovered that by diving the planes to low altitude they could attack staff cars, officers' clubs, and other military targets not protected by antiaircraft batteries. Although these attacks were highly inaccurate—no sighting devices were used to aim the missiles—they were very annoying to the Germans and had a great deal of nuisance value.

After completing the course at Kelly Field, Rowell was delegated to command VO-1M, the first marine aviation unit stationed on the West Coast. Upon his arrival at NAS, San Diego in August 1924, Rowell promptly decided to train the unit in the diving attack, believing, as he would later prove, that it would be a highly successful method of supporting ground troops. As a preliminary training measure, he had miniature bomb racks fitted to the fuselage of the squadron's vintage DH-4s and connected them to a bomb release, which he placed in the pilot's cockpit. VO-1M began to conduct experimental bombing practices with this gear while they awaited the arrival of the more advanced A-3 bomb rack, which Rowell had asked the Bureau of Aeronautics (BuAer) to obtain from the army. When these devices were installed, they enabled the squadron to continue their experiments using a range of standard navy practice bombs in place of the small miniatures they had been dropping.

In the spring of 1925, VO-1M conducted a series of air shows throughout the West Coast to demonstrate their flying prowess. Included in these displays was an exhibit of formation flying along with a demonstration of the diving attack, culminating in the dropping of smoke bombs which served to dramatize the potential impact on ground troops. Rowell was under the impression that a number of naval aviators had witnessed these exhibitions and had been impressed with the possibilities of the bombing technique demonstrated by VO-1M.

Navy flyers on the West Coast were quick to adopt the diving attack for their own needs. It is likely that Wagner was one of these. The arrival of the new Curtiss F6C Hawks allowed Wagner to try a succession of ever-steeper dives. Inevitably, he found himself diving almost straight down. The pilots in Wagner's squadron were soon approaching their targets at altitudes of more than 10,000 feet before pushing over in the near-vertical dives, which allowed them to keep the intended target in sight while they lined up to fire their machine guns.[6]

Early tests of this innovative tactic showed that it provided unparalleled accuracy in machine-gun and light-bombing ground attacks. These activities, apparently, were of great interest to CNO Eberle, for he requested that "light bombing"—as this tactic was to be officially termed in the coming months— be included in the annual gunnery exercises scheduled for the coming year.[7] In retrospect, it seems likely that the mock dive-bombing attack staged by Wagner was orchestrated by Captain Reeves to impress senior commanders, furthering the cause of aviation while "feathering his own nest," so to speak.

The gunnery exercises conducted in the late fall of 1926 were the first to include competition in dive bombing, though it should be pointed out that the dives, which were restrained to 45 degrees, were really an early form of glide bombing known as the "diving attack." Five squadrons assigned to the Battle Fleet participated in the practices preceding the actual competition. Three of these, VO-1, VO-2, and VO-4, were observation squadrons whose primary duty was to spot the fall of shot for the battleships. The UO-1 sea-planes they flew were not well suited for this task and had to limit the length and steepness of the dives called for in the orders outlining how the practice would be conducted.[8] Nevertheless, the results were staggering: of 311 bombs dropped during the entire practice, 44.5 percent were scored as direct hits.[9] And this on a target 200 feet long by 45 feet wide—an effective area one-third the length and 10 feet less than the width of a typical light cruiser, which was then considered the most likely objective in a real attack! The two fighter squadrons did even better. The new F6Cs and FB-5s with which they were equipped were much better suited to the task, and the pilots had more expe-rience in the diving maneuvers required for accurate bombing. Out of 105 bombs dropped, they made 70 hits, for an average score of 67 percent—more than double the accuracy of conventional aerial bombing, which at best could achieve an accuracy of about 30 percent! Although the bombs carried by the aircraft participating in the gunnery exercises of 1926 were small 25-lb. fragmentation bombs, the success of this gunnery practice proved that dive bombing could be used effectively to attack light surface craft, submarines, and personnel exposed on the upper decks of enemy battleships.

Though the orders for the aforementioned gunnery exercises had called for all squadrons to start their 45-degree dives at 1,000 feet, Lieutenant Com-mander Wagner took his squadron to 2,500 feet before descending toward the target.[10] During the course of the exercise, the pilots of VF-2 discovered that the target disappeared from view as they approached the point of release,

An unidentified pilot, perhaps Wagner himself, at the controls of the lead F6C-1 of
VF-2, taken in April 1927. *National Archives*

preventing them from lining up on the objective. Wagner believed that better
accuracy could be achieved if pilots were allowed to make steeper approaches.
He proposed changing the rules to permit descents at angles up to 75 degrees,
starting from an altitude of 10,000 feet. Wagner was not at all concerned
about the Hawk's ability to survive such a dive and was convinced that the
maximum speed and stresses encountered would be no more than that
which he had already experienced.[11]

As legend has it, one day in March 1927, Wagner "quietly added a little
more piano wire to the rigging of his plane, placed a hundred pound weight
under each wing, and started out on what was supposed to be a routine
flight." Climbing to 7,000 feet, he opened the throttle as far as it would go
and nosed over into a full-powered vertical dive. As the plane rocketed toward
the field below, the airport crew watched in horrified fascination, then scattered wildly before the onslaught which they saw hurtling out of the sky. At
the last moment, Wagner pulled up, nearly brushed the top of a hangar, and
landed triumphantly without a scratch.[12]

That spring, VF-2 began to practice bombing from near-vertical dives on

Ream Field, a fenced-in pasture surrounded by low trees near the south end of San Diego Bay. They dropped miniature practice bombs from A-3 bomb racks attached to the underside of the lower wing panels until they were regularly hitting a target laid out on the grass. To help develop the exact timing required to perfect this technique, Wagner frequently stationed Lt. Daniel W. (Indian Joe) Tomlinson and Lt. Edward (Eddie) Coyle close to the target to assess each plane's performance. Their comments helped each pilot to improve his technique so that the time of the attack could be compressed to the point were the planes were dropping their bombs within two-second intervals. Tomlinson, a superb flyer who had been experimenting with planes since 1920, would later organize the U.S. Navy's first aerobatics team, the Three Sea Hawks.

VF-2's executive officer at the time these experiments took place was Lt. Cdr. John E. Ostrander Jr., a naval aviator since 1921. In addition to his pilot's wings, Ostrander was an expert in aviation ordnance, the first officer in the navy to be so designated. Years later he would shudder as he remembered how close the planes come to crashing into the ground, leveling off below the tops of stunted trees surrounding the field. Though the dives could have caused casualties, no one died and the squadron made a high percentage of hits. After various trials they settled on an approach in a V formation in echelon, which allowed all planes to dive quickly from slightly different directions.

In April, Reeves organized a demonstration of the progress made by navy flyers on the West Coast for Gen. Italo Balbo of the Italian air force. Balbo, who was on an inspection tour of the United States to gather information for the Italian air force, received a telegram from Reeves inviting him to San Diego. Unbeknownst to the celebrated Italian airman, Reeves intended to impress his guest with a sensational display of dive bombing.

The invitation was accepted, and in due course the Italian general arrived in San Diego for an exhibition put on by the navy's best pilots. All through the morning Balbo watched as displays of various flying techniques were conducted for his benefit. Included were demonstrations of formation flying, stunting (aerobatics), and even a simulated torpedo attack. "Through it all he expressed the polite enthusiasm that was the Italian way of saying, 'It is not bad, but I have seen it all before.'"[13]

When the last of the scheduled flights was finished, Reeves, who found his guest to be a "handsome and likable chap," casually suggested a walk out onto the field. Suppressing his surprise, the Italian agreed, and the two men began to stroll along one of the runways. As they reached the center of the field Wagner's squadron appeared overhead flying in a perfect V of V's. "What a beautiful . . . ," the general began. But the sentence was never finished, for at that precise moment the pilot of the first plane began a dive that seemed destined to carry it straight down Balbo's open mouth. As the craft screamed overhead, seemingly intent on falling from the sky, the general's expression changed from one of casual interest to something very close to fear. "With visible effort he stood his ground, but he could not keep from ducking as each plane in the squadron pulled out of its dive and brushed past his head."

The cable which General Balbo sent home that evening was filled with superlatives: "I have seen today a type of bombing that I did not think possible."

Unknown to anyone in the Battle Fleet in the Pacific, a newly constituted squadron of fighters on the East Coast commanded by Lt. Cdr. Issac Schlossback was simultaneously experimenting with the same form of aerial attack which had startled and impressed General Balbo. Fighting Squadron Five (VF-5) was established on 3 January 1927 at the Naval Air Station, Hampton Roads, Virginia, and attached to the Scouting Fleet.[14] Equipped with brand new F6C-3s, the latest model Hawks, the pilots of VF-5s quickly discovered the virtues of what was undeniably the best airplane then in the fleet. On 4 May the squadron conducted exercises over Smithfield, Virginia, which ended in a impressive display of airmanship. Coming down from 11,000 feet, the squadron plunged toward the target in 70-degree dives akin to those of VF-2 on the West Coast.[15]

CHAPTER 3

Policy, Politics, and Procurement

THE SUCCESS OF THE BOMBING PRACTICE conducted in December 1926 by VF-2 caused Cdr. Eugene E. Wilson, then chief of the design section in the Bureau of Aeronautics, to suggest the need to develop a new class of aircraft: the light bomber or VB.[1] Until this point in its relatively short history, the Bureau of Aeronautics had concentrated on developing the four basic types of airplanes specified by the General Board of the Navy in 1922.

The General Board, which was established by the secretary of the navy in 1900 as a special advisory board, was frequently called upon to make recommendations concerning the design characteristics that were to be incorporated into new ships and aircraft. Though the General Board had no legal authority, it carried great weight due to the prestige of the high-ranking officers of which it was composed.

After the Bureau of Aeronautics was formed in 1921, the secretary of the navy instructed the General Board to frame a general policy to direct the activities of aviation within the navy. It took several months for the "Air Policy" drawn up by the General Board to work its way through the bureaucratic system. It was officially approved by the secretary of the navy on 1 December 1922.

Spotting was then considered to be the number one mission of aviation by the General Board, which recommended that the development of a spotting plane—the VO type—take first priority. Other planes included in the section of the Air Policy devoted to the advancement of aircraft included:

1. A plane for torpedo, bombing, and tactical scouting—the VT type, also known as the three-purpose plane;
2. A combat (fighting) plane for use afloat—the VF type;
3. A scouting seaplane of long range—the VP type.

Spotting planes were to be placed on all battleships, and modern cruisers and all aircraft, except for seaplanes, were to be capable of flying off ships.[2]

The General Board's policy with regard to aviation matters was consistent with its thinking on the strategic makeup of the fleet and the perceived mission of the U.S. Navy. The battleship was then considered to be the ultimate naval weapon, and most, if not all, of the high-ranking officers in the navy believed that the decisive action in the next war would be conducted by the dreadnoughts of the main battle line. Gunnery was the most important technical specialty in the navy, and membership in the "Gun Club," that nebulous fraternity of naval officers who believed in the supremacy of the big gun, was considered a prerequisite to high command. Spotting, an activity that involved observing the fall of shot, that is, observing the splashes thrown up by the large-caliber shells when they missed the target, was an essential element of gunnery. In order to bring the guns on target, the observer would provide gunners with any adjustments needed to correct errors in range or deflection. The desire for greater accuracy and the increasing range of engagement led to the development of sophisticated range finders and fire-control equipment, which were placed high up in the ship's superstructure.

Use of aircraft for this very important task had two significant advantages. First, the observer could be brought much nearer to the target, making it easier to observe exactly how close the splashes were to the intended victim. Second, placing the spotter in an airplane high in the air provided an unobstructed, smoke-free view of the action, which proved to be much more effective than trying to spot from a position atop a battleship's superstructure.

The tremendous advantage of using aircraft for spotting was undeniably demonstrated in March 1919 during gunnery exercises conducted by the battleship *Texas*.[3] Though the spotter in the observation plane lacked experience and was untrained in spotting, he was able to coach the big guns on target

In 1919 a launching platform with a Sopwith Camel was installed aboard the *Texas*, shown here in New York Harbor. *Naval Historical Center*

with an average error of only 64 yards. This was "many times better" than had previously been done by the ship's own spotters located high in the superstructure.[4]

The success of the *Texas* shoot convinced battleship men of the need to have spotting aircraft capable of accompanying the fleet. Though the big gun remained the sine qua non of warfare at sea, its effectiveness depended upon how quickly gunfire could be brought to bear on an enemy vessel. Studies conducted at the Naval War College had clearly shown that the fighting strength of a ship under attack would decline rapidly in conformance with the N-square law. Hence, the ship which struck first was most likely to be victorious. This concept became the driving force behind the navy's continual efforts in the interwar period to improve the range and fire control of its 14-inch and 16-inch guns.

If victory at sea depended upon naval gunfire, and if the effectiveness of gunfire depended upon spotting by air, then it was also essential to make sure that no hostile aircraft interfered with the spotting process! This concept had far-reaching implications for naval aviation and the doctrine of airpower at sea, for to control the skies above the battle required command of the air!

Cdr. Kenneth Whiting while serving as executive officer of the *Saratoga*, c. 1928. Whiting was one of the officers instrumental in defining the need to have aircraft carriers as a means of obtaining command of the air over the fleet. *Naval Historical Center*

This made the procurement of aircraft carriers essential for fleet operations, explained Cdr. Kenneth Whiting when he testified before the General Board in 1919.[5] Command of the air, Whiting pointed out, could not be won by seaplane fighters whose performance was impeded by the extra weight of the floats needed to recover the planes at sea. If seaplanes encountered land-based aircraft, a scenario already being predicted by the Office of Naval Intelligence, they would be shot down. "You, will find them floating in the ocean and the enemy [will] still [be] in the air," said Whiting. Though wheeled fighters could be launched from turret platforms or deck-mounted catapults in advance of a general engagement, they could not be recovered at sea and would be lost for the balance of the action once their fuel supply had been exhausted. Only the carrier could provide the landing, refueling, and rearming facilities needed to keep fighters continuously aloft; it alone could provide the fighter strength necessary to secure and maintain command of the air.

By the beginning of 1927, fighting had overtaken spotting as the most important mission for naval aviation. That year the staff within the Bureau of Aeronautics became heavily involved in studying the kinds of airplanes that would be best suited for use on the *Lexington* and *Saratoga,* the large aircraft carriers that would be commissioned later in the year. To some members of the staff it appeared that there was a definite need for a high-performance, two-place fighter in the fleet. The French and English had developed several two-seaters, and there was obviously some concern that the navy would be left behind if it didn't follow suit—this according to Lt. Ralph Ofstie, who was one of the first to advocate the development of this type of plane. Ofstie presented his thoughts regarding the design characteristics needed for a successful two-seat fighter to Admiral Moffett in a memorandum written on 26 January 1927.[6] He urged the bureau to prepare specifications for such a plane and recommended that development contracts be issued for at least two distinct experimental prototypes.

According to Ofstie, the mission of the two-seat fighter was primarily defensive. It could operate as a protective fighter for the spotting, bombing, or torpedo planes, or it could be used to defend the fleet (particularly the carriers) against enemy strafing attacks. Though Ofstie felt that it could be used for offensive work against enemy planes or light bombing, it would be unsuitable against enemy single-seaters.

The idea for a two-seat fighter appears to have originated on the Western Front in World War I. Diving out of the sun and gaining position on the enemy's tail when he wasn't looking emerged as the classic fighter tactic for shooting down enemy flyers. Adding a second seat and installing a rear gunner was thought to be a good way of countering such a maneuver. In those days the difference in speed between a single- and two-seater was practically nil, so that the performance between the two types was not an issue.

Ofstie's memo initiated a furious debate on the pros and cons of the two-seat fighter that would percolate through the naval aviation community for years to come. Widely circulated within the BuAer, it spawned a flurry of responses in the form of handwritten notations that were added to the routing slip which accompanied the document as it passed from desk to desk. It is evident from these comments that most airmen within the BuAer wanted a plane that could "fight and not just protect itself from air attack."[7]

Preparation of a specification like the one requested by Ofstie was the first step in the procurement of any new aircraft. These were prepared by BuAer's design section based on the nature of the mission to be performed by the particular aircraft type desired. Once drawn up, the specification was circulated throughout the aircraft industry in what amounted to an informal design competition. Each manufacturer was invited to submit designs and proposals to build a single airplane which would serve as an experimental model to be tested by the navy. After being evaluated on their engineering merits, contracts would then be issued to build the most promising designs. To promote competition and to ensure that the bureau was not accused of favoritism, contracts would usually be issued to more that one manufacturer. The competition was tough; it was the easiest way for a manufacturer to introduce its planes to the navy and only the best designs were selected.

While the bureau was busy debating the design characteristics of the two-seat fighter, students at the Naval War College in Newport were engaged in studying the operational factors that would determine the optimal mix of airplanes needed to carry out the missions assigned to the two *Lexington*-class carriers about to enter service.[8] Simulated exercises conducted on the game boards at the war college had revealed the difficult problem of aircraft stowage and handling. Arranging and rearranging an entire complement of aircraft so that the planes on the flight deck were positioned preparatory for a given mission, that is, scouting, bombing, fighter defense, and so on, was proving to be a very laborious task. Consolidating functions and limiting the types of aircraft assigned to a carrier's aircraft complement was one solution to this problem; another was simply to provide more carrier decks so that more planes could be launched simultaneously. Both solutions would play an important role in dictating the future direction of the navy's aviation program.

As the weeks passed, Moffett busied himself preparing BuAer's legislative program for the coming fiscal year. As chief of the bureau, he had spent the better part of the previous two years defending naval aviation in a series of pitched battles that began with Mitchell's scathing attack on the navy in the spring of 1925. Moffett, an astute politician, had skillfully conned naval aviation through the minefield of special boards and committees which had followed in the wake of the *Shenandoah* crash and had lobbied hard for a multiyear building program that would permit a twofold increase in the size of the navy's air force while providing much-needed stability to the nascent aircraft industry. The tenacity and determination which characterized

Moffett's tenure as chief of BuAer paid off handsomely for naval aviation when Congress agreed to authorize a five-year building program for aircraft. Signed by President Calvin Coolidge on 24 June 1926, the Naval Expansion Act authorized the procurement of 1,614 airplanes over a five-year period, enough planes to provide the navy with an operational force of 1,000 planes by 1931. Many consider passage of the Five Year Building Program Moffett's greatest accomplishment as head of BuAer.[9]

One result of the sweeping changes in aeronautical legislation passed by Congress in 1926 was the creation of a new position of civilian authority in the navy, the post of assistant secretary for aeronautics. The recommendation to strengthen the top-level aviation authority in both the navy and army emerged from hearings conducted by the Morrow Board set up by President Calvin Coolidge after the *Shenandoah* disaster to study the whole problem of "aircraft in national defense."[10] Edward P. Warner—a professor of aeronautical engineering at the Massachusetts Institute of Technology (MIT) who had won acclaim for his expertise in aviation matters while serving as a consultant to the Morrow Board—was quickly tapped to fill the new post. Taking office on 24 July 1926, Warner immediately threw himself into the work with "remarkable zest and enthusiasm."[11]

By December Warner was raising questions concerning the types of planes that were to be included in the aircraft building program. A month earlier he had attended a conference held in the office of Capt. James Raby, then commander, Aircraft Squadrons, Scouting Fleet (ComAirSctFlt) at NAS, Hampton Roads, Virginia, to discuss design changes needed for the T3M-2 that the Martin company was in the process of building for the navy. Other attendees included Glenn Martin, the plane's builder; Cdr. Holden C. Richardson, head of the design section in BuAer; and four of the pilots assigned to Bombing and Torpedo Squadron One (VT-1) who were currently flying the SC (upon whose design the T3Ms were based). During the discussions, Warner learned that the new plane was not considered suitable for scouting.[12]

In the first week of December, Warner wrote Moffett suggesting that perhaps the time was ripe to review the air policy set down in 1922. Moffett balked at this idea, believing that it was an inopportune time to review the navy's policy on aviation matters. It would be better, he explained in a memorandum addressed to the assistant secretary, to wait until more operational experience had been gained from the new carriers. The Bureau of Aeronautics was in constant communication with the operating units, and the con-

The squadron commander dropping a practice torpedo from one of the SC-1 aircraft assigned to VT-4. *National Archives*

tinual exchange of ideas frequently led to a design study for a new experimental type. In Moffett's view, only a radical departure from the existing types of aircraft being developed by BuAer would require a change of policy. Warner would have none of this. For the third time in as many months he brought up the subject of the three-purpose plane (the T3M type). "It has been made very clearly evident to me," Warner wrote, "that there is wide spread discontent with the existing plane and a wide variety of opinion about what should be done." Warner thought that it would be better to postpone purchasing the sixty-one three-purpose T3M-2s planned as part of the program for 1927. The "whole series of collateral questions" raised by this issue, he went on, warranted a further review of the navy's air policy. Furthermore, the General Board was the "most logically qualified body to give, or serve as a focus for such consideration."[13]

Moffett was dubious about the outcome of any BuAer matter presented to the General Board. From past experience he knew that the board would be "suspicious of BuAer's claims" and proposals; a better approach from his viewpoint would be to convene a special board whose members were more in tune with his ideas.[14]

By now, Moffett, who had been battling the foes of aviation for more than five years, was a master of using advisory boards to further his objectives for BuAer and the development of naval aviation in general. Unable to put off Warner's protestations any longer, Moffett did the next best thing: he wrote the secretary of the navy asking him to appoint a board to "review the situation in aviation, both ashore and afloat, particularly afloat, with a view to ascertaining how it [BuAer] can better meet the requirements of the Fleet." He included a list of personnel that would be suitable for selection to ensure that the board would not stray from the direction intended. To this list Moffett attached separate documents that outlined the principles and fundamentals of naval aeronautic policy, provided a proposed agenda, and contained a series of questions to be investigated.[15]

Moffett's request was implemented on 4 April 1927, when Secretary of the Navy Curtis D. Wilbur issued Order No. 2028-138 establishing the Board to Examine the Naval Aeronautic Policy for the purpose of recommending any changes that they found to be desirable.[16] Rear Adm. Montgomery M. Taylor, then director of fleet training, Office of Naval Operations, was assigned to head the new board. It appears likely that Moffett lobbied hard for Taylor's appointment knowing him to be broad minded on air matters and readily available. Other officers assigned to serve on the board besides Moffett were Capts. Joseph M. Reeves, Henry V. Butler, James J. Raby, Albert W. Marshall, Harry E. Yarnell, Cdr. Theodore G. "Spuds" Ellyson, and Lt. Cdr. Marc A. Mitscher. Except for Taylor, all were navy airmen. Moffett, Reeves, Butler, and Marshall had taken the observers course; Yarnell was scheduled to take it that summer; and Ellyson and Mitscher were pilots. How Moffett managed to achieve this feat is not known; nevertheless, it is an outstanding example of how he was able to manipulate the bureaucratic system for his own purposes.

Admiral Taylor's suitability for this task was enhanced by his experience as chairman of an earlier board set up to review the vexing personnel problems facing BuAer the previous year. Though Taylor attempted to strike a balance between the two opposing bureaus, that is, Aeronautics and Navigation, he was chastised by Moffett for not calling more aviators to testify during what has come to be known as the "First Taylor Board." To make matters worse, three members of this earlier board, all of them flyers, took issue with the majority's findings and submitted a separate report that was much more favorable to the aviation community.[17] Chagrined by this action and Moffett's unfavorable comments which followed, Taylor prudently called a host of navy airmen before the new board.

If Moffett wanted a counterweight to the General Board—as the writer Thomas Hone suggests—then the Second Taylor Board succeeded beyond his wildest dreams; the list of aviators who served or testified before it comprised a who's who of prewar airmen involving no less than eleven future admirals![18] It was an unqualified success from BuAer's point of view and directed the course of naval aviation for the next five years.

Of the many recommendations made by the Second Taylor Board, first in importance was the need to obtain additional aircraft carriers to both protect the fleet (i.e., secure command of the air) and carry on scouting and offensive operations. Though the board endorsed the continued development of airships, they were unequivocal in a desire to emphasize the development of aircraft that would operate from the ships of the U.S. Fleet; scouting and patrol from shore- or tender-based aircraft would be secondary. The need to both protect the fleet and carry out scouting and offensive operations far from the main battle force would greatly influence the design criteria used to construct the next generation of aircraft carriers.

The board also recommended that the number of shipboard aircraft types be reduced to a minimum. To most aviators it was becoming clear that the functions of tactical scouting, observation, defensive fighting, and perhaps even light bombing—missions currently accomplished by several different aircraft—could be combined into one type. The need to develop a light bomber, the VB type, was emphasized by Lt. Cdr. Bruce G. Leighton during his testimony before the board on 5 May 1927. Leighton, one of the growing cadre of technical experts on Moffett's staff, had overseen the development of the air-cooled radial engine. Now, as chief of the plans division and aide to Assistant Secretary Warner, he was heavily involved in preparing studies in support of the various carrier building programs being advocated by the Bureau of Aeronautics. Leighton viewed the light bomber as an essential element in the development of the light carrier, a vessel which he saw as a means of overcoming Japan's advantage in cruisers.[19]

Although the Washington Treaty limited the construction of capital ships and carrier tonnage, the failure to resolve the disparity in cruiser strength between the major powers resulted in a minor arms race with respect to this class of warship. The British lead in cruisers was an undisputed fact, and the "General Board perceived 'strong indications' that Japan was attempting to counter her inferiority in capital ships vis-à-vis the United States by constructing large numbers of . . . cruiser[s]."[20]

War planners preparing for war with Japan anticipated a multiphase advance across the Pacific that would culminate in a great naval battle that would result in ultimate victory. Although the five-to-three ratio of battleship tonnage established by the Washington Treaty seemed to ensure supremacy for the U.S. battle line, war planners feared attrition from attacks by the enemy's light forces. Raids by submarines, destroyers, and aircraft were expected to take place as the fleet steamed across the vastness of the Pacific. Aircraft carriers placed in advance of the main body, according to Leighton, offered the ideal method of screening against such attacks. Positioning light carriers 200 or 300 miles in front of the battle line would ensure that the enemy raiders were detected well before they could deliver an attack on the main body of the fleet. The plane needed for this mission, Leighton explained to the Second Taylor Board, was the light bomber:

> With the light fast bombing planes on board your carriers, not only can you discover enemy forces but if your light bombing is effective, you can hammer them long before they get in touch with your main body. Light bombs from light aircraft carriers appear to give promise of being extremely effective.

The plane Leighton envisioned to perform this task was the VB, a light, fast bomber capable of carrying a 500-lb. bomb. A plane of this type would be especially useful against destroyers and light cruisers—just the sort of ships that were expected to conduct surface raids on the main body.[21]

Leighton admitted that the above conclusions depended upon the accuracy and effectiveness of dive bombing. "An assumption," he explained, "that has not yet been definitely proved in service." Although the results of December's gunnery exercise involving the diving attack had been quite impressive, it had been conducted against a stationary target only. Trying to hit a moving ship from the air, especially one steaming at high speed, was another matter. Up to this point, the navy had only considered aerial bombardment for use against large combatants whose slow speed and large size made them attractive targets for the heavy bombers of the day. Underpowered and overloaded, these ponderous beasts were hard pressed to engage high-speed surface craft which could outmaneuver the slow bombers as they tried to line up for the bomb run.

The potential effectiveness of light bombing was so great that Leighton recommended that tests be conducted immediately to determine how accurately it could be done, the effectiveness of light bombs, and the effectiveness of the defenses against it. Though the board agreed with Leighton's assessment of the importance of dive bombing, they declined to endorse his suggestion for new tests. Instead, they included a watered-down statement recommending that

bombing should be developed from two angles—
(a) heavy bombing, wherein the bomb is dropped from an altitude based on available ceiling and effectiveness of antiaircraft fire and where its velocity is wholly due to gravity,
(b) diving bombing, wherein the bomb is delivered during a dive toward the target and its velocity is received from the speed of the airplane.[22]

Nevertheless, Leighton's suggestion caught the ear of someone higher up in the chain of command (Moffett seems the most likely), for the chief of naval operations soon issued a directive ordering a series of tests to evaluate the effectiveness of light bombing against moving targets.[23]

Well before these tests could be arranged, CNO Eberle directed the General Board (via the secretary of the navy), to review and comment on the report issued by the Second Taylor Board.[24] Though he endorsed its recommendations, Eberle cautioned against putting the new policy into effect until a thorough study of the changes necessitated in the present five-year program could be made. The General Board took several months before forwarding its recommendations to the secretary of the navy. In the interim, the "Red Rippers" of Fighting Squadron Five (VF-5S) conducted another startling demonstration of dive bombing that would prove to have far-reaching consequences for the future of naval aviation.[25]

In the early part of August 1927, Lt. Cdr. Osbourne B. Hardison assumed command of the relatively new squadron, which had eighteen pilots, two Reserve ensigns, a doctor, and a supply officer. At the time, VF-5S was the only squadron in the navy then operating with a full complement of eighteen aircraft—all new Curtiss F6C-3 fighters. Hardison's immediate task was to prepare the squadron to participate in the East Coast aircraft concentration period scheduled for October and November; thus he devoted August and September to gunnery practice.

In October the squadron received orders to undertake an experimental bombing practice against a target that was to be towed at 25 knots by a destroyer.[26] Hardison's squadron was the logical choice for this duty since it had already demonstrated a facility for conducting a diving attack, was flying one of the newest, most capable aircraft in the navy's inventory, and was at full strength. What followed was a series of experiments conducted under the auspices of the commander, Aircraft Scouting Fleet that included:

1. Perfection of a suitable target for towing;
2. A rehearsal with miniature bombs;
3. The record practice with 17-lb. fragmentation bombs; and
4. Simulated attacks on a destroyer.

The first concerned the selection of a suitable target that could be adopted for towing. Several experiments using empty 50-gallon gasoline drums and a number of spherical buoys linked together by short lengths of chain were conducted before the destroyer assigned towing duty, the *Putnam*, reached Hampton Roads on 11 October 1927. None of these items worked well enough to be used in the actual bombing exercises, and a decision was made to try a single large buoy painted bright yellow. Good results were subsequently achieved with a single 36-inch buoy towed at 20 knots.[27]

A preliminary bombing session was conducted nine days later when VF-5S dropped miniature practice bombs on the moving target from their F6C-3 fighters. The exercise, like the record practice to follow, was conducted by two three-plane sections under the command of the division leader, Lt. Wallace M. Dillon.[28] It proved to be a poor rehearsal for the next day's work, however, as the small splashes made by the tiny bombs could hardly be seen. The pilots were unable to judge the results of their initial bomb drops, precluding the possibility of improving their accuracy in succeeding drops by adjusting their aiming point based on experience. The small size of the target only served to further exacerbate this problem.

The official practice began on the following day. Instead of the miniature bombs used the day before, the planes were loaded with 17-lb. fragmentation bombs which made a bigger splash when they hit the water. Over the course of next two days each of the participating planes made a series of dive-bombing runs at various altitudes, with bomb releases timed to permit pullouts at 500, 1,000, and 1,500 feet. Each plane dropped five bombs per run, then when cleared of all bombs, made a simulated strafing attack on the *Putnam* from an altitude starting at between 1,000 and 4,000 feet. Aiming was done through the regular gunsights with which the planes were equipped. Bombing accuracy improved as the pilots gained experience and was slightly better on the second day. The accuracy was determined by recording the range and deflection errors of the bomb splashes made by each projectile as it impacted near the target. These were carefully plotted by observers on the *Putnam,* who measured the deflection error, and those on the destroyer *Breck* steaming 500 yards abeam the target, who measured errors in range. A total of 240 bombs were dropped during the two-day exercise.

As seen from the results tabulated in table 3.1, the most accurate bombing was done with pullouts at 500 feet, though there was very little difference in the results obtained at the other altitudes. The best results were achieved from the steepest dives of about 70 degrees. As indicated by the results shown in the table, zigzagging made bombing much less accurate and appeared to be a good defensive maneuver for ships under attack.[29]

Table 3.1 Results of Experimental Dive-Bombing Practice against a Moving Target, 21 and 22 October 1927

Recovery Altitude (feet)	21 October		22 October		Percentage of Total Hits
	Bombs Dropped	Direct Hits	Bombs Dropped	Direct Hits	
500	30	12	30	16	46.5
1,000	30	11	30	12	38.3
1,500	30	15	30	12	45
1,000*	30	4	30	5	15

Source: ComAirRonSctFlt to CNO, 15 Nov. 1927, File A5, BuAer Sec. Corr. 1923–38, RG 72, NA.
Note: Direct hits based on a target equivalent to a cruiser deck, 400 feet long with a 60-foot beam.
*Made while the Putnam was zigzagging.

Gun cameras simulating antiaircraft guns were positioned at various strategic locations on *Putnam* to record the possible effectiveness of antiaircraft fire as a defensive measure against dive bombing. The first camera (all except one were affixed to Scarff ring mounts) was placed on the flying bridge, another was placed on the galley deck house, a third on the starboard side of the after deck house, a fourth on the port side of the after deck house, and the fifth and last camera was mounted directly on the 3-inch antiaircraft gun located on the fantail. Trained aircraft gunners from the Aircraft Squadrons, Scouting Fleet were selected to man the gun cameras located on the galley and after deck house. The others were manned by personnel from the ship's crew, who had no previous training in this type of work.[30]

One of the F6C-3s flown by the pilots of VF-5S during the bombing exercises conducted against a moving target in October 1927. Note the centerline-mounted bomb rack under the fuselage and the split axle landing gear. The latter was a type designed for carrier landings that distinguished the -3 model from its predecessors. *National Archives*

During the two days of simulated strafing attacks made by the pilots of VF-5S, the gun cameras took 7,139 exposures. Of these, only 61 were recorded as possible hits, giving an effective accuracy of 86 percent. Even this percentage was considered too high by the commanding officer of VF-5S. He believed that even less hits would be made during actual warfare, since gunners in a real battle would not know when and where to expect the direction of attack, would undoubtedly be distracted by fear, and would be subject to the impediments of recoil, smoke, gun jams, and the need to reload ammunition.[31]

The dynamics of the "diving attack" and the difficulties that ships faced in defending against this form of assault had already been documented by BuAer:

In clear weather and high visibility, it is customary for the plane making a diving attack to begin its approach at an altitude beyond effective range of AA gunfire and to approach in such a direction that the defending gunners must fire directly into the rays of the sun . . . or to approach on such courses

that the sighting angles of the defending guns are constantly changing . . .
turning directly to the target at the last moment . . . due to the extremely
rapid change of range (upwards of 300 feet per second) accurate plotting,
spotting and fuse setting for AA shell is extremely difficult if not impossible,
and AA gun fire is likely to be of doubtful effectiveness . . . machine gun fire
does not promise to be accurate at ranges considerably in excess of 2,000
feet. The total time that a diving plane is within 3,000 feet of the target
will be of the order of 10 seconds or less. Wanting definite evidence to the
contrary it would appear that in a concerted attack of several machines
approaching from different directions the chances of getting home are very
good indeed.[32]

The bombing scores obtained during the light-bombing exercises against a
moving target showed the high degree of accuracy that could be obtained
through the use of dive bombing with relatively little practice. Though zigzagging made it much more difficult to obtain hits, the number of bombs
that had hit the target area was more than sufficient to sink a light cruiser or
destroyer had they contained the explosive power of a real 500-lb. projectile.[33] This fact was not lost on Rear Adm. James J. Raby, commander, Aircraft
Squadrons, Scouting Fleet. When Dillon recommended the installation of
bomb racks suitable for carrying 25-, 50-, or 100-lb. bombs after the exercise,
Raby, who had only recently achieved flag rank, suggested making structural
changes on the existing planes that would enable them to carry the much
more effective 500-lb. weapon.[34]

CHAPTER 4

False Starts: The F8C Helldiver

ADMIRAL RABY'S DESIRE TO REINFORCE the structural strength of the aircraft assigned to the Scouting Fleet so they could handle a 500-lb. bomb was predicated on his knowledge of the Bureau of Aeronautics' plans to develop a new type of aircraft capable of delivering this weapon in a diving attack. The idea to produce this new type of airplane—called the light bomber—originated in January 1927, when it was introduced by Cdr. Eugene Wilson as one of the new, experimental designs that he proposed for development in the coming year.[1] Wilson, who had recently been promoted as head of BuAer's design section, had previously been in charge of the engine section, where he had overseen the development of the second generation of air-cooled radial engines.

He knew that Pratt and Whitney Aircraft Company, developers of the revolutionary Wasp engine, was about to bring out an even more powerful radial in the 500-hp range. The new engine promised to provide as much power as some of the biggest in-line engines then in service. Wilson proposed that the new engine, which Pratt and Whitney had named the Hornet, be mated to the Curtiss Falcon, a two-seat army fighter that the navy was considering for its own use. The new engine was lighter and more powerful than the conventional 12-cylinder, 400-hp, water-cooled Curtiss D-12 that powered the army's craft. Substituting Pratt and Whitney's Hornet for the D-12 would produce "a light bomber [design] capable of carrying 500 pounds of bombs at high speed in excess of 150 mph, with such other characteristics as would make the machine a good carrier Observation airplane and a fair two-seater Fighter after the bomb load was dropped."[2] This combination, according to Wilson, would produce a plane that could be used as two-seat fighter, a scout, and a light bomber.

With Moffett's approval, the design section drew up specifications for the new plane, which would be designated as the F8C-2. The design was nearly identical to the F8C-1, the navy's version of the Curtiss O-1B then used by the army. Instead of the in-line D-12, though, it would be powered by Pratt and Whitney's new engine. For light bombing the F8C-2 would be equipped with four wing-mounted A-3 bomb racks, each capable of handling a single 100-lb. fragmentation bomb.[3]

Although the official specification called for an ordnance load of four 100-lb. bombs, Lieutenant Commander Leighton believed that the Hornet would provide enough power to carry 915 pounds of bombs. At least this was the figure he presented to the General Board as part of the data provided to further his arguments for the VB type.[4] This was only slightly less than the actual bomb load of the three-purpose plane, an aircraft that took up more deck space and required twice the takeoff run for lift-off.

To Leighton, "the high performance, good maneuverability and fine machine gun battery" of the F8C-2 made it a formidable fighter once its bomb load was released. He characterized the plane as a two-seater that

> is fully capable of defending herself against attack by any single-seater, and except for a small handicap in climb and speed and for an inferior degree of maneuverability is the equal of any single-seater in pursuit attack with machine guns against heavy machines or ground positions. It is only slightly inferior in bomb carrying capacity to the T3M-1 [three-purpose] machine, which inferiority is more than offset by its superior protection, and probable superiority in hitting accuracy if employed in the diving form of bombing attack.[5]

The diving attack had previously been considered only in connection with light bombs of 100 pounds or less as it had been considered impractical to build aircraft with the performance characteristics needed to perform the diving attack while delivering enough high explosive to seriously damage a major warship. Leighton, whose knowledge of power plants will be recalled from the previous chapter, believed that advances in engine technology were about to change this premise. As we shall soon find out, Leighton's ideas were a bit premature.

The combined recommendations coming from both Leighton and Wilson could not be overlooked. When the Bureau of Aeronautics awarded a three-plane contract to the Curtiss Aeroplane and Motor Company on 30 June 1927 for two navalized versions of the army's Falcon (designated as F8C-1s) it contained a provision to provide one Hornet-powered version, which was designated as the F8C-2.[6] Although the F8C-2 was primarily a fighter, scouting and light bombing would be secondary missions accomplished in an overloaded condition.[7]

What transpired in the next few months is not clear, but a new specification for a lighter, faster version of the new plane appeared within BuAer in early December.[8] Instead of the 525-hp Hornet originally specified, the new plane would be equipped with 450-hp Wasps, which were now coming off the Pratt and Whitney production line at the rate of fifteen per month. Development problems with the Hornet may have caused doubts about its availability.[9] Alternatively, BuAer may have felt that a Wasp-powered Curtiss plane would provide a more useful trial horse for the XF2U-1, an experimental two-seat fighter also being developed for the navy by the Chance Vought Corporation. In any case, it was clear that BuAer wanted a different airplane than it had originally specified in May when it had issued a contract for the first F8C-2 design.

The Curtiss company responded with a promise to build an entirely new, two-place fighter powered by the smaller but readily available Wasp engine.[10] The company also agreed to absorb the added expense of redesigning the plane, which amounted to about half the actual production cost, with the understanding that the added expense could be recovered as part of any production order which might be placed by the navy in the event that the plane proved satisfactory. The question now arose as to whether Curtiss should design the new fighter along the lines of the specifications furnished Chance Vought for the XF2U-1, or to a new set of specifications for an entirely new plane which would sacrifice fuel capacity for better performance along with the ability to carry 500 pounds of bombs. The company wanted to make sure beyond a shadow of a doubt that their "ship" when finished, if satisfactory, would meet the current need of the Department. From the Navy's standpoint the production of a plane along the lines of the Chance Vought specification would fulfill its declared policy of purchasing airplanes for a single purpose from two different manufacturers, but would not add a radically new design to its inventory of aircraft.

These issues were discussed with the contractor on 16 December 1927 at BuAer's offices. The meeting was chaired by Capt. Emory S. Land.[11] Land, who was then assistant chief of the Bureau of Aeronautics, would later rise to fame as head of the U.S. Maritime Commission, becoming Roosevelt's World War II "Shipping Czar." Under Land's astute leadership the participants agreed that it would be best to proceed with the latest specification, which would then be reviewed by Curtiss and incorporated into an airplane of an entirely new design. The revised design was designated XF8C-2, using the letter prefix X, which the bureau had recently adopted to differentiate prototypes from production models. Plans for the new plane were quickly drawn up by Curtiss and submitted to the navy for approval in February 1928. The bureau then issued a change order authorizing Curtiss to install the Pratt and Whitney R-1340-B Wasp engine in place of the Hornet.

The XF8C-2, designated as company design number L-117-1, was constructed at the Curtiss plant in Garden City, New York. Although the plane's lines were based on the original Falcon, a number of features were incorporated from other aircraft, including the location of the main fuel tanks, which were built into the fuselage along each side of the front cockpit. Except for the tail surfaces, which were framed from aluminum, the craft was built from conventional materials, including welded steel tubing for the fuselage, wood-framed wings, and doped cloth, which was applied to the fuselage, wings, and tail surfaces. Armament consisted of two forward-firing .30-caliber machine guns mounted in the center section of the upper wing outboard of the propeller arc, two flexible guns on a Scarff ring mount in the upper cockpit, plus a centerline bomb rack. The power plant was the 450-hp Pratt and Whitney R-1340-B Wasp engine.[12]

Testing Prior to Acceptance

Before any new plane was accepted by the navy it had to pass a series of flight tests specified by BuAer as part of the procurement contract. The first of these was a preliminary test at the manufacturer's own facility to demonstrate

the craft's air worthiness and endurance. These first tests were usually conducted by a company pilot flying from an airstrip adjacent to, or close by, the
facility that had constructed the plane and were observed by a naval officer
assigned to the bureau as an inspector of naval aviation. The company's test
pilot would put the plane though various maneuvers and attitudes in order to
determine if it was structurally safe and aerodynamically sound. Once this
was proven, the company had to demonstrate the plane's stamina by successfully completing an endurance flight of one hour. Later on, the standard test
program was expanded to include stability tests and a second endurance flight
at altitude. After satisfying these requirements, the plane would be flown or
otherwise delivered to NAS, Anacostia for further testing. There, a company
pilot would be required to conduct another series of demonstration flights
designed to verify that the new plane had met all of the requirements specified in the government's procurement contract. When these were successfully completed, the navy would officially accept the plane and ownership
would be transferred to the government, assuming of course that it met the
various performance requirements specified in the contract. It was not uncom-
mon for an aircraft to be returned to the manufacturer after acceptance for
minor modifications, which were expected to further enhance the craft's performance.

Once the plane was officially in navy hands, it was turned over to the flight
test section at Anacostia for further testing to determine the full extent of the
plane's capabilities and its suitability for the various military missions for
which it was intended. When an aircraft was received by the flight test section it would be carefully inspected to make sure that there were no defects
and that it was ready for flight testing. It was then instrumented and loaded
with lead weights to simulate the various pieces of equipment, armament,
and ammunition that would normally be carried in a combat situation. This
was mandatory in order to test the plane's performance, stability, and suitability for military service.

By the early 1920s the suite of tests for carrier aircraft included evaluations
of the plane's handling and stability at various speeds and altitudes. Its rate of
climb, service ceiling, dive to terminal velocity (power off), and performance
in a spin were also tested, as was delivery of ordnance, which included the
firing of guns and the delivery of bombs. Cockpit suitability, including visibility for various functions and suitability of gun and bombsights, was also
tested and evaluated. Carrier landings were conducted too, though these

were done at Chambers Field in Norfolk, which had a simulated carrier deck laid out on its airstrip.[13]

Few of the forgoing tests had been officially established when the completed XF8C-2 was flown to the Naval Air Station at Anacostia in late November 1928 for acceptance testing as a carrier fighter. Since it was intended for use as bomber, BuAer requested that test flights be performed to determine the craft's maximum speed and climb characteristics while carrying a 500-lb. bomb.[14] Tests to determine its suitability as a diving bomber were also expected, though the bureau left the details up to Lieutenant Tomlinson, who now headed the flight test section. Tomlinson, who had succeeded Ostrander as the commanding officer of Bombing Two, had only recently been assigned to Anacostia as chief test pilot for the navy. A position awarded, no doubt, as a reward for his stellar performance while leading the Three Sea Hawks in the spectacular aerial maneuvers which were conducted at the National Air Races the summer of 1928. Tomlinson decided that the final test should be a terminal velocity dive. If the plane held together after that they "would give it a whirl" as a dive bomber.[15]

The manufacturer's demonstration took place on 3 December 1928 and was conducted, as Tomlinson later recalled, before the "crowned Heads of the Bureau of Aeronautics and other Navy Department Officials . . . Admirals, Captains and Commanders—enough gold braid to paper the Mint." Once the plane was in the air, the manufacturer's test pilot began to put it through a series of acrobatic tests that included slow rolls, square loops, inverted loops, and every combination thereof, interspersed with inverted flights, turns, and climbs.

Tomlinson marveled at the maneuverability of the new plane, which, in his highly qualified opinion, performed exceptionally well for a two-seater. Then, in accordance with the plan, the plane began to climb for the final test until it became but a dot high in the sky. "We were getting stiff necks from staring up at it," explained Tomlinson, when someone shouted, "Look! He's Starting his Dive!" Then

> the dot headed straight down. It was traveling at tremendous speed. From a tiny speck, high in the heavens, it grew in the twinkling of an eye into a silver bullet, racing earthward. Then we heard the roar of the motor. From the time the dive started until that roar became audible we estimated the plane had dropped at least four thousand feet.
>
> Terminal velocity! That point in the dive at which the head resistance

equals the combined weight and power of a plane. The roar continued but his speed so far as we could determine, remained about the same. Terminal velocity had been reached; his downward speed was somewhere between 350 and 400 miles an hour [not likely for a plane with fixed landing gear]!

Suddenly the thing we had all been dreading happened. No one spoke. First a flash of something bright and shining left the plane. Then, almost at once, we saw a bare fuselage, dragging behind it a tangled ass of wreckage, which had been the wings but a moment before. The roar of the motor changed to a sickening whine.

Hearts beating like trip-hammers and scarcely a man breathing, we stood transfixed, staring mutely upward. Somewhere in the wreckage which was hurtling earthward was a brave and skillful pilot. *Good god, would he never jump?*

Then a small object detached itself from the wreckage. From our position and at that distance we could not be sure whether it was the pilot, or merely some part of the plane floating down. A white streamer shot out from the object. It was the pilot! . . . For a sickening moment it strung out behind him, a mere strip of rag. Then the huge silk bag opened above him, like a white flower bursting into bloom.

Fortunately, the pilot had been able to get out of the plane without injury and made a safe landing by parachute. As for the cause of the failure, it appeared to the onlookers that the tail section had simply fallen apart due to some fault or weakness in the airframe.[16]

A few days after the crash, Capt. Ernest J. King, who succeeded Land as assistant bureau chief, chaired another conference at the Bureau of Aeronautics to discuss what design changes were necessary to correct the plane's defects. Representatives of the Curtiss company who were present agreed to replace the wrecked prototype with an improved version with a redesigned tail section based on new strength factors recommended by the bureau.[17] No other changes would be made in order to minimize engineering work and speed delivery, provided the navy issued a change order covering the necessary modifications.[18] The plane was to be a "dog ship" (meaning a test plane, from the then-popular euphemism "trying it on the dog") relative to a production version which was to function as a two-seat fighter and dive bomber. Curtiss promised to have the plane ready by May.

When the second prototype was delivered to Anacostia on 22 April 1929, the company had already began to refer to the plane as the "Helldiver," a name befitting its intended role as a dive bomber. During the next three weeks the XF8C-2 underwent a series of trials as a two-seat carrier fighter fully equipped with all of the extra gear (including emergency flotation gear, oxygen equipment, machine guns, ammunition, arresting gear and hoisting sling, etc.) deemed necessary for routine operations at sea. Unfortunately, the plane failed to meet the performance guarantees specified in the contract for top speed and rate of climb. Thus BuAer had no choice but to return the prototype to Curtiss as it tried to figure out what to do next.[19]

The idea of using the XF8C-2 to test the concept of a two-seat fighter that could be used for dive bombing was quickly forgotten in the rush to correct the plane's other defects before its source of funding ran out. The problem was serious enough to warrant Moffett's personal attention. Less than a week after the XF8C-2's failure, Moffett sanctioned a number of changes in the plane's design that were obviously intended to improve its performance during the required trials. Included in the list of modifications were recommendations to: (a) install one of the NACA type cowlings, (b) remove the axle hooks which were no longer needed in light of the decision to eliminate the fore and aft carrier landing wires, (c) remove the flotation bags, and (d) fair and clean up the airplane as much as possible.[20] These changes were accomplished as quickly as feasible, and the plane returned to Anacostia so that a new set of trials could be run before the fiscal year ended on 30 June 1928.

BuAer was under considerable pressure to secure a suitable design for a two-seat fighter that could be used as the basis for the production model that Moffett had promised to include in the procurement program for 1929. Chance Vought's entry in the competition, the F2U, was way behind schedule and could not possibly be delivered before the end of the fiscal year. The General Board and the secretary of the navy had both recommended that at least one squadron of two-seaters be deployed in order to evaluate the tactical potential of this type fighter, and the fleet wanted to take delivery of the planes as soon as possible.[21]

To expedite delivery of these desperately needed aircraft, Moffett approved the procurement of a production prototype that would be equipped with brakes, a tail wheel, and under-wing racks for 100-lb. bombs, and the other gear that would normally be needed for actual service. Eliminated from the new prototype, which the bureau was now calling the XF8C-4, was the centerline bomb rack, which had become superfluous now that the plane was considered unsuited for use as a dive bomber.[22]

These and other minor design changes delayed delivery of the first aircraft until April 1930. Curtiss eventually received orders for thirty-six production models, of which twenty-five were outfitted for carrier use. These went to the navy under the F8C-4 designation. The other nine were delivered to the Marine Corps as F8C-5s, though they were redesignated O2C-1s once in service.[23]

The navy planes were delivered to San Diego in August and were placed into operation with VF-1B aboard the *Saratoga,* which was soon equipped with a full complement of eighteen planes. After six months of service, however, it was clear that the aircraft's performance was marginal at best. In addition, the roomy gunner's cockpit provided an unexpected problem: the rear seaters found that they had trouble bracing themselves during the radical maneuvers for which the plane was designed. So many of the gunners became air sick that one-third of the aviation mechanics assigned to this duty had requested that they be taken off the flying roster.[24]

Although the pilots liked the plane, it could not keep up with its single-seat contemporaries.[25] Unfortunately for both Curtiss and the navy, the F8C-4 did not perform as well as the XF8C-2 on which it had been based, being deficient in rate of climb and speed.[26] This was largely due to the added weight of the extra military equipment carried during operations at sea and the additional fuel, which had been added to extend the plane's range. Reeves, who had been against the two-seater from the start, had not changed his opinion on the value of this type of aircraft.[27] The feisty admiral (who had been promoted in the fall of 1928) had taken over command of the Carrier Divisions after a two-year hiatus and was once again the senior aviator afloat. Although Reeves disliked the two-seater concept, his comments were tempered by the knowledge that his immediate superior, Vice Adm. Frank H. Schofield, still favored the development of this type.[28]

While production of the F8C-4 model was in process, Curtiss began to design an improved version that would have much higher speeds. To provide more power they installed the new Wright 9-cylinder R-1820 Cyclone engine rated at 575 hp. Although based on the same airframe as the previous Helldivers, the new model had more streamlining, a Curtiss-designed engine cowl to reduce drag, and sliding cockpit hoods that were carefully faired into the fuselage to cut down air resistance. To reduce drag even further, the wheels were covered with aluminum fairings known as "spats."

The navy ordered two prototypes for evaluation. The first, designated the XF8C-7, was intended for the personal use of the assistant secretary of the

The F8C-2 did not live up to expectations as a two-seat fighter and had a short service life. Wing-mounted bomb racks and an auxiliary fuel tank have been fitted to this aircraft, which bears markings signifying that it is the ninth plane in VF-1, as well as the squadron insignia that designates Fighting One as the "High Hat" squadron.
National Archives

navy for air. It was tested in October 1930 without any military equipment. The second plane, designated the XF8C-8, was tested in December. It was fully equipped for service but lacked the "spats" installed on the first prototype.

Acquired on an expedited basis, both were equipped with radios and flown to San Diego in late January 1931 so that they could participate in Fleet Problem XII as command planes. Few carrier planes were equipped with radios at the time, and it was hoped that these "Command Helldivers" would provide a useful means of coordinating fighter tactics. Although they proved suitable for radio liaison and command, the planes did not possess the flying qualities needed for carrier use. The extra weight carried by these planes necessitated such a long takeoff run that they were totally useless as scouts, which had to be spotted ahead of all other airplanes on the flight deck so that they could be launched first. Other shortcomings included a low rate of climb, poor visibility for the pilot, and unfavorable landing characteristics.[29]

As two-seat navy fighters, the Curtiss Helldivers had short lives. By the end of 1931 all had been withdrawn from first-line service or reassigned for observation duty. Though unsuccessful in the navy, they made a name for themselves as dive bombers serving with the marines, who found the wing-mounted 100-lb. bombs quite satisfactory for their ground-support needs.

In 1932, Maj. Ross E. Rowell established a special dive-bombing unit as part of his command in Marine Air Group One, then located in Quantico, Virginia. The squadron was composed of O2C-1 Helldivers, which had originally been ordered under the F8C-5 designation.[30] In September, Rowell took this squadron to Montreal, Canada, where they put on an air show that ended with a thrilling dive-bombing exhibition conducted in front of the grandstands. The Canadian show was followed by a similar exhibition of flying skills at the National Air Races in Cleveland, Ohio. In the following year Rowell's squadron performed additional shows at Chicago, New York, and Miami. These displays added further mystique to the Helldiver, which had already staged a prominent appearance in the Metro-Goldwyn-Mayer movie of the same name released in 1931. Written by the legendary naval aviator "Spig" Wead, the picture was filmed with the cooperation of the navy using planes from VF-1B and VF-2B photographed at North Field and on board the *Saratoga*.[31]

As discussed in Chapter 2, Rowell had first begun to experiment with this method of attack in the mid-1920s while he commanded Marine Observation Squadron One (VO-1M) in San Diego. When VO-1M received orders to proceed to Nicaragua in February 1927, they were still flying the remodeled DH-4Bs that the marines had purchased from the army in 1922.[32] The planes were armed with a single fuselage-mounted Browning machine gun with A-3 bomb racks affixed to the wings. VO-1M loaded their planes, along with all their fuel, ammunition, and equipment, on two navy transports and were ready to sail within forty-eight hours. The wings of the DH-4Bs were detached, though the planes were shipped otherwise intact. Disembarking at the port city of Corinto, they proceeded to Managua by narrow-gauge railroad, where the planes were unloaded and then dragged through the streets of the city to the baseball park on the outskirts of town which was to serve as the squadron's airfield.

From February to May the seven DH-4Bs under Rowell's leadership flew daily patrols to provide aerial reconnaissance and intelligence information for the occupation forces. This was done by visual observation, supplemented by aerial photography. Although Rowell was ordered to avoid involving the squadron in any action, elements of his unit were forced to return fire on two occasions, though it did not do any bombing until 17 July 1928, when a contingent of thirty-seven marines came under attack. The marines, then garrisoned with a contingent of the Nicaraguan National Guard at the remote town of Ocotal, 125 miles from Managua, were surrounded by insurgents. The marines' plight was discovered at about 1000 by the morning air patrol. Rowell got the bad news when the patrol returned at noon. He immediately reported the situation to the commanding general of the Marine Expeditionary Force in Nicaragua, who directed Major Rowell to take whatever action was deemed necessary to aid the besieged marines.

All of his pilots had been trained in the diving attack, and Rowell had given orders for the five DHs available to be armed, fueled, and ready for takeoff. Returning to the airfield, he immediately ordered the squadron into the air equipped with full magazines for both fixed and flexible guns. Rowell did not dare load all the bomb racks, since the DH-4Bs needed to take off with a full load of fuel too, if they were to make it to Ocotal. The airstrip was only about 400 yards long and the heavily loaded planes made it off the runway with little room to spare. Arriving over the besieged garrison, Rowell made a quick circuit over the town to reconnoiter the situation. A weather front full of lightning, wind, and rain was approaching rapidly from the east, which, along with fuel limitations of the DH-4Bs, dictated immediate action. A light rain was falling as Major Rowell formed the squadron into a column at 1,500 feet and then led the diving attack with machine-gun fire and 17-lb. fragmentation bombs. The insurgents, who had never been subject to this form of aerial attack, failed to take cover and were cut to pieces. The diving attack was a highly effective tactic that never failed to disperse the enemy during the numerous engagements which followed over the next two years.

Rowell's action is generally acknowledged to be the first dive-bombing attack on a hostile force, though it should be remembered that the tactics employed involved a swallow dive, which was quite different from the near-vertical dives then being perfected by the navy. Nevertheless it earned Rowell the first Distinguished Flying Cross ever awarded to a marine pilot for action against an armed enemy.[33]

Rowell's attack followed close on the heals of another startling demonstration of the offensive potential of aircraft—a surprise air raid on Pearl Harbor conducted by planes launched from the aircraft carrier *Langley*.

CHAPTER 5

First Carrier Strikes

Dуring the winter of 1927–28, Rear Adm. Reeves, who had been in command of the aircraft squadrons of the Battle Fleet since October 1925, made sure that the *Langley* was kept busy training the pilots and flight-deck crew that would be needed to fill out the complements of the *Lexington* and *Saratoga,* which were scheduled to join the fleet in the spring. The new ships had originally been laid down as high-speed battle cruisers but had been converted to aircraft carriers under the treaty agreement worked out during the Washington Conference of 1922. Their size—888 feet overall on a standard displacement of 33,000 tons—would make them the largest vessels then in the fleet. Unlike the *Langley,* whose paltry speed of 14 knots relegated her to a trailing position, the new carriers would also be among the fastest ships in the fleet. What's more, their combined air complement—each was scheduled to handle seventy-two aircraft—would be more than quadruple the number of combat planes in the Battle Fleet. Whoever commanded these ships in the coming months would enjoy the chance of a lifetime.

Reeves knew that his three-year tour of duty as commander of Aircraft Squadrons, Battle Fleet was scheduled to come to an end that summer, but he did not want to pass up this unique opportunity. In mid-February he

Left to Right: Then Captain Reeves, an unidentified officer, and Rear Admiral Moffett observing flight operations on board the *Langley*, c. 1927. *Naval Historical Center*

wrote Moffett to solicit the bureau chief's support for an extended tour of duty.[1] Reeves wanted to remain in command for another year to work on the problem of how best "to handle and operate several carriers in fleet operations." Moffett wrote back, stating that Reeves was the "one to carry on this important work."[2] Moffett believed that Reeves could "make more progress and accomplish more than anyone else" and promised to take the matter up with Adm. Charles F. Hughes, the incumbent CNO, and Rear Adm. Richard H. (Reddy) Leigh, chief of the Bureau of Navigation, which handled all matters regarding personnel.

As spring approached, the *Langley* began preparations for Fleet Problem

VIII. Instead of the twelve planes "officially" authorized, Reeves, to the horror of the senior flyers on board, insisted that the ship embark thirty-six aircraft.[3] While the *Langley* had ample hangar space and quarters to accommodate these planes and their crews, the restricted size of her deck limited the number of planes that could be spotted on the flight deck at one time. None of the officers on board believed that this could be done, but Reeves, taking personal charge of the flight deck, began to direct the placement planes for takeoff.[4] One by one he moved them closer and closer together until all were aligned on deck and ready for launching, a procedure which all aboard, save Reeves, unanimously agreed would be an extremely dangerous undertaking!

In mid-April, *Langley* sortied from San Francisco with the rest of the Battle Fleet for the waters off Hawaii, where the fleet would stage the maneuvers that constituted Fleet Problem VIII. The objective of the exercise was to seize Honolulu, which was being defended by the Scouting Force beefed up with air units based in the Hawaiian Islands. The *Langley*'s singular mission during this exercise was to provide airborne scouts in advance of the main force. To accomplish this task she was ordered to take station 6,000 yards astern the battleships, an order which irked Rear Adm. Reeves to no end, since it required the *Langley* to leave her station and head into the wind every time she wanted to launch or recover aircraft, which made it almost impossible to keep up with the fleet.[5]

Flying operations were conducted each morning and afternoon during the cruise across the Pacific to Hawaii. The planes would take off, conduct their scouting mission, and return for landing. As each plane dropped down onto the deck, it would be caught by the arresting gear and brought to a sudden stop with a jolting jerk. Squads of deck handlers would swarm out of the protective nettings surrounding the flight deck to free the tail hook from the arresting wire, then quickly push the aircraft forward to clear the deck for the next plane coming in to land.[6] Reeves was always pressing for more and more speed. Though quick to condemn a miscue, he was also willing to praise a smart action. Reeves practiced the old gunnery axiom that safety precautions were written in blood; there would be accidents, even deaths, but that was the price the aviators would pay to advance the state of the art.

By 29 April the *Langley* had reached the island of Oahu. As she steamed toward Pearl Harbor, she was greeted by a gaggle of army pursuit planes that suddenly dived on the six planes from VF-1B that were patrolling above the

An F2B-1 aboard the *Langley* showing the extra arresting gear in use at the beginning of 1928. In addition to the traditional tail hook, carrier planes of the day had a series of anchor-shaped hooks attached to the undercarriage axle, which engaged a series of fore and aft wires that kept the aircraft from a series of "grasshopper" jumps when the tail hook caught one of the arresting wires. This arrangement was no longer required after oleo struts and steel wires replaced the bungee cords used previously. *Naval Historical Center*

ship. On previous cruises to Hawaii the navy had been cursed with planes that were decidedly inferior to those flown by the army flyers stationed at Wheeler Field. Now, as the other pilots on *Langley*'s flight deck watched with glee, the radial-engined F2Bs of Fighting One easily outmaneuvered the army planes.[7] Among those watching the show was Lt. Cdr. Daniel Tomlinson, the commanding officer of VF-6B. He had just landed aboard after a four-hour patrol flight and was furious at having to stand by while VF-1B tangled with the army flyers.

When the *Langley* docked later that afternoon, Reeves ordered all planes ashore, as was standard procedure when the carrier was in port. Air operations resumed on Monday morning, with Tomlinson chasing his pilots into the air with orders "to run every army pursuit plane to the ground," though army observation planes and bombers were not to be molested. As his squadron approached Wheeler Field, Tomlinson saw three army PW9s flying a Lufbery circle, a defensive maneuver in which the planes flew a ring-shaped pattern, each covering the tail of the other. The army planes began to climb for altitude as soon they saw the navy planes, which immediately began to climb too. The navy planes were much faster than the army craft, enabling Tomlinson to outclimb the PW9s, thus gaining the height advantage which allowed him the luxury of diving on the helpless army planes. "It was one grand picnic," exclaimed Tomlinson. "The PWs squirmed and twisted." Every time the army boys looked back there was a Pratt and Whitney–powered navy plane all set to chew off his tail.[8]

During the remainder of their stay in Hawaii, the *Langley* participated in a number of drills and training exercises that were conducted to test the ability of the army and the navy to defend the islands from hostile attack. During one of these occasions, Reeves was asked to attack Pearl Harbor with his carrier planes in order to provide the army with an opportunity to practice air defense. To fulfill this request *Langley* sortied from Pearl Harbor with other elements of the fleet late on the evening of 16 May. By 0305 she was steaming toward Oahu at 10 knots and could see the searchlights of Diamond Head. At 0437 she turned into the wind, rang up full speed, and began launching a deckload of planes. In seven minutes thirty-five planes had taken off and were on their way to Pearl Harbor. Arriving over Honolulu at daybreak, they attacked Wheeler Field and the other army installations in simulated attacks, using the strafing and light-bombing maneuvers they had been practicing for months. Though the army had been forewarned, the navy pilots caught their army contemporaries "flat on their backs in bed," just as their successors were destined to be caught some thirteen years later. *Langley* did not go unscathed, however. At 0551 she was sighted by three torpedo planes that conducted a mock torpedo attack on the vulnerable carrier.[9]

Lexington, the first of the big carriers to reach the West Coast, arrived while the *Langley* was still engaged in the exercises around Hawaii. Instead of allowing her to leisurely await the fleet's return, Reeves ordered the new ship to make a high-speed run from San Francisco to Oahu, making the 2,225-mile passage in a record-setting time of 72.6 hours at an average speed of 30.6 knots. While *Lexington* was in Pearl Harbor, Reeves shifted his flag and the *Langley*'s planes to the new carrier so that he could use the big flight deck to test large-scale, high-tempo flight operations on the return voyage. These were conducted on a regular basis and consistently included simulated dive-bombing attacks which allowed both the pilots and the antiaircraft gun crews to gain practical experience in this new form of combat at sea.

After executing several attacks, it became evident that the concentrated

The *Langley* at Pearl Harbor on 28 May 1928, showing thirty-four planes spotted on her deck, ready for takeoff. *Naval Historical Center*

fire of the ship's antiaircraft battery could be nullified if the diving planes approached from several directions at once.[10] If the squadron split up and dived on the carrier simultaneously from at least three different angles, the antiaircraft batteries would be unable to concentrate on any one section of planes. The dive-bombing tactics which they devised to achieve this goal began with a high altitude in a V of echelon. As the formation passed over the carrier the squadron leader would roll over and pull back on the stick, executing the beginning of a split S turn that would wind up as a dive aimed at the forward flight deck of the carrier below. Each of the other two section leaders in the formation would immediately lead their groups into opposing (left and right) crossover turns. The leader of each of these six-plane sections waited for the squadron leader to reach the halfway point in his dive before executing a split S of their own, followed by the other planes in their section, all diving together on the carrier with the right-flank planes aiming at the elevator in the center of the flight deck and the left-flank planes aiming at the arresting gear on the stern. This maneuver resulted in three groups of planes attacking the carrier in rapid succession from dead ahead and from each beam.

Like other navies throughout the world at this time, the U.S. Navy viewed the "decisive action" of the next war in terms of what had happened at the Battle of Jutland in the First World War. It continued to focus on the gunnery duel that was expected to be the determining factor in the outcome of the great battle that would ensue when two opposing fleets met on the high seas. Many of the fleet exercises, board games, and tactical studies conducted during the 1920s were designed to evaluate various aspects of this engagement. In most scenarios, the gunnery duel would be preceded by a destroyer torpedo attack initiated in an attempt to damage at least some of the opposing battleships. The destroyers did not have to sink any of the dreadnoughts to be successful. Their job was to slow down the enemy's battle line. One or more torpedo hits on a major warship in the vicinity of a boiler or engine room would cause enough damage to impair the ship's ability to steam at maximum speed. If this occurred, the undamaged battleships in the battle line would have to slow down or risk leaving the wounded vessel behind. Not only would this reduce the firepower of the capital ships forming the main battle force, but it would place the unprotected straggler in a dangerous position, for it could easily be picked off by marauding destroyers or submarines. The only other alternative was to reduce the speed of the entire line, which would give the opposing force a decided tactical advantage.

The success of the dive-bombing exercise conducted against a moving target in the fall of 1927 opened the door for light bombing to be used as a means of countering the dreaded destroyer attack that was expected to precede the main engagement. The importance of this mission—the first offensive use of aircraft in support of the battle line—did not go unnoticed by the high command. The Bureau of Aeronautics was then in the process of developing both single- and two-seat fighters for the light-bombing role, and there was a great deal of interest in determining how to make the best tactical use of these aircraft.[11] Accordingly, it was decided that two of the fighting squadrons assigned to the *Lexington* and the *Saratoga* be redesignated as light-bombing squadrons at the beginning of the new fiscal year. Thus on 1 July 1928, Fighting Squadron Six (VF-6B) was officially renamed Bombing Squadron One (VB-1B) and Fighting Five (VF-5B) became Bombing Two (VB-2B). The primary mission of the new units—the light-bombing VBs—was to develop dive bombing as a method for attacking the light surface forces which were expected to engage the Battle Fleet at the start of any major fleet action before they come within torpedo range. After dropping their bombs on the enemy destroyers, the light bombers would be free to go after whatever enemy aircraft were in the air.

The changeover coincided with the start of the summer concentration period which Reeves had instituted as a means of training the new batch of pilots that arrived at the beginning of each year while continuing to develop the aerial tactics that would be used when the squadrons rejoined their ships in the fall. Although service in the squadrons constituted sea duty, the planes themselves were based on shore at NAS, San Diego. It was customary to rotate personnel just before the start of the concentration so that half of the squadron leaders were usually new, a fact that dictated a fresh start on fundamental tactics each year.[12]

In August, the aircraft squadrons began to train for the gunnery exercises that would be conducted in the autumn. For the VBs this included extensive practice in bombing and gunnery to prepare them for the individual battle practice and squadron advanced battle practice that the squadron was to "fire" for the record.[13] In the fall these activities were interspersed with weekly tactical exercises and participation in the monthly maneuvers conducted by the fleet.

In November 1928, Bombing Squadron Two participated in a fleet exercise set up to test the offensive and defensive capabilities of aircraft during the destroyer attack phase of the main engagement. The drill was designed to provide the fleet with experience in repelling a coordinated attack by enemy destroyers and torpedo planes. For pilots in the torpedo planes playing the role of the enemy it would provide practice in coordinating their torpedo attacks with those of the destroyers.[14]

The two heavy-bombing squadrons that were involved in the exercise, VT-1B and VT-2B, were then flying a mixture of T3M-2s and T4M-1s. These heavy planes were the only aircraft in the fleet capable of lifting the 1,650-lb. Mark VII torpedo, which carried a 400-lb. warhead—enough explosive to damage even the most heavily armored warship. In a general naval engagement, the singular mission of the VTs was to attack the heavy ships of the battle line whenever an opportunity presented itself.[15]

The tactical doctrine for conducting such an attack had been worked out a year earlier during the 1927 concentration period.[16] It would be coordinated with the destroyers and launched from the enemy's disengaged side so that the intended victims would be caught in a cross fire. The planes were to approach the target in line abreast and on a steady course at low altitude in order to release their weapons from the dropping height of 10 to 25 feet recommended for the Mark VII torpedo. A smokescreen was to be laid "in all possible cases," during the approach and retreat phase of the attack to protect the planes from the withering antiaircraft barrage that was expected be thrown up by the secondary batteries of the enemy ships.

For the November exercise the Battle Fleet was divided into two opposing forces: the Green Force, made up of the various battleship divisions plus the *Langley*, operating one squadron from VF-2B and five scouts from VS-1B, and the White Force, consisting of the Destroyer Squadrons, Battle Fleet, along with four squadrons of shore-based attack aircraft flying from North Field. In the plan of action submitted before the simulated battle began, Fighting Two was assigned the unenviable task of trying to defend their own forces from the enemy's air attack while simultaneously trying to bomb the enemy destroyers before they could come within torpedo range of the battle wagon. At 0855, the first division of VF-2B, which had been circling over the *Langley*, launched a simulated light dive-bombing attack against a squadron of White destroyers which were preparing to launch a torpedo attack. After attacking the destroyers in the division, it broke into several sections and engaged the enemy smoke layers, torpedo planes, and light bombers, but were hopelessly overwhelmed by the White Force, which numbered seventy-four attackers.

Neither the *Lexington* nor the *Saratoga* participated in the engagement. Fleet Problem IX would be the first exercise in which the new carriers played an active role. As in previous problems, the fleet would be divided into two opposing forces. The Black Force, commanded by Adm. William V. Pratt, would consist of the Pacific-based Battle Fleet with *Saratoga* and *Langley* for air support. Their task was to attack the Panama Canal. The Blue Force, commanded by Vice Adm. Montgomery Taylor, would try to defend it. It would be composed primarily of the vessels assigned to the Scouting Fleet, then based in the Atlantic, plus *Lexington*'s air group, which would be reinforced by land based aircraft stationed in the Canal Zone.[17]

Previously, these exercises had stressed the importance of the battle line and its bombardment of the Panama Canal. The battleships would maneuver in range of the canal, fire a few blank charges to simulate a long-range attack, and then proceed to the fleet anchorage in the Bay of Panama, where "all hands would go ashore for a big bust at the Union Club."[18] Though a simulated bombing attack had been conducted on the canal two years earlier, it involved few planes and was not representative of the airborne striking power available now that the *Lexington* and *Saratoga* had joined the fleet.

When the orders for the exercise were first published, they made no mention of the carriers. According to Eugene Wilson, Reeves's chief of staff at the time, the ComAirBatFlt immediately sent a message to Adm. William V. Pratt urgently requesting a conference.[19] The next morning the bearded admiral and his staff took off for San Pedro, home base of the Battle Fleet. Arriving at San Pedro, they made their way to Pratt's flagship, the battleship *California*. Once on board they were shown into his cabin and seated at the usual billiard-cloth table provided for important conferences. Reeves convinced the commander-in-chief to allow him to conduct a coordinated air attack on the installations at both ends of the Panama Canal. To ensure the element of surprise, the *Langley* would approach the canal from a position outside the normal range of her aircraft, which would be launched on a one-way journey. After bombing installations on the Atlantic side of the canal, the pilots would be instructed to land at a nearby airfield and burn their planes (simulated) before surrendering. While the planes from *Langley* were attacking the northern end of the canal, *Saratoga* would attack the Miraflores Locks on the Pacific side in coordination with the bombardment scheduled by Pratt's battleships.

When Admiral Pratt suggested that it would be wise to assign a squadron of battleships to escort the carriers within striking range of the canal, Reeves came up with an alternate proposal. To avoid being discovered by the defending air forces he recommended that *Saratoga* be detached from the main force. After a detour to the southwest he would head for the canal, making a high-speed run-in to the launching point. To placate Pratt's concerns about the danger of being caught by Blue's surface forces, Reeves suggested that a rendezvous be set up at the launching point with one of the battleship divisions.[20] Pratt wasn't all that enthusiastic, but he slowly warmed to the plan. It was too late to change the orders already issued, but he liked the idea of a surprise attack. It would be better, he explained, if they kept the plan a secret until after the fleet had sortied. Once under way he would issue new orders so that Reeves could execute his plan.

As the Black striking force proceeded southward toward Panama on the morning of 22 January 1929, *Saratoga* turned toward the southwest, headed in the direction of the Galapagos Islands. She was accompanied by the light cruiser *Omaha*, the only ship in Pratt's force that had the speed and endurance to keep up with the big carrier. The light cruiser was the flagship for Rear Adm. Thomas J. Senn, commander, Destroyer Squadrons, Battle Fleet, who remained aboard with his staff. Though Senn was senior to Reeves, he turned tactical command of the *Omaha* over to the ComAirBatFlt and was content to travel aboard as an "interested and enthusiastic observer" while his ship served as *Saratoga*'s plane guard.[21]

The two ships continued to steam south for the next three days, making sure that they were well beyond the prying eyes of any Blue scouts. The morning of 25 January they turned toward Panama and began the high-speed run-in that would place the ship 140 miles from the canal at dawn the next morning. Squally weather restricted air operations until the late afternoon, when a three-plane section of scouts was launched as a precautionary patrol. As the fighters raced off, Admiral Reeves stood alongside his operations officer, Frank Wagner, on *Saratoga*'s bridge wing and watched them vanish into the distance. At 1605 one of the planes suddenly reappeared and dropped a message on the flight deck advising the presence of an enemy destroyer (the *Breck*) ahead.

Most carrier planes were not equipped with radios at this time because of the extra weight and complexity involved. Thus the only way the pilots could communicate with the ship was to drop handwritten notes enclosed in a protective container. Wilson claims that short lengths of garden hose were used for this purpose.

When the *Breck* appeared on the starboard bow seven minutes later, *Saratoga* opened fire (simulated) with her 8-inch guns at 20,000 yards, theatrically disabling the "enemy" destroyer. Though Wilson states otherwise, *Breck* was able to get off a radio message reporting the carrier's presence and relaying her course and speed to the rest of the Blue Force. This information was picked up by the light cruiser *Detroit*, commanded by Capt. R. Drace White. White, an old friend of Admiral Reeves, stood in at high speed, finding the big carrier just before dusk. The *Detroit* was promptly engaged by the *Omaha*, and both cruisers were ruled "out of action" by the local umpire, Cdr. Ken Whiting. Nevertheless, the Blue cruiser continued to shadow the *Saratoga* throughout the night, providing a play-by-play account of the big carrier's moves. *Omaha* had been forced to slow down to conserve fuel and, according to Wilson, her place was promptly taken by the *Detroit*. This explanation seems highly probable in light of the need to have a suitable vessel present during the morning's launch to serve as a plane guard. Though the *Detroit* was part of the Blue Force, Reeves would have been hard pressed to explain the loss of a pilot had such a vessel not been available. This was not wartime, and the brass higher up would have frowned upon unnecessary breeches of safety.[22]

The *Saratoga*'s troublesome problems were minor annoyances compared to those encountered by her sister ship *Lexington*. She was ordered to attack the Black striking force which had been detected approaching the Canal Zone. *Lexington* was preparing to launch her planes when the intermittent rain squalls through which she was passing suddenly parted, revealing the presence of Black battleships on the far horizon. The enemy battle wagons immediately opened fire at the extreme range of 30,000 yards and continued to pummel the *Lexington* for twenty minutes, closing to within 16,500 yards until the carrier was obscured by another squall. *Lexington* continued to launch her planes, which promptly began to bomb the enemy warships in an effort to protect the carrier previewing the action that would take place during the Battle of Samar some fifteen years hence. Under actual conditions the *Lexington* would have been sunk and her planes stranded as they did not have the range needed to reach the nearest landing field, which was 300 miles away. Although it was clear that the *Lexington* would not have survived, the umpires allowed her to remain in the games though her speed was reduced to 18 knots.

While the rain squall provided protective cover for the carrier, it made landing conditions extremely difficult for the pilots, who could barely make out the flight deck. Nevertheless, the recovery went ahead without incident and was accomplished so well that her pilots and flight-deck personnel were later commended for the manner in which they brought all the squadrons aboard without loosing a single aircraft.

With the fall of darkness, *Saratoga* began a 30-knot dash toward the Miraflores Locks. By dawn the big carrier was 140 miles from the Panama Canal. At 0458 *Saratoga* began launching a full deckload of aircraft for the initial attack against the Miraflores Locks. She was now carrying more than one hundred aircraft, her air complement having been increased by the addition of the three squadrons from the *Langley*.

The first wave of seventy planes consisted of one eighteen-plane squadron of F3B light bombers from VB-2B plus their O2U-2 liaison, two fighter squadrons for aerial protection consisting of fourteen F2Bs from VF-1B and eighteen F3Bs from VF-2B, plus the seventeen T4M heavy bombers of VT-2B accompanied to their three liaison planes. With the flight deck clear, a second

The first wave of F3B-1 fighters and T4M-1 torpedo bombers taking off from the *Saratoga* to attack the Panama Canal during Fleet Problem IX. Note the difference in the size of the two aircraft. *Naval Historical Center*

wave of thirteen O2Us from VS-1B and VS-2B were spotted for launching which commenced at 0656. By then the planes from VB-2B had arrived over the Panama Canal, where they conducted a simulated dive-bombing attack on the Miraflores Locks. They then proceeded to attack Fort Clayton and Albrook Field with machine-gun fire.

While the attack was in progress, a section of the squadron's planes were assaulted by six army pursuit planes which had been patrolling at high altitude. A dogfight broke out which was intensified by the arrival of three additional army craft. Though casualties would have been experienced on both sides in a real fight, the army planes were soundly defeated by navy's fighters, whose air-cooled engines provided superior performance over the army types, which still relied on the much heavier, liquid-cooled D-12 engines. The navy planes broke off the engagement at 0700 and set a course back to their carrier.

The second attack on the locks occurred at 0805 when VT-2, accompanied by the escorting fighters of VF-1 and VF-2, conducted a high-altitude attack on the Miraflores and Pedro Miguel Locks from an altitude of 11,000 feet.

Planes from Scouting Squadrons One and Two added to the destruction when they too bombed the Miraflores Locks at 0950.

Between launchings, the *Saratoga* ran into a division of Blue battleships. Her planned rendezvous with her escort of Battleship Division Five did not taken place due to an error by the division's navigator, who underestimated the strong current off Cape Mala, thereby delaying the timely linkup.[23] Operating without a screen, the big carrier came under heavy fire from the three Blue dreadnoughts. Under real conditions she too would have been sunk. Her loss would have represented a serious setback too, as she carried 30 percent of all the navy's planes afloat and 60 percent of all officer pilots trained for carrier operations.[24]

Though officially disabled, *Detroit* trailed the *Saratoga* all night, reporting her position to the *Lexington,* which was ordered to find and attack the enemy flattop. She began launching aircraft at 0604. First off were the planes of Fighting Squadron Three. Attacking from 10,000 feet, they dove toward the enemy carrier, strafing her flight deck with simulated machine-gun fire. The *Saratoga,* which had eighty-eight planes in the air at the time, had not retained any fighters for self protection and her flight deck was clear of aircraft. An hour later she was assaulted a second time by Torpedo Squadron One, which conducted a horizontal bombing attack after being intercepted by a section of fighters returning to the *Saratoga.* After completing their bomb runs, VT-1B returned to the *Lexington,* where they were refueled, rearmed, and launched again to conduct a second bombing attack.

While this action was furiously taking place between the carriers and battleships of both forces, the *Aroostook,* a First World War minelayer that had been converted into a seaplane carrier, advanced undetected toward the coast of Panama. She was substituting for the *Langley,* which had suffered a mechanical breakdown before the fleet had sortied from the West Coast. With *Langley* indisposed, *Aroostook*'s single amphibian would have to impersonate the twenty-four plane *Langley* attack group. The plane took off at 0600 so that she would arrive over the northern part of the canal just as the planes from *Saratoga* were attacking at the other end of the canal. Taking the defending forces completely by surprise, *Aroostook*'s single plane conducted simulated bombing attacks on the Gatun Locks and spillway, the naval air station, and the army installations on the Atlantic side of the canal. After completing his mission the pilot landed as ordered and surrendered, to the surprise of the army defenders. Regrettably, the navy failed to inform the army that this one plane represented a whole squadron of attackers, mitigating the immediate impact of this otherwise spectacular mission.[25]

After the exercise was completed a critique of the problem was conducted at the motion picture theater annex attached to the Officers' Club in Balboa, the only facility large enough to accommodate the seven hundred officers in attendance. The attack staged by *Saratoga*'s air group proved to be the high point of the discussion. Every phase of the air operation had gone off like clockwork and was, in the words of the commander-in-chief, "an epic in the history of aviation." The rapid launching of planes, their ability to establish a rendezvous in the dark, and the efficiency and precision with which they carried out their assigned missions were especially praiseworthy. The eighty-three planes launched by the *Saratoga* were a "vast mobile force" that spoke "eloquently of the advanced state of the development of aviation as an integral part of the Fleet."[26]

As the airmen basked in the glamour and enthusiastic fervor which followed the success of the air operations, which were conducted on a scale and intensity greater than in any previous series of maneuvers, they were reminded "of the inherent limitations and weaknesses in the [navy's] Air Arm!" The surface navy, or the "Black Shoes," as they were euphemistically called by their "Brown Shoe" counterparts in the air force (uniform regulations dictated the shoe color which differentiated the two groups), were still not convinced of the superiority of aircraft. For one thing, the ordnance load carried by all planes during the operation had been theoretical and did not represent the actual capabilities of the light aircraft then in service. As for the heavy bombers, horizontal bombing was notoriously inaccurate and presented the defenders with a relatively easy target since the attackers had to fly straight and level during the bomb run. Neither the dropping altitude nor the maximum speed of the heavy bombers presented much of a problem for the anti-aircraft crews, providing a false sense of security to the battleship men.

The problem of quickly rearming planes with bombs and torpedoes as they stood on the crowded flight deck was one of many difficulties which had yet to be surmounted. Another unsolved problem was the long takeoff run needed by the torpedo bombers: the T4Ms were the first of their kind to be used extensively and were proving troublesome to handle. They needed so much deck space that they had to be spotted just ahead of the arresting gear, making it difficult, if not impossible, to structure any kind of coordinated attack with light bombers and fighters.[27]

A much bigger problem for the airmen was the extreme vulnerability of the carrier with her unarmored flight deck, a problem exacerbated by the limited number of carriers then available which necessitated a dangerous concentration of aviation resources afloat. It was essential to ensure the security of such a vessel, since the fighting fleet could ill afford to lose the high percentage of aircraft and crews assembled in such a large carrier.

Though Reeves's recommendation to provide a mobile screening force of escorting cruisers and destroyers was a sensible solution that would later become doctrine, the fear of surprise surface attack would affect the development of carrier tactics for years to come. Eleven years later, one of the leading aviators in the fleet, Capt. Marc Mitscher, still believed that it was essential for the big carriers to retain their main battery of eight 8-inch guns for self-protection in the event they were surprised by surface forces at night or in low visibility.[28]

The results of Fleet Problem IX proved beyond doubt the important role of aviation in the fleet. In spite of the adverse criticism of certain phases of their operations (mainly maneuvering and navigation) the commander-in-chief stated that the operation of both carriers during the problem demonstrated "careful training, thoughtful preparation and skill in the formation and execution of plans."[29] It was imperative that new aircraft be developed to further the mission of the fleet in war. Control of the air was still the primary mission of the airplane and fighters were considered to be the most important type of craft followed by the VO or observation plane. Though cruiser-based float planes had made important contributions to the fleet, the need to stop and pick them up was a tremendous detriment. Instead, they should be based on small carriers, which most high-ranking officers felt were separately needed additions to the fleet. Both the VBs and VSs were essential additions to the carrier complements. The light bomber was held to be of particular importance because of the extremely difficult antiaircraft problem it presented to the enemy.

While the results of the after-action critique reaffirmed the place of aviation in the U.S. Fleet, the battleship continued to dominate naval thinking. As Admiral Taylor stated in his report to the CNO, all studies of the actions conducted during Fleet Problem IX continued "to point to the battleship as the final arbiter of Naval destiny."[30]

The only carrier planes then capable of damaging a surface warship were torpedo bombers. Yet these planes lacked the speed, range, and punch to do

much more than assist the destroyers, which were expected to conduct torpedo attacks on the enemy battle line just before the main engagement.
Lacking a truly offensive weapon, the aircraft carrier was still seen as an auxiliary which could provide and protect aerial scouts and spotters needed by
the Battle Fleet. What was needed to enhance aviation's value to the fleet was
a new type of plane—one suited to the role envisioned by Lt. Cdr. Leighton in
his statement to the Second Taylor Board.

CHAPTER 6

Perfecting the Dive Bomber

THE IMPRESSIVE DIVE-BOMBING scores achieved during the various exercises conducted in the 1927–28 gunnery year created considerable interest in the development of a light bomber specifically designed for carrier use. The need for this new type was further underscored by the conclusions reached by the General Board of the Navy while conducting a study of the military characteristics of aircraft carriers in the latter half of 1927.[1] A number of recommendations concerning the development of a light bomber type quickly followed. Eventually these reports landed on Moffett's desk for endorsement by the Bureau of Aeronautics. While Moffett affirmed the concept of light bombing, he saw no need to develop a "special" plane as some had suggested. As he reported to the CNO:

> From such studies as have thus far been made it appears that the construction of a special machine to be used exclusively for diving bombing attacks is not desirable. It seems preferable to proceed with the continued development of higher performance single-seat or two-seat fighters and to incorporate in these planes the ability to handle bombs of various weights.[2]

The Bureau of Aeronautics, Moffett went on to explain, had already taken steps to include dive bombing as one of the functional requirements for its new two-seat fighter (the ill-fated XFC8-2) by including the ability to carry a 500-lb. bomb in its specification. BuAer had just completed a design study for a "special type of bomber" designed to deliver a 1,000-lb. bomb in the diving attack and was looking into the possibility of fitting a 500-lb. bomb to a new high-performance, single-seat fighter that was going to be evaluated in the near future.

The fighter which Moffett alluded to was being constructed by the Boeing Airplane Company at its own expense in the hopes that it would provide a replacement for the F2B/F3B/P-9 line of fighters that it had successfully sold to both the navy and the army. The company decided to construct two prototypes: one version (Boeing Model 83) for the navy, and another (Boeing Model 89) for the army. Except for the undercarriage and some minor details, the two planes were nearly identical. The navy plane was intended for use on carriers and was the first to be completed. It was fitted with arresting gear and had a spreader-bar undercarriage. This arrangement precluded the installation of a centerline bomb rack for a 500-lb. bomb like the one installed on the second prototype intended for evaluation by the U.S. Army Air Corps.[3]

Model 83 first took to the air on 25 June 1928. It was briefly tested at the Sand Point Naval Air Station in Seattle before being sent to San Diego for further evaluation in actual service aboard a carrier. The second prototype, Boeing's Model 89, was later sent by rail to the navy test center at Anacostia, making its maiden flight there on 7 August 1928. Although the navy's paperwork referred to both planes as XF4B-1s, they were still Boeing property and did not carry official military markings, though the Model 83 did have the words "U.S. NAVY" painted on its fuselage.[4]

A trial board composed of Lts. Daniel. W. Tomlinson and Thomas P. Jeter and Lt. (jg) William V. Davis Jr. was established on the West Coast to conduct tests of the XF4B-1 that had been delivered to San Diego. The first order of business was to equip the plane with two .30-caliber machine guns and a gunsight. Each of the pilots assigned to the trial board along with five others selected from the various squadrons stationed at North Field made one test flight in the new plane to evaluate its performance and suitability for military service. After putting the craft through its paces and landing, each pilot recorded his comments on the plane's performance in a special logbook set up by the trial board to record the results of the test program. Lieutenant Jeter made the only carrier landings, setting down and taking off from the Langley's deck three times.[5]

The XF4B-1 shown here is the Model 89 version delivered to Anacostia. Note the 500-lb. bomb which Reeves insisted fighters be able to carry. *National Archives*

While the plane proved a delight to fly and was well suited for carrier operations, the split-axle landing gear precluded the installation of a center-line bomb rack, and no provision had been made to add wing racks, two features that Reeves wanted in any carrier fighter so that they could carry either one 500-lb. bomb or a number of smaller bombs. Reeves was obviously peeved when Capt. Ernest J. King, then Moffett's assistant chief, suggested that two types of landing gear be procured for each F4B: one for bombing and one for carrier landings. Reeves saw no reason for this and wanted to know why the plane could not be fitted to carry either rack as needed. He was adamant about the need to carry as many lightweight bombs as possible, which he believed could be used defensively on attacking enemy bombers and torpedo planes or offensively to strike exposed personnel on surface craft. As he stated in his tersely worded reply to King's memo, it was essential that the F4B be able to operate from a carrier at all times while carrying a number of light bombs and, if possible, to carry one 500-lb. bomb in place of the numerous light bombs.[6]

Reeves's insistence that multiple bomb racks be mounted on all fighters was not universally accepted by all aviators, many of whom felt that the added weight and increased drag of the racks was bound to adversely affect a plane's performance. Though Reeves emphasized that loading a single-seat fighter with bombs did not change the type of plane nor the service for which it was intended, there was a growing feeling among the most fervent pilots that a fighter's aerial capabilities should not be compromised by adding additional equipment. Towers, the most senior aviator in the navy, also held this view, leading to yet another verbal confrontation with Reeves. This incident occurred in early October during Towers's appearance before a special board (of which Reeves was a member) investigating the allowance of aircraft bombs on carriers.

"We are becoming rather convinced in the bureau," stated Towers, "that the necessary weight and reduction in performance which go with equipping a fighter to carry 500-lb. bombs will spoil it as a fighter." When Reeves pressed Towers about the F4B's bomb load, the latter insisted that it was impossible to combine the functions of a dive bomber and a fighter into one plane without sacrificing performance. The fleet, Towers concluded, was going to want superior performance and you couldn't do that with a plane carrying a 500-lb. bomb.[7]

A decision had already been made within BuAer to press ahead with the development of a production model of Boeing's new plane in the hopes that the new fighter could be operational by the beginning of May. To save procurement time the bureau decided that the West Coast plane should be returned to Boeing as soon as possible and modified in accordance with a long list of minor changes that the design section wanted to incorporate in the production version. The Model 89 plane would remain at Anacostia so that its power plant, cowling, and arresting gear could be subjected to an exhaustive series of tests before being returned to the manufacturer. After completing this work the navy sent the Model 89 back to Boeing, which then modified both prototypes to conform to the configuration of the twenty-seven F4B-1s subsequently ordered. The production models were delivered with provisions for both bomb racks, and had the undercarriage of the Model 89 and the arrester hook of the Model 83. Ironically, it was Towers who recommended retaining the centerline bomb rack in addition to the A-3 bomb racks fitted under each wing.[8]

By the beginning of 1929, a number of high-ranking officers within the fleet were becoming increasingly concerned about the danger of dive bombing. There was a growing awareness of the menace that this new form of attack represented, particularly with respect to the thin-skinned destroyers.

An F4B-1 of Light Bombing Squadron One taking off from the *Lexington* in 1930 with an auxiliary fuel tank in place of the 500-lb bomb. *Naval Historical Center*

These lightly plated ships were extremely vulnerable to small bombs or machine-gun fire and could easily be disabled by one or two well-placed hits. As was vividly demonstrated in the experimental bombing practice conducted by VF-5S in the fall of 1927, such attacks were unlikely to be stopped by the defensive fire of the antiaircraft weapons then available.

The problem of trying to hit a diving aircraft with conventional antiaircraft fire was articulated by Rear Adm. Luke McNamee, then director of fleet training. In a memo to the CNO he requested that the General Board conduct an investigation into the problem of how to defend ships against the diving attack. As McNamee explained in his memo, if a squadron of airplanes approached its intended target from an altitude of 15,000 feet it was likely that they would remain undetected "by reason of sun glare, cloud protection, or the like," until after the planes commenced their attack. From this altitude a diving plane would quickly reach a terminal velocity of around 240 mph. At this rate of descent the diving plane would reach the 1,500-foot level of bomb release in about thirty-six seconds. If a gun projectile having an average velocity of 2,000 feet per second was fired at the instant the plane started its dive, six seconds would elapse before the projectile reached the point in its trajectory at which it would meet the diving plane. Even if the defensive fire began at the earliest possible instant, the defenders would have thirty seconds or less to hit the attacker before the bombs began to fall. When one considers that such an attack would be made by a number of aircraft approaching on different bearings on line of approach between 70 and 80 degrees from the horizon, it was not surprising for McNamee to conclude that

> the prospects of stopping even a small proportion of them by gun fire are not good to say the least. . . .
>
> Such planes may attack with demolition bombs, with gas filled containers, or with light-case high-explosive bombs against auxiliaries, transports, or unarmored vessels such as cruisers or destroyers. The effect of such an attack on even a heavily armored vessel is bound to be disastrous to fire control parties, secondary and antiaircraft gun crews and other exposed personnel and materiel.

McNamee's claim that there were already sixteen types of aircraft in service capable of making a dive-bombing attack was an exaggeration, though it is uncertain whether this was done through ignorance or as an intentional ploy to emphasize the danger of aerial attack to the fleet. Though the 100-lb. bomb was the heaviest that had actually been released in a diving attack to date, several new types of aircraft capable of dropping 500-lb. bombs were just about to enter service.

McNamee, and others no doubt, realized that the increasing performance of aircraft was bound to result in the development of new planes that could deliver larger weapons of even more destructive power.[9] Indeed, BuAer had already placed orders for two experimental bombers that were intended to have the capability of delivering a 1,000-lb. projectile via the diving attack.

In late spring of 1928, the design section had drawn up specifications for an experimental plane it called a "diving bomber," which would theoretically be capable of delivering a 1,000-lb. bomb from a vertical dive akin to those that had been achieved by lighter aircraft carrying much smaller projectiles. Developed as BuAer Design No. 77, the plane would be a metal-framed biplane having fabric-covered wings and an all-metal fuselage. The design prepared by BuAer was powered by a new radial engine, the 500-hp R-1750, which Wright Aeronautical had under development. As in all aircraft purchases conducted by BuAer, the engines would be purchased under separate contract and furnished to the airframe manufacturer under the category of government-supplied material. Since the new plane weighed in excess of

5,000 pounds, it would be designated as a VT type and be classified within BuAer's "heavy" category of aircraft. The plane would also be capable of carrying a torpedo, a provision (later waived) intended to satisfy the ongoing policy of producing multimission aircraft.

In keeping with its plan to encourage competition within the aircraft industry, BuAer awarded separate contracts for two different versions of the experimental plane. The first contract went to the Naval Aircraft Factory, which received an order on 18 June 1928 in the amount of sixty thousand dollars to produce the XT2N-1. Twelve days later, another contract was issued to the Glenn L. Martin Company for the second plane which was designated as the XT5M-1. Martin would be paid fifty thousand dollars for the prototype and would receive an additional thirty thousand dollars to cover the cost of development and a set of production drawings. Paying for the design rights up front would eliminate any confusion regarding ownership of the design and would permit the navy to solicit bids from other manufacturers to produce the plane if it proved suitable for service.[10]

The twenty-thousand-dollar difference between the two contracts illustrates the inequity of trying to use the Naval Aircraft Factory as "a yardstick for gauging the cost of private suppliers" and the dilemma facing the airplane manufacturing companies, which had to compete with the navy's own facilities.[11] Because it was a government facility, the Naval Aircraft Factory did not need to show a profit and was not bound to account for the manufacturing overhead accrued during the normal course of business. Thus, they were able to build their plane for less money.

As was customary during this period, BuAer began to issue change orders almost immediately. On 12 July 1928 it advised Martin's representative that it might be necessary to install a Pratt and Whitney R-1690 until the Wright R-1750, which was apparently undergoing teething problems, became available. Both engines were expected to be rated at 500 hp at 2,000 rpm. The navy wanted Martin to design the plane so that either might be installed. After Martin advised the bureau of the added costs this would entail, they were advised to stick with the R-1690.[12]

Before actual construction could start, the contractor was required to build a mock-up of the airplane which would be inspected by a board made up of a representative from each of the engineering sections (engine, ordnance, and design) within BuAer. Work on a mock-up of the XT5M-1 proceeded rapidly at the Martin plant, which was then located in Cleveland,

Ohio. It was inspected at the end of August by the inspector of naval aviation at Cleveland (a naval aviation officer detailed to oversee that the navy's contracts were properly fulfilled). The inspector was highly critical of the downward visibility afforded the pilot due to the location of the lower wing and the bulge of the fuselage. He couldn't understand how the pilot would be able to judge the position from which to commence his dive and was doubtful that "the pilot would be able crane his neck far enough to be able to see directly downward." This was a serious problem that warranted immediate attention.

In September Holden C. Richardson, now a captain, traveled to Cleveland for a firsthand view of the problem.[13] As head of the design section, Richardson had ultimate responsibility for overseeing the design process. He was a trained engineer and pilot who had been involved in the operation and design of aircraft for over sixteen years. Richardson had commanded the NC-3 during her abortive attempt to cross the Atlantic and was widely respected throughout the aviation community. While in Cleveland he discussed the problem at length with Lessiter C. Milburn, Martin's chief engineer.

Milburn was already hard at work on the problem and had several solutions in mind. He traveled to Washington, D.C., a week later with drawings showing two possible remedies. The first was a design change that would improve the downward view from the cockpit by decreasing the width of the top part of the fuselage. The second was a redesigned version of the plane that improved visibility by moving the lower wing back and the pilot forward. After discussing both approaches, both parties decided to stay with the original layout improving the pilot's view by changing the shape of the gasoline tanks so that the top side of the fuselage could be made narrower.[14]

In February 1929, Commander Towers, in his capacity as head of the plans section, Bureau of Aeronautics, was called to testify before the General Board with regard to question of providing a defense against the diving attack. Towers informed the board that while the tactics of dive bombing had proceeded quite rapidly, the material aspects of its development were proving to be more difficult to accomplish than first thought. The Bureau of Aeronautics, he explained, had discovered that the diving attack put more strain on the plane than had previously been thought. As a result it had been necessary to greatly increase the strength of the aircraft involved in carrying out this form of aerial attack.[15]

Indeed, two crashes during the initial testing of the ill-fated XF8C-2 had shown the need to reinforce the tail structure of planes intended for use as dive bombers. It appears that this information was passed along to both the Martin company and the Naval Aircraft Factory (NAF) in the form of a change order that further delayed the delivery of the experimental dive bombers being developed simultaneously by both organizations.[16]

Towers even thought that it might be necessary to restrict the dive angle of the new planes in order to reduce the stress on the wings, which had grown larger in order to lift the heavier bombs now required. The forces acting on the structural components of a wing increased rapidly as the wing got bigger, and no one in the Bureau of Aeronautics was sure whether or not the new planes would survive a pullout with a 1,000-lb. bomb. Limiting the dive angle, though, would reduce bombing effectiveness because it complicated the aiming process. In less steep dives the pilot had to compensate for the forward motion imparted to the bomb by the horizontal component of the plane's velocity as it dived toward the target. In a very steep dive the plane's horizontal speed was practically negligible; all the pilot had to do was place his sight on the target and keep it there. This principle is what made dive bombing so effective! Even at this early date, navy pilots knew that "to make hits, the dive had to be within 10° or 15° of vertical."[17]

While Towers testified before the General Board, both manufacturers continued to work on their respective versions of the experimental dive bomber. Martin's XT5M-1 was the first to be completed. It was ready for its first flight in the early weeks of May 1929.

The NAF had planned to complete its entry by July, but the XT2N-1 would not take to the air until March of the following year. When it finally did fly it proved to be totally unsuitable for service; its engine tended to overheat, the fuel tanks leaked, and the plane exhibited structural weakness in the tail components that limited both dive angle and pullout load.[18]

As specified in all contracts, the navy expected the manufacturer to demonstrate the air worthiness of the craft before delivering it to NAS, Anacostia for further testing. As part of this requirement the navy expected the plane to undergo a one-hour full-power flight test. The Martin company, which had recently relocated to a new plant in Baltimore, asked the navy if this test could be conducted at Anacostia since its new airfield was still under construction.

While this request was being processed, steps were taken to schedule the performance trials at Anacostia, which would be conducted under the auspices of the Board of Inspection and Survey convened there for that purpose. As a draft of the letter outlining the guarantees expected to be fulfilled during the trials was circulated throughout the various design sections, it was suddenly brought out that the contract contained nothing about the plane's diving abilities.[19] Richardson suggested that a conference be called to determine what tests should be made. Though these were not part of the plane's specifications, the Martin company agreed to hire a pilot to demonstrate the diving qualities of the plane after it had been accepted by the navy.

In the meantime, the bureau agreed to let the Martin company conduct its one-hour power test at Anacostia. These took three days to complete as the plane's engines suffered severe overheating, which required Martin's technical crew to fiddle with the cowling until sufficient cooling could be achieved. While these changes were being made, a number of other minor modifications were requested by the navy. These were completed by mid-June, and the XT5M-1 was turned over to the navy for the required acceptance trials. Although the plane was received at the beginning of July, testing did not commence until 13 August due to the high priority of other work at Anacostia.[20]

Several more weeks passed before the bureau formulated a plan for testing the plane's capabilities as a dive bomber, which was to be conducted in accordance with the following schedule:

(a) Dives up to as near vertical as possible with and without power, without bomb load, to demonstrate the action and controllability of the airplane in a dive and in recovery. The dives should be started at sufficient altitude to permit holding the airplane in a diving attitude for a distance of at least 8,000 feet with sufficient altitude remaining to effect a safe pull out. Twenty-five hundred (2500) feet should be allowed for recovery.

(b) Repeat with 500-lb. bomb load.

(c) Repeat with 1,000-lb. bomb load.

The last was to be made in as near a vertical dive as was possible! Realizing the inherent dangers involved, BuAer urged caution and recommended a step-by-step approach using as many preliminary tests as was deemed necessary.[21]

This was a pretty severe test according to Lt. Cdr. John E. Ostrander Jr., an experienced pilot and aviation expert then in charge of the armament desk in the design section of BuAer. "Pretty tough!" he wrote on the routing slip. "I'll bet $5 to 50¢ the plane does not" hold up under the worst condition, he continued. Others, notably Cdr. Sydney M. Kraus, believed that even if the plane failed the test it would be of value, since few of the so-called diving bombers had been tested under actual service conditions. As long as this condition persisted, argued Kraus, the design of dive bombers would be hampered and there would be no clear definition of their utility.[22]

Because of the danger involved, the Martin company agreed to conduct these tests (which were not included in its contract) with the understanding that the risk to the plane would be borne by the navy. If the plane crashed, which was a definite possibility, the company would still receive payment.

Martin hired William H. McAvoy, then senior test pilot for the National Advisory Committee on Aeronautics (NACA) at Langley Field to conduct the special dive tests demanded by BuAer. On 14 October 1929 McAvoy made an orientation hop to get the "feel" of the plane and test its controllability. He was able to get in one steep dive before the engine started acting up, curtailing flight operations for the rest of the day. The plane reached a maximum speed of about 200 knots and "felt good," according to McAvoy, whose remarks were made to the assembled onlookers.[23]

Testing resumed two days later. McAvoy took off from the Naval Air Station at Anacostia and climbed to 10,000 feet, nosed over, and put the plane in a vertical dive. He began with the throttle closed, carefully observing the rpms and airspeed. At 190 knots the plane began to vibrate. McAvoy immediately pulled back on the stick and looked back over his left shoulder to see if anything was wrong. Everything was OK on that side of the plane so he turned to his right to take a look at the other side. What he saw must have sent a chill up his spine! Portions of the fabric covering the right wing surface had been torn off the ribs and were tattering in the slip stream. Pulling out of the dive, he brought the plane down to 65 knots, gliding slowly to an uneventful dead stick landing.

An examination of the plane afterwards showed that a good bit of fabric on the lower wing panel had been torn away along with one of the trailing edge ribs. Several other ribs and spars were also damaged or deformed. The structural failure exhibited by the wing was apparently caused by high local stresses along the leading edge. This was confirmed by NACA, which had recently discovered that the local stresses built up on the leading edge of a wing during a high-speed dive were much greater than expected.[24]

This unexpected mishap canceled further testing of the plane, which was returned to the Martin plant for modification and repair. At the factory the wing was rebuilt and strengthened by reinforcing the leading edge and pro-

Shredded wing section showing damage experienced during test pilot William McAvoy's harrowing terminal velocity dive in the XT5M-1. *Author's collection*

viding closer rib stitching of the fabric. The XT5M-1 was then brought back to Anacostia, where testing was resumed on 20 March 1930.[25]

McAvoy was once again at the controls as he put the plane through a series of test dives under three different conditions: first without a bomb, then with a 500-lb. bomb, and finally culminating with two dives with a 1,000-lb. bomb attached. The latter were initiated from an altitude of 9,800 feet, with pullouts at around 5,000 feet. The plane responded well throughout the tests, obtained an airspeed of 225 knots, and easily handled the 4-G pullout. Although all three dives were conducted at less than full load—the aircraft was 360 pounds lighter than specified for maximum load—the board of inspection considered the plane's performance to be favorable and recommended it as a service type suitable for use in the further development of dive-bombing tactics. More work was still needed to strengthen the plane, however, as a cursory inspection after the flight revealed that some of the wing components had been slightly distorted from the severe stresses encountered.[26]

While the Martin company was engaged in preparing the XT5M-1 for the foregoing, a new problem cropped up which threatened to hold up the development of dive bombers. While conducting routine bombing exercises in the fleet, it had suddenly been discovered that under certain circumstances bombs were unexpectedly striking the airplane as they were released. During the previous year a number of accidents had occurred while dive-bombing exercises were being conducted in which airplanes were struck by their own bombs! There were several cases of practice bombs striking the landing gear of F6C-4s and in one instance a miniature bomb struck the propeller. In one extreme instance a live 17-lb. bomb lodged between the wheel and landing-gear strut of an F3B. Miraculously, the pilot managed to land the plane unharmed. Yet another plane landed with a bomb hanging by its arming wire.[27]

When Rear Adm. Henry V. Butler, commander, Aircraft Squadrons, Battle Fleet, learned of these problems he ordered that all planes engaged in practice missions with live bombs be carefully inspected before landing to ensure all bombs had been jettisoned. In cases were bombs failed to be properly released, pilots were to make every effort to discard them into the sea before a landing was attempted. Butler's memo also included a series of instructions spelling out the proper conditions for bombing. No bombs, for example, were to be released while the plane was in a severe skid, nor were they to be dropped from a plane which had been thrown on its back—two actions which had been implicated in the previous accidents.[28]

The Bureaus of Aeronautics and Ordnance immediately established a joint program to discover a remedy that would remove as many hazards as possible from what was quickly becoming a very dangerous endeavor. The first step was to determine the actual trajectories of the bombs as they were released from various dive angles. An extensive series of drops were soon conducted at the Naval Proving Ground in Dahlgren, Virginia, where motion picture cameras were used to photograph the bombs as they were released from an F7C-1 airplane. The pilot for these flights was Lt. John J. Ballentine, a naval aviator in charge of the aviation detachment at Dahlgren.

Ballentine's recollections of the events which took place during this period reveal just how little the navy knew about the structural weaknesses of the aircraft it employed for dive bombing and the extreme danger facing the pilots engaged in this activity. At one point the program involved such urgency that Ballentine was required to drop a bomb, land, pick up another, and climb to

10,000 feet without interruption. This heavy schedule sometimes went on all day long.

While in the midst of this very intensive program, an F7C-1 based at the Marine Air Station in Quantico, Virginia, lost one of its wings in flight. The pilot escaped by parachute, but the plane disintegrated in the air and came down a total wreck. Concerned about the implications this might have for his own plane, Ballentine flew to Quantico to see if he could determine the cause of failure. While looking over the wreckage, he discovered that one of the two main fittings that normally held the plane together had failed. Returning to Dahlgren, Ballentine immediately inspected his plane and was unpleasantly surprised to find the fittings on his ship cracked![29]

After the defective fittings were replaced, Ballentine took the plane for a test flight just to make sure that it had been reassembled properly. As he entered his first dive, the plane began to shake as if the wings were ready to come off. Ballentine instantly began to pull up ever so gently and was relieved when the vibration ceased as soon as his speed dropped off. After climbing to regain lost altitude, he tried it once again, this time putting the plane into a shallower dive and slowly gaining speed until it began to vibrate. He held onto the dive just long enough to look over the wing structure to find out what was wrong. The problem was caused by a piece of metal fairing that had slipped down one of the bracing wires to a point were it crossed another. Perhaps this had resulted from a slight oversight during reassembly or maybe the fairing had simply pulled loose. In any case, the problem disappeared once the mechanics tightened the fairing. Ballentine later admitted that it had given him quite a thrill when the wings began to shake, especially after seeing what had happened to the plane at Quantico.

In the meantime, a trio of engineers that included Lt. Cdr. Arthur C. Miles, head of BuAer's design section, Cdr. C. L. Schuyler, the Inspector of Ordnance at the Naval Proving Ground, and George A. Chadwick, a civilian employee of BuOrd, came up with the idea for a new type of release mechanism that would swing the bomb free of the aircraft structure.[30] The bomb-displacing gear which they invented became the prototype for the bomb "crutch" later used on the SBD Dauntlesses and SB2C Helldivers of World War II fame. It consisted of two arms hinged under the plane with attachment lugs on either side of the bomb. When the bomb was released, the arms forcibly moved the bomb away from the fuselage, ensuring that it would clear the propeller. As the bomb disengaged, a spring-loaded retracting device

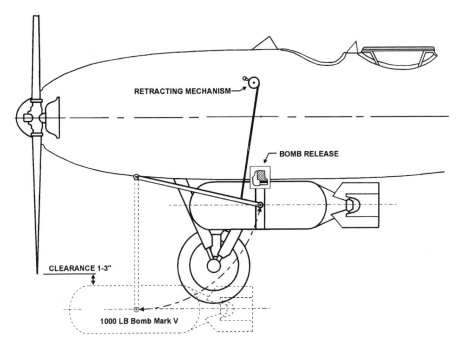

Figure 6.1 A reproduction of the original engineering drawing submitted by the Glenn L. Martin Company for the displacement gear installed on the XT5M-1.

pulled the arms back into position. It was decided to suspend further testing of the XT5M-1 until such a device could be installed on the new dive bomber.

Contracts issued by the Bureau of Aeronautics for the construction of aircraft almost always contained some provision with respect to the plane's ordnance requirements, though all gear of this nature (machine guns, sights, bomb racks, flares, and so on) were usually supplied to the contractor. In the case of the XT5M-1 this included the bomb release mechanism, which was to be manufactured and installed by the manufacturer under separate contract from the Bureau of Ordnance.[31]

By July the Glenn L. Martin Company had produced a detailed blueprint showing the design and installation arrangement of the displacement gear suggested by Lieutenant Commander Miles and company.[32] It took several more months for review and approval, however, before Martin could proceed with fabrication and installation of the new device so that testing of the XT5M-1 could proceed once again.

In late December 1930, Lt. Cdr. John E. Ostrander Jr. received orders directing him to proceed via air to the Naval Proving Ground at Dahlgren to flight test the special ordnance gear now installed on the Martin plane. Ostrander wrangled the assignment so that Ballentine, who had a wife and child, would not have to test the new mechanism in what was clearly a hazardous undertaking.[33] The two men had become friends while they were both engaged in an earlier assignment at the Naval Proving Ground.

Final testing was planned for 7 January 1931. Preliminary tests had been conducted the day before using partially loaded practice bombs that Ballentine had dropped in shallow dives. Now Ostrander was scheduled to make a series of drops using fully loaded practice bombs that would culminate in a bomb being released from a near-vertical dive. The first two dives would be made at 45–55 degrees, two more would be made at 60–65 degrees, and another two at 65–70 degrees. If everything worked well, Ostrander would then attempt to make two more drops at 75–80 degrees.[34]

Fortunately the tests were conducted without incident. The displacement gear worked perfectly and the tests were successfully completed. The Naval Proving Ground was so pleased with the results that Ostrander received a letter of commendation endorsed by both the chief of the Bureau of Ordnance and the chief of the Bureau of Aeronautics. There was even talk within the Bureau of Aeronautics about awarding Ostrander the Distinguished Flying Cross, but this never came to pass.

The success of the tests conducted by Ostrander was the crowning achievement in BuAer's efforts to develop the first dedicated dive bomber.[35] In April, the XT5M-1 with its wings strengthened and new displacement gear installed was officially accepted by the Board of Inspection and Survey. Moffett immediately ordered the procurement of twelve BM-1s from the Martin company, making them the first airplanes purchased in the new VB category. The production version was nearly identical to the prototype, but had a larger, 625-hp R-1690-44 Pratt and Whitney engine.

While the first production model was being tested at Anacostia, a fatal accident occurred which revealed the existence of an undetected design defect in the BM-1. Lt. Edward Richie, the test pilot assigned to check out the first plane, was conducting a routine test flight over Anacostia when it "just came apart at 8,000 feet."[36] When he attempted to jump to safety, Richie's parachute became entangled in the aircraft and he went down with the plane, which crashed on Oxon Hill, dangerously near a crowded school yard. Mirac-

The XT5M-1 experimental dive bomber shown here was the first plane designed to drop a 1,000-lb. bomb in a near-vertical dive. NAS, Anacostia, c. 1930. *Author's collection*

ulously, none of the children playing nearby were hurt, albeit the incident pointed out the need to move the flight test work further downriver.

An analysis of the wreckage showed that the design of the tail structure was flawed, causing harmonic vibrations in flight which were severe enough to rip the tail apart. Martin had to redesign the tail section around a two-point suspension. Though this corrected the vibration problem, it created another; navy personnel assigned to BuAer's flight test section discovered that the changes made by Martin had shifted the BM-1's center of gravity, making it into a "flat spinner."

This undesirable characteristic was confirmed by Lt. Robert B. Pirie during flight tests of the redesigned aircraft. As Pirie put the plane into a spin he discovered that the BM-1's nose would come down instead of going up, as desired. This dangerous attribute made it almost impossible to recover from a spin. Pirie told Lt. Cdr. Ralph Ofstie, head of flight testing at Anacostia, that he "didn't want any more of that airplane, that it was dangerous, and it had to be corrected before we could use it in the fleet." When Ken Ebell, Martin's test pilot, took the plane up to duplicate the problem, he was unable to recover from the uncontrollable spin that ensued and was forced to bail out. Although

Ebell had to struggle out of the cockpit a few hundred feet above the water and was hit by the wing as he exited the plane, he was saved by his parachute, which opened just before he hit the water.[37]

Once again a conference was held in BuAer's offices to fix a flawed design. After considerable discussion the powers at large decided not to abandon the plane. Instead, the representatives of both the Material Division and the flight test section were directed to cooperate with Martin in order to improve the plane's stability by readjusting the distribution of weight. This must have corrected the problem for no more adverse incidents were recorded and a second order for sixteen more planes was placed on 17 October 1931.[38]

Aircraft design was very much a trial and error procedure in those days and was governed by the philosophy of "fly and try, then fix it."

CHAPTER 7

Like Blind Men Armed with Daggers

IN MARCH 1930 elements of the U.S. Fleet sailed to the Caribbean, where not one but two fleet problems would be conducted in as many months. The first of these, Fleet Problem X, was an exercise designed to give fleet commanders experience in obtaining tactical superiority over an enemy force of approximately the same strength. These maneuvers were designed to provide the fleet with practice in deploying its light forces and aircraft while conducting search operations to seek out the opposition. It was a five-day affair that started at midday on 10 March 1930.

As in Fleet Problem IX, both of the big carriers were assigned to an opposing force. Each was directed to search for the other flattop continuously during daylight hours and to attack it once located. Flight operations were nowhere near as extensive as in the previous year's problem because of bad weather encountered during the first three days of the exercise. Although scouting operations were conducted on both sides during this period, no aerial contact was made until 14 March, when a section of Blue fighters from the *Langley* sighted three of Black's scout planes headed toward the *Saratoga*. They were unable to engage this small force, which soon conducted a successful dive-bombing attack on the *Saratoga,* putting her forward flight deck out of commission according to the umpire, who ruled that it would take at least two hours to repair. In a determined effort to maintain air operations, *Saratoga*'s handling crews immediately began to respot her aircraft as far aft as possible so that they could take off from the undamaged flight deck. As they were still engaged in this activity, more enemy planes suddenly appeared overhead and began to dive on the now defenseless carrier. Within thirteen minutes these forty-two planes, launched earlier from the *Lexington,* conducted five more dive-bombing attacks on the *Saratoga,* putting the rest of her flight deck out of action and destroying half her aircraft.[1]

After finishing off the big carrier, *Lexington*'s planes switched targets and attacked the *Langley.* Minutes later the vulnerable ship received another pasting from twelve more *Lexington* fighters. As a result of these air strikes, the chief umpire stationed on *Saratoga* ruled that the flight deck and all planes of both Blue carriers had been put out of commission. In one quick stroke the Black Force had gained complete control of the air and with it superiority in long-range gunnery. Having annihilated Blue's carriers, Black's fighters were now free to conduct unmolested attacks on the enemy's battleships.

The second problem conducted that year, Fleet Problem XI, was held in April. Less structured than the first, it was intended to be an exercise in making quick estimates and decisions. During this problem, *Saratoga,* in a reversal of roles, attacked the *Lexington,* destroying thirty-eight planes on her flight deck. As in the first problem, the carrier which was the first to locate and attack its counterpart in the opposing force was able to achieve air superiority, gaining an overwhelming advantage for its own fleet.[2]

Air commanders, especially those in positions of high command, were beginning to realize both the extreme vulnerability of the carrier, whose unarmored flight deck could be easily damaged by light bombing, and the difficulties of trying to defend against attacking aircraft. None of the anti-aircraft measures which we now take for granted—radar, proximity fuses, remote control gunnery—existed, and it appeared as if it would be impossible to stop an aerial attack once the enemy had launched its planes. Rear Adm. Henry V. Butler, the commander of the Aircraft Squadrons, Scouting Force, described the situation now facing carrier commanders at the critique following the conclusion of the problems. The opposing forces, he explained, were "like blindfolded men armed with daggers in a ring, if the bandage over the eyes of one is removed, the other [was] doomed." The only solution,

The *Saratoga,* identified by the vertical stripe on her funnel, conducting air operations in the early 1930s. *Naval Historical Center*

exclaimed Butler, was to locate the enemy carrier and attack while the latter's planes were still on deck.[3]

In those days conducting long-distance flights over water in a plane not equipped for a water landing was considered a highly hazardous undertaking. Not wishing to lose pilots during this peacetime era, the navy severely limited the extent of the scouting operations which could be conducted from carriers. During the two problems discussed here, the pilots assigned to fly scouting missions were ordered to stay within 25 miles of any surface vessel to safeguard the crew in the event of a water landing. This limited the scouting range to a small area just ahead of the two escorting destroyers, which were directed to steam 25 miles in advance of the carrier. Although the O2U, which was the most numerous of the planes assigned to the scouting squadrons, had a range of over 500 miles, the longest scouting operation ever conducted had been limited to 75 miles. Tactical scouting beyond this point was considered quite dangerous, due to the small range of the radios (50–100 miles at best) carried by these aircraft and the difficulties of trying to navigate over water. Nevertheless, experienced pilots such as Wagner felt that scouting could be conducted up to 300 miles out.[4]

These and the other shortcomings of the current crop of carrier scout plane were discussed during the routine critiques which were held at the conclusion of each problem. Although the O2U could carry up to ten 30-lb. bombs if necessary, the added weight limited the amount of fuel they could carry when fully loaded, restricting the plane's flying time to about five hours. In this condition they had an effective combat radius of only 175 nautical miles. A better-armed, longer-ranging aircraft was needed for the scouting role if enemy carriers were to be bombed before they had the opportunity to launch their planes. Butler wanted BuAer to develop a VS that had short a takeoff run, high cruising speed, and folding wings. These features would enable more aircraft to be carried and hasten the process of locating the enemy.[5]

Mastery of the air, Butler concluded, could not be overemphasized. Though many high-ranking officers agreed with this assessment, others remained unconvinced of the importance of aviation. Among the most out-spoken of the latter was Rear Adm. Frank H. Clark, commander of the Blue carrier group. Clark was skeptical, if not openly hostile, to the assertions of the other aviators present. "What planes can observe from the air has been much exaggerated," he exclaimed.[6] Even the twelve fighters flying combat air patrol over the *Lexington* were completely unaware of two bombing attacks taking place on their ship. How he asked, are we to achieve supremacy in the air? As yet no aviator or force commander had solved the problem of how to engage enemy planes before they attacked.

Poor visibility, no doubt, contributed to Clark's negative assessment of aviation's value to the fleet. Even during clear weather a haze had extended over the entire Caribbean during the course of the exercise, making observa-tion from aircraft actually worse than from surface vessels. Aerial scouting was further complicated by a layer of broken clouds that formed at 2,000 feet on most days, forcing the planes to fly at low altitudes.

Lack of adequate radio communication was yet another problem. Neither the fighters nor the light bombers carried radios. The Bureau of Engineering was working on the development of a lightweight radio telephone set that could be used by a pilot alone, thus eliminating the need for a second crew member to operate the "key," but these were unavailable as yet. As a stopgap measure, Butler recommended that two high-speed radio liaison planes be added to each fighter and light-bombing squadron. The only model suited for this task was the Curtiss XF8C-4, which led to the expedited purchase of the special prototypes mentioned in Chapter 4.

On the positive side, the exercises of 1930 had been the first to study the "carrier group," which Vice Adm. Carey Cole defined as a complete tactical unit consisting of one carrier, four cruisers, and two destroyer squadrons. How could such a group avoid attack by surface ships? he asked. Could it escape a night torpedo attack? What were its full possibilities as a means of reducing the enemy strength before a major engagement? Could it hold control of the air long enough for its support to arrive? All were favorably answered by Rear Adm. Frank Brumby, who again emphasized the importance of obtaining control of the air.[7]

These and other questions about the potential value of the aircraft carrier would to be severely tested in the following year during Fleet Problem XII. Conducted in the Pacific-Panama area in February 1931, it saw the return of an old hand in aviation matters, Rear Admiral Reeves, as well as a newcomer to the Battle Force, Capt. Ernest J. King.

Reeves returned to sea after Rear Adm. Richard H. (Reddy) Leigh, the chief of the Bureau of Navigation, offered him the choice of either going to Newport, Rhode Island, as president of the Naval War College or back to the fleet as commander of carriers (Battle Force). Preferring sea duty to shore duty, Reeves, who had just completed an unsavory tour of duty as a member of the General Board in Washington, quickly chose the latter.[8]

King, a former submariner, was one of a number of senior officers in the interwar period who saw aviation as an opportunistic means of furthering their careers during the late 1920s and early 1930s when stagnation in the seniority list limited the availability of good commands. An extremely ambitious officer, he would later become the first and only officer in the U.S. Navy to hold the dual posts of commander-in-chief, U.S. Fleet and CNO. Though King had recently won acclaim by salvaging the sunken submarine S-51, he lacked the seniority for the cruiser command he really wanted.

King was enticed to enter aviation in return for a carrier command that Moffett promised King in April 1926 if he would be willing to learn to fly, even though King was close to fifty years of age. Moffett knew that Congress was about to pass legislation mandating that all aircraft carriers and seaplane tenders be commanded by qualified naval aviators.[9] The *Lexington* and *Saratoga* would soon be commissioned, but none of the really experienced pilots had been in the service long enough to accumulate enough seniority to warrant these important commands. The only solution, Moffett told King, was to make flyers out of the older officers. After several months of thinking it over, King, desperate to secure a decent command, accepted Moffett's offer to take over the seaplane tender *Wright*.[10]

The *Wright* was an important aviation command at the time. In addition to functioning as a mobile base for seaplanes, it also served as the flagship for the commander, Aircraft Squadrons, Scouting Force. King arrived in June for the change in command ritual that included a cursory inspection of what was then considered an "easy ship," that is, loosely disciplined. According to King's biographer, he saw his predecessor over the side before addressing the assembled crew. "And now, gentlemen," he is said to have exclaimed, "we are going to have an inspection that is an inspection." King then proceeded to "tear" the ship apart.

After six months on the *Wright*, King was ordered to Pensacola to take the mandatory five months of flight training needed to qualify as a naval aviator. King's training turned out to be an awkward reversal of roles, with the younger flight instructors teaching the "old fuds" who outranked them! Everyone was treated fairly yet impartially; favors were neither sought nor given, and pulling rank was forbidden. King's flying lessons ended as soon as he had accumulated enough hours in the air (two hundred was the minimum required by law) needed to meet the requirements of a naval aviator—just enough to qualify him for a carrier command. When King received his wings on 26 May 1927, he had only completed seventy-five hours of solo flight. Though he would frequently take the controls when accompanied by another pilot in later years, he never flew alone again, for he had acquired only the most rudimentary of flying skills.

Nine months later, while King was on detached duty salvaging yet another sunken submarine, Moffett offered King command of the *Langley*. King thought it was best to stay where he was and declined the offer. After a three-month struggle in brutal weather, King raised the S-4, for which he received a second Distinguished Service Medal. After his return to the *Wright*, Moffett recommended that King be assigned as next commander of the *Lexington*. A week after they were issued, however, King's orders were changed again! Instead of the *Lexington*, he was disheartened to learn that he was to report to the Bureau of Aeronautics for duty as assistant chief.

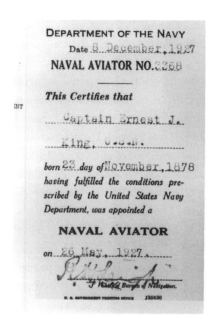

DEPARTMENT OF THE NAVY

Date 8 December, 1927

NAVAL AVIATOR NO. 3368

This Certifies that

Captain Ernest J.

King, U.S.N.

born 23 day of November, 1878 having fulfilled the conditions prescribed by the United States Navy Department, was appointed a

NAVAL AVIATOR

on 26 May, 1927

Chief of Bureau of Navigation.

(Seal)

Received E.J. King

Captain, U.S.N.
(Rank and Service)

Card certifying Ernest J. King's appointment as naval aviator number 3368, on 26 May 1927. *National Archives*

After Moffett had nominated King for command of the *Lexington,* Moffett had unexpectedly learned that Capt. Emory S. Land, the highly regarded assistant chief of BuAer, had requested a leave of absence from the navy to serve with the Daniel Guggenheim Fund for the Promotion of Aeronautics. Moffett's first choice to replace Land was Cdr. John Towers. The two men were "of one mind on practically everything, including their contempt for the crusty old guard," but Towers was too junior to be acceptable to the Bureau of Navigation, so Moffett requested King instead. King arrived in Washington in August 1928, bitter and disappointed at the lost opportunity. Both men were used to having their own way, so a clash of wills was inevitable. "King did not like being assistant to anyone, and he was uncomfortable with Moffett's demands for absolute loyalty and the admiral's seeming unwillingness to listen to opposing opinions."[11]

The showdown came after Moffett returned from the London Naval Conference early in 1929. In his absence, Moffett's personal pilot and protégé, Lt. Alford J. Williams Jr., was earmarked for duty at sea. Williams, who had gained considerably notoriety as a winning air racer, didn't want to go, and threatened to resign if so ordered. In King's mind, Williams was a "prima donna" who was shirking his duty as a naval officer. Although aviation assignments had been a jealously guarded prerogative of Moffett's, King believed that the Bureau of Navigation should control personnel assignments. Thus with King's approval, Rear Admiral Leigh, chief of the Bureau of Navigation, cut orders assigning Williams to the *Saratoga*. Williams was so mad that he impetuously resigned his commission. Moffett was furious. He felt that King had exceeded his authority. Worse, the action smacked of personal disloyalty. As Moffett later told Joseph (Jocko) Clark, "It came to a point where either King was going to be Chief of the Bureau or myself." So in May 1929, he transferred King to the Naval Air Station at Hampton Roads and elevated Commander Towers to assistant chief even though this was normally a captain's billet.[12]

Although the air station at Hampton Roads was a large and important base, King had to mark time for another year before he would get the carrier command he yearned for. When Moffett offered *Saratoga*, King replied that he would prefer the *Lexington* as she normally would not have an admiral aboard to look over his shoulder. King soon got his wish, taking command of the ship in June 1930.

King, a tall, thin, wiry man with "a deceptive twinkle in his eyes" had a reputation for being a tough disciplinarian. He ruled *Lexington* with an iron hand and was a perfectionist who was aware of every detail of the ship's operation. The doctrine of carrier operations was still in its infancy and the relationship between the captain and the commanding officers of the embarked aircraft squadrons was ill defined. It was not unusual for squadron commanders, who regarded the carrier as no more than a temporary airfield, to resent being told how to fly. King would have none of this; the squadrons would be under his command and conform to his standards. The carefree attitude and ragtag appearance he observed at their base in North Island would not be tolerated aboard *his* ship. While under King's command, each pilot would be required to inspect his aircraft both before and after every flight.[13]

Early in February 1931, the *Lexington* went to Coronado Roads to take on planes and supplies in preparation for Fleet Problem XII. She joined *Saratoga* and *Langley* on the fourth and sailed in company with the rest of the Battle Fleet toward the Panama Canal. Reeves's dashing carrier attack two years earlier had shown the canal's vulnerability to assault from the air. Assigned as the commander of the Blue Force for this problem, Reeves now found himself charged with defending the very shore installations he had been assigned to destroy in Fleet Problem IX.

The problem began with the assumption that a Pacific power was attacking both the Panama Canal and a hypothetical Nicaraguan canal at a moment when the United States was doubtful about the neutrality of a European power. This made it necessary to keep the bulk of the U.S. Fleet off the coast of New England and leaving it up to the two big carriers to defend the canal. The *Saratoga* and *Lexington,* along with three light cruisers and their accompanying destroyers, were all that Reeves had to oppose the enemy battleships of the Black Force.

At the start of the problem, Admiral Reeves, suspecting that the enemy might try to capture the Galapagos Islands, ordered King to scout the islands to make sure that no hostile forces were lurking there. King, who may have felt he was being sent on a wild goose chase was placed in tactical command of a small task force that included two light cruisers in addition to the two plane guard destroyers that usually accompanied every carrier. He sent both cruisers to the Galapagos, directing one to proceed at high speed with orders to launch her catapult planes as soon as possible. Both ships were recalled after the scouts reported that no "enemy" ships were visible in any of the island's harbors. By this time one cruiser had burned so much oil that she had to be replenished from the *Lexington.* The big carrier had recently been modified for this in response to the fuel problems uncovered during Fleet Problem IX.[14]

Secure in the knowledge that the Galapagos were free of the enemy, King turned his force to the northeast, where he suspected the enemy would be. Late in the morning of the following day, the navy airship *Los Angeles* succeeded in sighting Black's only carrier, the *Langley.* This was the only useful thing the big dirigible accomplished during the entire exercise, for she was promptly discovered by enemy planes and shot down. An hour later, at midday, King received orders directing the *Lexington* group to execute its strike mission. King immediately began to close on the *Langley* and began making preparations for the air strike which would be launched later that afternoon.[15]

At 1520 King launched an attack group consisting of ten fighters, six scouts, and seventeen bomb-laden torpedo planes, holding one squadron of fighters over the *Lexington* as a combat air patrol.[16] Each plane carried a simulated bomb load of one 500-lb. bomb, except for the torpedo planes, which were armed with two. Although the reported position of the *Langley* was only 40 miles away, the "enemy" ship was actually 75 miles distant. Standing orders demanded that all planes be back on board a carrier by sunset, thus King instructed the attack group to fly north-northeastward for an hour and then return. Unless they located the enemy, in which case they were free to attack.

In due course the first group of planes returned on board the carrier. They had neither seen nor heard anything of the *Langley* or the second group of planes which they had preceded. They were soon followed by the six scouts of the second group that had found and bombed the *Langley* before returning to the *Lexington*. But what of the other two squadrons of the attack group?

With dusk approaching King initiated the lost-plane procedure. He ordered that the ship's searchlights be turned on and directed the engineering crew to make smoke. Just before dark lights were sighted to the southeast and the missing planes began to approach the carrier. The emergency was far from over, however, as the carrier pilots now had to land in the darkness, a feat they had not done before. The ten fighters, nearly out of gas, landed first and were followed by the torpedo bombers. Except for a few blown tires, all of the planes were successfully brought aboard without incident.

When the lost sheep had been found, King in great relief could only ask the flight commander, "Where in the hell have you been?" Departing from his orders, the commander had left his original course, turned toward the northeast for ten minutes then eastward for another ten. Just as he was about to make for the *Lexington* he sighted the *Langley* and attacked. With only a small plotting board and a magnetic compass as navigation aides, the pilot had quickly lost his way over the featureless ocean.

After the planes landed an army observer on board asked King how he felt when he realized that the planes were lost. King replied, "Hell, I was too busy to worry about how I felt. What I had to do was to figure out how to get those damn planes back aboard!"[17] With all planes safely aboard, King darkened ship and headed south at reduced speed.

On the following day, both the *Lexington* and *Saratoga* used their high-speed capabilities to escape from enemy cruisers which were pursuing them. The limited range of the carrier aircraft then available meant that the carriers had to steam to within 40 to 75 miles of their objective before they could launch an aerial attack. This made them vulnerable to enemy marauders, leading senior officers to conclude that it would be too dangerous for carriers to operate without the support of battleships. Though this was probably a correct assessment in 1931, it was this type of thinking by the non-aviators that would severely hamper the future development of the fleet's carrier tactics.[18]

The results of Fleet Problem XII were a disappointment to the airmen. By the end of the exercise both large carriers were low on fuel, had nearly exhausted their supply of aviation ordnance, and had theoretically lost half of their aircraft. Worse were the navigation difficulties experienced by pilots as they tried to relocate their carrier after an extended flight of any duration. Admiral Pratt, now CNO, believed that the exercise had shown that air attack as a defense against approaching fleets had less value than had been expected, forcing Reeves to admit that the air force alone could not stop the advance of battleships.[19] Nevertheless, Reeves continued to argue vehemently for mutual dependence, claiming that only airpower could extend the maximum range of gunfire via spotting from the air. He wrote a "strong and carefully worded report" to the Navy Department after the critique in support of the air force, which kept aviation from receiving severe budget cuts in the next year.[20]

This was to be the last major act in the drama of Reeves's direct association with naval aviation. Upon his return to San Diego he received orders to report for shore duty after the normal rotation in commands at midyear. Had Reeves been a qualified naval aviator it is likely that his next assignment would have been command of one of the naval air stations on the Pacific Coast. Reeves preferred to stay on the West Coast near his home in the San Francisco Bay area and was temporarily appointed as senior member of the Pacific Coast Section of the Board of Inspection and Survey before becoming commandant of Mare Island Navy Yard while he awaited the return to sea duty. On 10 June 1933 Reeves jumped from the relative obscurity of the Mare Island Naval Yard to take over as commander, Battleships, Battle Force, a required prerequisite to command of the Battle Force, a full admiral's billet, which Reeves assumed twenty days later! As the noted historian Gerald Wheeler explained in his biography of CNO Pratt, "This late recognition of Reeves reflected both Pratt's friendship for this splendid officer and his desire to give aviation a more prominent role in the U.S. Fleet."[21] But this is getting ahead of our story.

When Rear Adm. Harry Yarnell relieved Reeves on 27 June 1931, he immediately assumed the duties of commander, Aircraft Squadrons, Battle Force. The new title was in line with the reorganization which had just been instituted by Admiral Pratt. Pratt wanted to emphasize the training mission of

An F4B-2 landing on the *Saratoga*, showing the split-axle landing gear and the cowl ring which distinguished the -2 from its predecessor. Note the bomb racks and auxiliary fuel tank. *National Archives*

the navy and was seeking to create subordinate commands within the fleet that were better suited for developing the unified doctrine and tactics.[22] The solution, which went into effect on 1 April 1931, was to rearrange the U.S. Fleet into four major commands—Battle Force, Scouting Force, Submarine Force, and Base Force—with type commanders that would be responsible for the training and administrating of specific ship types. When Yarnell assumed command of the Aircraft Squadrons, Battle Fleet, he automatically became "type" commander for all fleet aviation. In time Pratt hoped to raise this position to a vice admiral's billet.

That summer, a new wrinkle was added to the exercises conducted during the annual aircraft concentration. For the first time, fighters and light bombers could practice their dive-bombing attacks on a maneuvering ship, for the *Stoddert,* a World War I vintage destroyer had been converted into a remote-controlled target ship. The crewless ship was equipped with radio control so that she could be pummeled with dummy bombs without fear of injuring any of her personnel. The *Stoddert* proved to be difficult for the airmen to hit. Her small size and the high degree of maneuverability which she exhibited under remote control left little margin for error on the part of the attacking pilots. The target ship had another advantage; the officer conning her from a trailing destroyer knew exactly when the attack would take place, the direction from whence it would come, and the number of planes involved. Since this officer had no other mission than to avoid being hit, he was free to maneuver the ship at will.[23]

Unfortunately, the first bombing exercises involving the *Stoddert* were marred by a tragic accident that resulted in the death of a pilot. On 30 July 1931, Lt. T. G. Fisher was killed while attempting to drop a water-filled practice bomb in a simulated dive-bombing attack on the moving ship. As he entered his dive, the target ship began a high-speed turn to the left. Fisher twisted the plane with ailerons, trying to keep the *Stoddert* in his sights, dropped his bomb at release altitude, and pulled back on the stick. What happened next is not known for sure, but the flotation gear under his wing accidentally inflated as he began his pullout, ripping the top wing off the F4B-2 he was flying. The rest of the plane plunged to the sea with the pilot still in it; all that was recovered was Fisher's helmet and a part of his brain. Ironically, Fisher, who was VF-2's commanding officer, had stressed the need to get good scores, telling his squadron before the flight that steep dives got hits.[24]

At the end of January 1932, the fleet sailed for the Hawaiian Islands, where they would participate in the joint Army-Navy exercises which would take place before Fleet Problem XIII. Enroute to the islands, Yarnell, flying his flag aboard the *Saratoga*, assembled his two big carriers and their escorts into a separate task force. Breaking away from the main body, he headed for a position off the island of Oahu, where he planned to launch a surprise attack on the army installations at Pearl Harbor.[25]

During the night of 6 February, Yarnell ordered a high-speed run-in that would place the carriers within launching range before daybreak. The raid was led by Lt. Cdr. Joseph J. "Jocko" Clark, commander of *Lexington*'s Fighting Squadron Two. A crack unit, VF-2 was the only carrier-based squadron in the navy composed of enlisted pilots, though all of the six three-plane sections in the eighteen-plane squadron were led by an officer. Clark took off one hour before dawn of the seventh, a Sunday, and headed for Oahu in the still dark sky. Finding the island in the huge expanse of the Pacific was made easier by the battery of searchlights at Kahuku Point, which served as a homing beacon and navigation aid.[26]

Clark attacked just as dawn was breaking over Pearl Harbor, catching the army pilots completely by surprise. He made simulated dive-bombing and strafing runs on hangars, storage tanks, and aircraft parked on the army's field. Though theoretically destroyed on the ground, the umpires allowed the U.S. Army Air Corps planes to take off. Unable to locate the attacking carriers, the army planes returned to base and were promptly struck by the second wave of navy raiders that Yarnell's air staff had perfectly timed to trap the army flyers. The army, in an effort to save face, tried to minimize the damage which would have been inflicted in a real attack, exaggerated its claims about striking the carriers, and had the gall to protest the legality of attacking on a Sunday!

After attacking Pearl Harbor the carriers spent several more days in the waters off Oahu covering marine landings that followed. At the completion of the joint exercises with the army they steamed the short distance to Lahaina Roads to await the arrival of the Scouting Fleet enroute from the Atlantic for participation in the Fleet Problem to follow. Pearl Harbor couldn't handle the big ships of the fleet at that time, so Lahaina Roads served as the main anchorage when the fleet journeyed to Hawaii.

For the carriers, Fleet Problem XIII turned out to be a repeat of the experience gained in 1929 and 1930. Once again the *Lexington* and *Saratoga* were pitted against each other. The *Lexington* and her two plane guard destroyers were assigned as a unit of the Black Force, which included the cruisers of the Scouting Force, *Langley* and the patrol planes normally assigned to the Base Force. *Saratoga* remained with the battle line, which was designated as the Blue Force for the duration of the problem. When the two big carriers were on opposing sides, as in most of the previous problems, they normally went after each other first. Once air supremacy was obtained, the surviving air group was then free to go after the ships of the other side. *Saratoga* struck first, the heavy bombers of VT-2, commanded by John J. Ballentine, attacking the *Lexington* while she was still in the process of launching her own strike group. Both carriers then launched strikes against the other. After the attacks, the chief umpire, Adm. Frank H. Schofield, arbitrarily assessed the damage as 38 percent for *Lexington* and 25 percent for *Saratoga*. Admiral Schofield later claimed that he had received conflicting reports from the observers stationed on each ship. He also wanted to keep both carriers in action so that they might continue to gain operational experience. Frank R. McCrary, the *Saratoga*'s captain, would later complain bitterly that *Lexington* should have been put out of action. The consensus of opinion among carrier

The *Saratoga* and *Lexington* off Diamond Head in February 1932. The two ships were the only large aircraft carriers in the fleet during the early 1930s and were frequently pitted against each other during the annual fleet problem. *Naval Historical Center*

personnel was that the carrier which suffered the first combined bombing attack would be devastated. McCrary couldn't see how *Lexington* had managed to escape the seven tons of bombs dropped by his ship's planes during the attack on her nemesis! But *Lexington* had over thirty planes in the air at the time, including twenty-five fighters. King claimed that his planes would have destroyed *Saratoga*'s heavy bombers long before they reached his ship since the enemy fighters that accompanied the heavy bombers were engaged in trying to dive bomb the defending carrier.[27]

After the first series of engagements King sent word to Adm. William H. Standley, the Blue commander, asking for permission to operate independently. With Standley's approval King withdrew at high speed to the south and then turned west so that the *Lexington* would be in a better position to attack the *Saratoga* while he himself remained undetected. King always wanted to win, and it was said that "he would change the rules or do anything to insure victory."[28]

King carefully monitored the reports of *Saratoga*'s movements, then timed his attack so that *Lexington*'s planes would reach *Saratoga* just as the last of her planes were coming aboard. *Lexington*'s planes caught *Saratoga* with all but six of her aircraft on deck, and, as these were preparing to land, they were not in a position to offer any resistance. They swept in to inflict more damage on the *Saratoga,* putting her out of action for the rest of the day. The next day King sent out another attack on the chance that the *Saratoga* might have been "rebuilt," a technique frequently employed in these maneuvers to reconstitute important combatants, but they could not find the enemy carrier.[29]

For the airmen, the most important lesson to be learned from these exercises was the need to add more carriers to the fleet. Fleet Problem XIII and its immediate predecessors showed that when there was only one carrier in each force, the primary objective became the destruction of the other carrier. An all-out effort ensued to accomplish this task, the usual result being that both sides lost their carriers. The obvious lesson to be learned was the need to procure more flight decks, that is, build more aircraft carriers.

CHAPTER 8

Tail Hooks and Tin Fish

WHILE THE FLEET was busy testing the equipment and tactics needed for war, Moffett and his staff were battling to protect the aircraft-building program from the wave of cost-cutting measures which began to permeate through the government after the stock market crashed in 1929. In May 1930, the aviation budget that Moffett had submitted for the coming fiscal year was slashed by 33 percent. Though Moffett lobbied hard to get more money allocated for aircraft procurement, the budget for the "Aviation Navy" was reduced even further in the first of a series of belt-tightening measures that BuAer was forced to take during the Depression. Nevertheless, Moffett made sure that enough money was included to procure the 279 new airplanes which would be needed to reach the goal of 1,000 planes by the end of the 1931 fiscal year.[1]

In the meantime, delays and uncertainty in the development of the XT5M-1 made it impossible to proceed with the acquisition of a production version of the "heavy" dive bomber—now dubbed the VB type—until it had been officially passed by the Board of Inspection and Survey. Once this obstacle was cleared Moffett would be able to authorize procurement of enough planes to equip a small test squadron so that the effectiveness of the heavy dive bomber could be proved in actual service.

Where to put the new planes created somewhat of dilemma for Moffett now that the light-bombing squadrons had reverted back to fighting units. He would have liked to have established a separate squadron for the new bombers, but budgetary constraints would not permit the addition of a new unit unless cuts were made someplace else. Eager to test the practical utility of this new type of aircraft, Moffett wrote to the assistant secretary of the navy suggesting that the number of carrier-based torpedo squadrons be cut in half so that a squadron of these newly developed dive bombers could be assigned to one of the carriers. Moffett's plan must have been approved, for a contract for twelve BM-1s was issued shortly after the XT5M-1's acceptance. The number of aircraft was just sufficient to keep one nine-plane squadron at full strength for at least a year.[2]

The original order was later expanded to include a total of sixteen planes, which entered service with Torpedo Squadron One aboard *Lexington* in 1932. Sixteen more aircraft, designated as BM-2s, were ordered in October 1931. They too were assigned to Torpedo One as they became available, filling out the squadron's complement of eighteen planes. The dive-bombing tactics demonstrated by VT-1 were so successful that the squadron's name was changed to Bombing Squadron One in 1934.

The conversion of VT-1 into a bombing unit left the carrier force with only one squadron of torpedo planes, VT-2 aboard *Saratoga*. By 1933 it looked as if even this squadron would be dissolved due to the lack of a suitable aircraft. The slow speed, large size, and generally low performance of the ungainly torpedo planes then in service made them extremely unpopular with both carrier commanders and their superiors.

Virtually no progress had been made in the development of the torpedo plane since the introduction of the Martin three-purpose T4M-1 plane in April 1927. Although the third version of this aircraft, the Great Lakes Aircraft Corporation's TG-2, was now in service, its performance was actually poorer in some respects than that of its predecessors.[3]

Experience gained during Fleet Problem IX had shown that torpedo bombers were not well suited for carrier operations. The exceedingly long takeoff run of these planes made spotting them extremely difficult. In a no-wind condition the T4M-1 needed 674 feet of deck to take off. Under these conditions torpedo planes waiting to be launched had to be spotted as far

A T4M-1 of Torpedo Two circling to land on the *Saratoga*. *National Archives*

back as the arresting gear. This made it impossible to schedule any kind of a rapid turnaround in the order in which squadrons of lighter aircraft could be recovered and relaunched. Even with a moderate 15-knot wind over the deck, a fully loaded torpedo plane required more than 300 feet for takeoff. This precluded their use on either the *Langley* or the new carrier *Ranger,* both of whose flight decks were considerably smaller than that of the *Lexington* and *Saratoga.*[4]

The advanced battle practice conducted off the coast of California in March 1933 only added increasing concern to the growing doubt about the value of carrier-based torpedo bombers and the viability of the torpedo as an aerial weapon. The Mark VII-2A torpedo, the only aerial torpedo then available, weighed 1,737 pounds but contained only 319 pounds of TNT.[5] This was a huge load for an aircraft designed to lift off from the short decks of a carrier. To many it was also an uneconomical use of the torpedo bombers' ordnance-carrying ability since the torpedo's warhead amounted to a relatively small percentage of the weapon's total weight. A number of senior officers were beginning to question whether it was prudent to sacrifice such a large proportion of the military load carried by an aircraft to the compressed air flasks, fuel tank, and propulsion machinery needed to drive the torpedo

Rare shot of a T4M-1 lifting off from the *Saratoga* with a 1,740-lb. Mark VII torpedo. *National Archives*

toward its intended target. The capability of hitting under the waterline did not appear to be much of an advantage for the torpedo either, inasmuch as tests conducted in 1924 on the incomplete battleship *Washington* had shown that a heavy bomb falling close alongside would produce the same underwater damage as a torpedo hit.[6]

The Mark VII-2A torpedo, 18 feet long and 18 inches in diameter, was produced by the Bureau of Ordnance (BuOrd) for aerial use in the early 1920s by modifying a standard Mark VII torpedo. When it entered service in 1922 it was restricted to a dropping altitude of less than 25 feet, with 15 feet recommended. The first gunnery exercises using the new weapon were conducted by Torpedo Squadron One in April 1922. The exercise took place 7 miles south of the Key West harbor entrance on a torpedo range laid out by the squadron's gunnery officer, Lt. John E. Ostrander Jr. The torpedoes were fitted with practice heads which were supposed to keep the torpedo afloat at the end of its run. To ensure recovery of the $10,000 weapon—a princely sum in those days—a second plane followed the dropping plane down the range to mark the torpedo's final position with a smoke bomb. A recovery boat was supposed to locate and retrieve the spent device so that it could be

The PT-1, shown here launching a torpedo, was the first operational torpedo plane to enter service with the U.S. Navy. Though the plane had a wingspan of 74 feet, it was unable to get airborne carrying a full load of gas, the torpedo, and its crew of two. *Naval Historical Center*

overhauled, recharged with compressed air, and refueled for reuse. When a torpedo sank, as they frequently did, divers would attempt to locate the weapon, the loss of which was considered to be the responsibility of the operating personnel. Ostrander, who was well aware of this policy, spent many hours looking for and recovering sunken torpedoes.[7]

The aircraft flown by VT-1 during these exercises were PT-1 float planes powered by the 330-hp Liberty engine. These were very large planes for their day, with a wingspan of 74 feet and a maximum takeoff weight of 7,075 pounds. They were woefully underpowered, however, and were further handicapped by a small fuel tank and tiny oil reservoir. It had a maximum cruising speed of only 45–55 knots when loaded, and you couldn't get them off the water with a full load of gas, both crew members, and the torpedo! Thus, it was nearly impossible to exceed the launching parameters BuOrd had established for the Mark VII torpedo.[8]

Although the engineers at the Naval Torpedo Station at Newport, Rhode Island, had successfully launched Mark VIIs at ground speeds up to 95 knots from heights to 32 feet, pilots were instructed not to drop the weapon at speeds above 75 knots or at an altitude greater than 25 feet. Even under these conditions the Mark VII-2A performed poorly. It had a number of material deficiencies which caused many of them to sink or run erratically unless "properly prepared and properly launched at a perfect attitude from low altitude . . . in comparatively smooth water." As described by one exasperated pilot, it was a "mechanical contrivance of extreme delicacy" that showed a marked tendency to dive and run too deeply.[9]

Torpedo exercises conducted by the Scouting Fleet showed that the Mark VII could not be successfully launched from an aircraft at an altitude in excess of 10 feet! The torpedo was so fragile that mechanical failure rates of 25–30 percent were commonly encountered during many of the gunnery exercises conducted with the Mark VII-2A in the late 1920s and early 1930s.[10]

The deficiencies and the limits of the Mark VII-2A were not ignored by the naval aviators who would have to employ these weapons in wartime. In March 1928, the commanding officer of VT-9S courageously wrote a scathing letter to the director of fleet training denouncing the use of torpedo planes unless a better weapon could be produced. In wartime, he explained, a torpedo plane pilot would be expected to drive in at high speed and to launch his torpedo while being harassed by antiaircraft fire and enemy aircraft. Under such circumstances, he continued, it would be unusual for a torpedo to be dropped from an altitude much under 25 feet at low speed. The Navy Department was deluding itself, he wrote, if it feels that it has a war weapon in the torpedo presently issued to aircraft. In his opinion, "the torpedo plane should be abolished" unless the Navy Department developed a torpedo rugged enough to permit it "being launched at 125 knots from an altitude of 25 feet, and slightly nose up or slightly nose down."[11]

This letter was transmitted to BuAer via the commanding officer of the aircraft tender *Wright,* the commander of Aircraft Squadrons, Scouting Fleet, and commander of the Scouting Fleet, all of whom endorsed the need for a torpedo of a more rugged design. In due course these comments were passed on to the Naval Torpedo Station, which reminded all concerned of the program to develop a special aircraft torpedo, now defunct, which had been discontinued so that the limited funds available could be used to adapt torpedoes already on hand. From the station's standpoint it made sense to continue to try to improve the Mark VII torpedo as opposed to starting from scratch on a new design. The Bureau of Ordnance concurred with this notion, insisting that the best course of action would be to continue to use whatever funds were available to improve the existing weapon.[12]

While the question of whether or not to develop a new torpedo worked its way through the bureaucratic organization of the navy, Moffett wrote to the commander-in-chief of the U.S. Fleet (CinCUS) to solicit the opinions from the forces afloat as to whether the design of a torpedo plane of small dimensions to carry a relatively short-range torpedo should be undertaken. Though the pilots favored the development of a short-range torpedo that could be carried by a small, fast two-seater, Reeves was against this concept, arguing that it would only reduce the offensive firepower of the carrier. "We should not walk back in the range capacity and offensive power of armament until every other resource has been exhausted," he reported.[13]

In Reeves's professional opinion the impetus to decrease the size of carrier aircraft resulted from a desire to increase the number of planes from a given landing platform. This was a fine idea, so long as it did not result in the reduction of total offensive power. Reeves, who was about to depart the fleet for shore duty, assigned his chief of staff, Cdr. Eugene Wilson, the task of responding to Moffett's memo. According to Wilson's report, Reeves, the departing commander of the Aircraft Squadrons, Battle Fleet, believed that

1. Production of a single-purpose torpedo plane was not warranted;
2. The T4M could be modified to permit material increases in performance;
3. Torpedo planes should be built to accommodate pilot and gunner only;
4. Present torpedoes could be improved to permit high dropping altitude and high dropping speed;
5. Present torpedoes could be shortened while maintaining present range via the use of more efficient engines;
6. Every naval aircraft must be built for several major capabilities;
7. Torpedo dropping and heavy bombing were not incompatible.

The above recommendations were duly forwarded to Admiral Pratt, who undoubtedly received a similar communication from the commander of the aircraft squadrons in the Scouting Fleet. Admiral Pratt, then CinCUS, took it upon himself to respond directly to Moffett's original request concerning the need for a new torpedo plane. The fleet, he reported, held that speed was an essential element in the success of an aerial torpedo attack, thus requiring the development of an aircraft torpedo capable of being dropped at a speed greatly in excess of that permitted by the Mark VII. This in turn required a marked increase in the ruggedness of torpedoes to permit higher dropping velocities from higher altitudes while keeping the present effective range and explosive charge. While Pratt agreed that the faster torpedo plane was needed, he was vehemently against squandering resources on the small torpedo plane which Moffett had suggested. Instead, he felt that BuAer should build improved aircraft better able to handle the heavier weapons. "The safest guide to follow with respect to a development program for all types of naval aircraft," proclaimed the commander-in-chief, was "to endeavor to reduce size, save weight, and increase performance [of the aircraft]."[14]

The opinions solicited by the Bureau of Aeronautics on the subject of the development of an aerial torpedo were submitted to the General Board of the Navy in September 1929. After due consideration, the board recommended the development of a new aerial torpedo that was capable of being launched at 100 knots from 50 feet. It was to have a range of 7,000 yards at a speed of not less than 30 knots. The weight was to be 1,700 pounds, length 13 feet 6 inches, and diameter 23 inches, with a 400-lb. warhead and a range of 4,000 yards at 35 knots. These specifications led to the design of a new 13.5 feet by 22.5 inch aircraft torpedo which BuOrd designated as the Mark XIII in August 1930.[15]

While the Naval Torpedo Station worked on developing the new torpedo, it continued its efforts to improve the performance of the Mark VII with the goal of obtaining a maximum dropping speed of 125 knots from an altitude of 50 feet. In July 1932, the aviation detail at Gould Island, Rhode Island, conducted test launchings to compare the performance of modified Mark VII-2A torpedoes to the standard design. Drops were made from 60 to 80 feet at from 65 to 132 knots with angle of entry from 5 to 49 degrees down by the head. Out of the ten standard torpedoes dropped, three were considered successful, but only one failure occurred in the thirteen drops made with the modified version. This led to a conversion project to change forty Mark VII-2A to 2B types, at a cost of $785 per torpedo. The new model had a nontumble gyro, a better depth mechanism, and a heat-treated nose cone, modifications which would enable the torpedo to be successfully dropped from 50 feet at 100 knots.[16]

The new models would not be delivered to the fleet until September 1934. By then the aerial torpedo was considered a weapon of restricted use that should only be employed on occasions when low ceilings precluded the use of bombers.[17] In the eyes of both the pilots and their superiors, the low-level approach and slow speed needed for a successful torpedo launch made torpedo planes extremely vulnerable to enemy gunfire. Experience with torpedo planes in various fleet exercises had shown that unsupported torpedo attacks were foredoomed to failure. As one torpedo squadron commander pointed out, ships armed with multiple machine guns could smother any attack that approached within the present range of the Mark VII torpedo.[18] The only solution was to provide a protective cover of smoke just before the scheduled attack. Not only was this difficult to coordinate and achieve due to the vagaries of the winds, but it required the use of additional aircraft, which limited the number of attackers, or worse, took planes from other needed duties.

Although the Bureau of Aeronautics had made every effort to improve the performance of the torpedo plane, it had not been able to develop a successor to the TG-2 that could keep up with the new planes entering the fleet. The last prototype was the Douglas XT3D-2. Delivered to Anacostia in 1932, it had a top speed of 153 mph. Though this was 25 mph faster than the TG-2, it was not anywhere near the 65-mph increase demonstrated by the latest two-seat fighters and scouting planes. In spite of the BuAer's best efforts, the development of the torpedo plane had lagged behind that of the other carrier types. It did not appear as if this situation would improve with the introduction of new Mark XIII torpedo either, as BuOrd was now predicting that this weapon would weight about 1,859 pounds. This was 119 pounds more than the existing Mark VII-2B, further exacerbating the weight problem in the design studies for the new VT-VB type, which BuAer hoped to solicit bids for in the near future.[19]

The Bureau of Aeronautics continued to push for the development of a 1,000-lb. aerial torpedo. Though this involved a material reduction in the explosive charge and range of the weapon, BuAer still believed that this was the only solution that would permit the use of torpedoes from carrier-based aircraft whose performance was consistent with the rest of the carrier complement. The new BMs were proving quite successful in service, and it was suggested that these planes could also be used for horizontal bombing by equipping the lead plane in each squadron or division with a bombsight and having the remaining planes drop on the leader. If a 1,000-lb. torpedo was developed, the BM could also be used for launching torpedoes, thereby eliminating the need for the VT type altogether. BuOrd had investigated the feasibility of producing a weapon of this size, but had found the concept impractical based on the current state of the art in propulsion technology. No funds were available for its development either, as the country was now in the midst of the Great Depression and the navy's budget had been severely restricted.[20]

Lacking a lighter weight torpedo, BuAer was forced to go ahead with plans for a new torpedo bomber capable of 180 mph with a full load of bombs. Only one experimental prototype was procured, the XTBG-1. It was not deemed suitable for service and no production order was issued. For the time-being, the fleet would have to make do with the inadequate torpedo planes at its disposal.

CHAPTER 9

Advances in Fighter Performance

U NTIL THE LATE 1920s most of the advancements in the design of naval aircraft came as a direct result of the Bureau of Aeronautics' efforts to improve airplane performance. Its endeavors to encourage the advancement of engine technology quickly led to the development, improvement, and adoption of the air-cooled radial engine for naval service. Once this was accomplished, the bureau set about to increase airframe strength so that its planes would be capable of enduring the greater stresses incurred by the bigger ordnance loads and more strenuous aerial maneuvers made possible by the new engines. Toward the end of the 1920s the design effort began to shift from the navy's engineers to the aircraft manufacturers, who began to introduce a series of technological breakthroughs that would radically improve the performance of propeller-driven aircraft. The streamlined engine cowling was the first of the innovative features introduced by the aircraft industry.

In late December 1929, the Boeing Airplane Company delivered an enhanced version of the F4B-1 fighter to the navy for testing as an improved carrier fighter. Although designated a fighter, the F4B-1 was a dual-purpose type that combined the best features of a fighter and a dive bomber. It was initially assigned to Bombing (VB) One-B on board the *Lexington*. The improvements incorporated into the F4B-1 were intended to significantly increase the plane's speed. To achieve this end, Boeing added a Townend-type ring cowling, installed a high-compression engine, and substituted smaller, drag-reducing wheels. These modifications were made by the manufacturer at its own expense, and the airplane was delivered free of charge to San Diego, California, for testing and evaluation by the pilots of VB-1B.[1]

The increase in performance was spectacular. The experimental plane was 20 percent faster than the current production model (182 mph at sea level) and delivered an impression speed of 196 mph at 8,000 feet. By far, the most important new feature was the cowl ring, which drastically reduced the drag generated by the otherwise exposed engine cylinders. While the Townend ring dramatically improved the F4B-1's performance, it reduced pilot visibility and made engine maintenance more difficult. Despite these disadvantages, the F4B-1 was so superior—it could outmaneuver and outfight any other aircraft in the fleet—that BuAer decided to purchase twenty-seven of the modified Boeing fighters, which were then classified as the F4B-2.

In addition to the Townend ring, the planes were equipped with Frise ailerons and a strengthened spreader bar–type landing gear. Though the latter precluded the release of a center-mounted 500-lb. bomb, it was an improvement over the original F4B-1 design, which, the navy soon discovered, could not take the severe punishment experienced during carrier landings.[2]

During one unfortunate exercise at sea, a flight of F4B-1s equipped with 55-gallon auxiliary fuel tanks was unexpectedly recalled to the carrier at the start of what was to have been a three-hour flight. The fully loaded planes were forced to land on *Lexington*'s rolling deck. The added weight of the fuel tanks and the extra fuel which still remained in them was simply too much for the landing gear, which failed as four of the planes touched down.[3]

The next major jump in airplane performance resulted from the introduction of retractable landing gear. Ironically, this major innovation was introduced in the last of the two-seat fighters. The company responsible for this innovation, the Grumman Aircraft Engineering Corporation, was a newcomer to the aviation industry.

In 1929 Leroy Grumman, the company's founder, was working for the Loening Aeronautical Engineering Company in New York City when he learned of Loening's plans to move to New Jersey. Rather than relocate, Grumman and a small cadre of key Loening employees decided to start their own company, which they decided would specialize in amphibians and flying boats.[4]

Grumman's long relationship with the U.S. Navy began with a modest proposal to build a new type of seaplane float with a fully retractable wheel-retracting mechanism. The all-metal design Grumman intended to use was based on the monocoque construction technique in which the aluminum outer skin provided much of the structure's strength. The new float would be considerably lighter than previous designs, offered better streamlining, and had a simple device for retracting the wheels that could be operated from the pilot's cockpit.[5]

The navy was enthusiastic but skeptical of Grumman's ability to produce the new design, since none of the new features had been tried before. Nevertheless, Grumman's proposal was attractive enough to warrant issuing a contract in the amount of $37,700 for the construction of two prototypes. These were delivered to the test unit at Anacostia, where they passed the catapult trials with flying colors. The new floats weighed less than existing navy types *without* wheels, and was the first to incorporate retracting gear. BuAer was so impressed with the results that it immediately placed an order for six more.

As Richard Thruelsen explains in his book *The Grumman Story,* the success of the retracting mechanism impressed those within BuAer's plane division. On his next trip to Washington, Leroy Grumman was asked to consider the possibility of adapting his design for the F4B. Grumman stated that the slender fuselage of the Boeing plane wouldn't take the retractable gear without a complete redesign. But what about a Grumman plane? Would the navy be interested in a new high-performance, two-seat fighter? Grumman had been working on the design of just such a plane and he would be glad to submit a bid to build the plane if the navy was interested.

Within two weeks Grumman had drafted a preliminary proposal for an experimental two-seat fighter, which he duly forwarded to BuAer on 10 March 1930. Along with the preliminary specifications, Grumman's proposal included design data, a suggested price, a balance diagram, and a three-view drawing. Two weeks later he received an informal letter from BuAer expressing interest in discussing the possibilities of the new plane. During the year-long dialogue which ensued, Grumman responded to an endless number of questions ranging in scope from the plane's fuel capacity and endurance, to modifications for a new engine, to preliminary pricing and delivery schedules.

The final design that emerged from these discussions didn't look like any previously built military fighter. Instead of a slender body, it had a thick-waisted, pot-bellied fuselage whose appearance of bulk and solidity was accentuated by the short-legged retractable landing gear upon which the plane rested. The fuselage would be constructed using the same monocoque technique which Grumman had successfully used on its floats. It would have Grumman's retractable landing gear and a powerful 600-hp Wright engine—the largest yet to power a navy fighter. Other advanced features included a NACA cowling, enclosed cockpits, and a NACA airfoil.

On 28 March 1931, a contract for the new plane, officially designated as the XFF-1 (the second *F* stood for Grumman, as BuAer had already assigned Great Lakes Aircraft the letter *G*), was formally issued in the amount of $73,975. The payment was broken down as follows: information for approval and design, $9,000; miscellaneous data, $8,900; (1) model XFF-1 airplane, $46,875; and final drawings, $9,200. The performance guarantees specified that the plane was to achieve 190 mph at sea level, a landing speed of 65 mph, a climb rate of 12,000 feet in ten minutes with full load, and a ceiling of 22,000 feet. The option to purchase a scout version was also included in the navy's contract.

The next nine months were extremely busy ones for Grumman, as it began to construct its first airplane. By May the company completed a wooden mock-up, which was duly inspected and passed by a gaggle of BuAer officers who journeyed to Grumman's plant on Long Island to critique the general layout of the plane and the arrangement of its instruments and controls. In June, Grumman received an unexpected bonus when the navy exercised its option on the scout version, designated the XSF-1. Now they would be building two planes instead of one. By November Grumman had completed the wings and fuselage and was ready to install the engine—a process which would not be completed until the third week in December. The finished aircraft was then readied for flight.

Before the plane could be turned over to the navy and final payment received, the XFF-1 would have to demonstrate its stability in flight and pass the two one-hour endurance tests now mandated by BuAer. To complete the manufacturer's test program, Grumman hired William McAvoy, the NACA test pilot who seemed to have cornered the market for testing new navy planes.

The flight was conducted at Curtiss Field, Long Island, on the morning of 29 December 1931. McAvoy stepped into the cockpit and made some taxi runs to check out the plane's ground-handling characteristics before taking to the air. Half an hour later he returned to the field and was forced to land, his windshield covered with oil. The ground crew quickly discovered that one of their members had failed to tighten the cap on the oil fill line, which had allowed a fine mist to escape once the oil pressure built up. The cap was tight-

Mock-up of the XFF-1 two-seat fighter taken at the Grumman factory on Long Island. *National Archives*

ened, and McAvoy took off once more to complete the interrupted test flight! The plane performed well thereafter, passing the manufacturer's test with ease.

Several days later, McAvoy flew the XFF-1 to Anacostia, where it was turned over to the flight test section, whose pilots would evaluate the XFF-1's flying characteristics while verifying the performance criteria specified in the contract.[6] The test results showed beyond a shadow of a doubt that Grumman had produced a tough, fast, agile airplane. It raced over the measured mile at 195 mph—faster than the newest single seater, the F4B-3, which was clocked at 167 mph under the same conditions (sea level). The XFF-1 either equaled or outperformed the best single-seat fighters in every category but two (rate of climb and ceiling).

The exceptional performance of the XFF-1 added to BuAer's growing concern about the design of a new single-seat fighter. The desirability of procuring a pure fighting plane unfettered by the bombing requirements heretofore deemed essential for all VF types was recognized by Cdr. Marc Mitscher. Mitscher, now in his second tour of duty at the Bureau of Aeronautics, was one of the most experienced carrier pilots in the navy. He had completed his carrier qualifications on the *Langley* in June 1926 and was in command of her

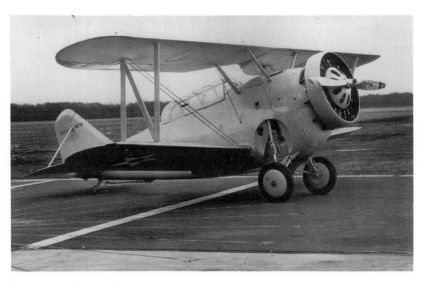

The XFF-1, shown here at Anacostia, was the first successful fighter prototype to have retractable landing gear. *National Archives*

flight deck the day a record-setting 127 landings were made. Mitscher made the first landing on the *Saratoga* and was her first air officer.[7]

By 1931 the requirement for dropping a 500-lb. bomb in a dive was now routinely included in the specifications for all new single-seat fighters. Mitscher, along with others, believed that this requirement had a detrimental effect on the characteristics essential for a fighting plane's primary mission—the destruction of enemy aircraft—which had seemingly become secondary to the bombing mission. Mitscher wanted to reverse these priorities. The time had come, he wrote, to initiate a design study of a "special" VF free from the dive-bombing encumbrances that hindered flight performance.[8]

Mitscher's idea was endorsed by the views of Rear Adm. Harry Yarnell, commander, Aircraft Squadrons, Battle Force. "It is becoming increasingly evident," Yarnell wrote, "that if the performance of fighters is to be improved . . . bombing characteristics of fighters must be made secondary to fighting characteristics." Although Moffett concurred, no planes of this "special" class were ordered in 1932. Instead the design section was instructed to evaluate potential designs for a single-seat fighter that was at least 8 mph faster than the new two-seater with a minimum range of 500 miles.[9]

After several weeks of study the material division recommended that the bureau proceed along two separate lines of development. The first was to procure an experimental aircraft based on the design for a new single-seat dive bomber that it was already working on. The specifications prepared by the design section called for a biplane of clean design, using the lightest type of fixed landing gear with an internal fuel tank large enough to satisfy the requirement for a range of 500 miles. Though this aircraft would be capable of dropping a 500-lb. bomb in a dive, it would still be considered a fighter.[10] This was a conservative approach which relied on the traditional type of landing gear rather than the retractable kind which Grumman had pioneered. Grumman's gear had the disconcerting habit of folding when it hit a particularly rough bump and was not yet considered fully reliable.[11]

A contract for two prototype VFs based on this first scheme was issued to the Curtiss company on 16 April 1932. Curtiss designed the new plane around the tried and true airframes that it had used on the earlier Hawks, attached new wings, and made provisions for mounting either of the two new powerful engines that Wright Aeronautical Corporation was developing: a huge 700-hp single-row radial and a 600-hp twin-row radial. The smaller physical size of the latter was expected to generate less drag, justifying the lower power output. To ensure the most speed possible they installed streamlined pants over the wheels, which were mounted at the end to a single streamlined strut. The first to fly—the XF11C-2—was equipped with a 700-hp Wright Cyclone engine. It had a top speed of 192 mph at sea level and 202 mph at 8,000 feet. The plane passed its acceptance tests, and a production order was issued for twenty-eight planes in October 1932.[12]

The second scheme called for BuAer to develop a new specification based on a scaled-down version of the XFF-1. The material division recommended that Grumman be encouraged to submit an unsolicited bid for an experimental model of such a plane. Although contrary to the intent of the Aircraft Procurement Act of 1926, the practice of issuing production contracts for experimental aircraft without competitive bidding was frequently used by the bureau to circumvent the time-consuming bidding process, which involved the creation of specifications, soliciting bids, and then evaluating the proposals submitted by each manufacturer. This was a procedure that BuAer had neither the time nor the money to conduct for every aircraft it wanted to try out. To get around some of the more restrictive aspects of competitive bidding, the bureau entered into an estimated price contract with the manufacturer for a prototype with the understanding that unforeseen technical difficulties or design changes could be handled through the expeditious issuance of a change order. Moffett justified the use of these negotiated contracts by claiming that they were in the best interests of the government.[13]

While the XFF-1 was still undergoing trials at Anacostia, Grumman began work on the design for a single-seat fighter that would outperform the XFF-1 and occupy less deck space. The first step was to reduce the overall dimensions and weight of the plane. Grumman opted to design the craft around the new Pratt and Whitney R-1535-44 engine, which had two rows of cylinders instead of the customary single row. This important innovation in engine technology reduced the frontal area of the power plant and allowed the cowling to be faired into the fuselage, improving its drag-reducing properties. To obtain the maximum speed possible, Grumman streamlined the fuselage, enclosed the cockpit with a sliding canopy, cleaned up the landing-gear housing, and added a retractable tail wheel and arresting hook.[14]

A contract for a prototype was issued on 2 November 1932. Like its predecessor, the XF2F-1 had fabric-covered wings and an all-metal fuselage, though the latter was designed with watertight compartments that would keep the plane afloat in the event of an emergency landing at sea. This was thought to be more reliable than the inflatable flotation bags then installed on carrier types and would eliminate the added weight (rubber bags, carbon dioxide bottle, and release mechanism) of this extravagant safety device. Two synchronized .30-caliber machine guns were mounted above the forward fuselage, and 100-lb. bomb racks were attached to each wing.

The plane was flown for the first time on 18 October 1933. After the manufacturer's demonstration flight it was ferried to Anacostia for more detailed testing. The plane turned out to be an exceptional performer; it had a top speed of 229 mph, was highly maneuverable, and was ideal for carrier operations. In aviator parlance it was a "hot ship" which required careful handling in light of its marginal stability and the tendency to whip into a spin when stalled. This wasn't a problem at altitude since a quick recovery could be made once the nose dropped and speed increased. To correct the problem, Grumman lengthened the upper wing by 6 inches to increase stability.

By the following year the XF2F-1 had received more favorable comment than any single-seater tested by the navy.[15] Although it was one of five experimental single-seat fighter models then being evaluated for service with the fleet, it was the only plane to have successfully completed its trials. These two factors made the plane the overwhelming choice for procurement.

The success of BuAer's efforts to improve fighter performance was made in the face of the growing monetary predicament confronting the navy due to the effects of the Depression.

CHAPTER 10

Expansion Begins

As the economic crisis continued throughout the early 1930s, Moffett faced the daunting task of trying to maintain the Bureau of Aeronautics' aggressive program of aircraft procurement and development in the face of the stringent budget cuts continually demanded by the Hoover administration. By the spring of 1932 the problem of providing enough aircraft to meet the growing needs of aviation in the fleet was reaching crisis proportions. In April 1933 the bureau submitted a preliminary aviation budget for the 1934 fiscal year that amounted to $29.8 million, down $3 million from the previous year's budget. In the months that followed, the Bureau of the Budget trimmed this figure to $26.5 million, forcing additional action on Moffett's part. On 27 September Moffett urged that this amount not be reduced any further. It was impossible, he explained, for his bureau to tighten its belt further without jeopardizing its ability to provide the new aircraft that would be needed to equip the *Ranger,* four new cruisers, and the three modernized battleships that were scheduled for recommissioning in 1934. The addition of these ships would necessitate the procurement and added operating costs for no less than 150 more navy planes.[1]

Despite these arguments, the Bureau of the Budget cut another $5 million from BuAer's request for 1934. In the hearings that followed, Moffett complained bitterly of the lack of funds which necessitated the elimination of many projects important to naval aviation. Reductions in expenditures had been made whenever and wherever possible, he testified, but they were now reaching the danger point, and any further decrease in the budget would seriously impair the efficiency and usefulness of naval aviation. Moffett's efforts resulted in a slight restoration of operating funds for naval aviation, which, when combined with an $8.1 million appropriation sufficed to provide just enough aircraft to meet the immediate aviation needs of the fleet, albeit some reductions had to be made in the number of shore-based aircraft.

Less than a month after passage of the 1934 budget, Moffett was dead, having perished aboard the *Akron,* when the airship crashed into the sea on 3 April 1933. The news stunned the nation, the navy, and the naval aviation community. After eleven years at the helm of BuAer, Moffett was abruptly gone.

For three weeks the powers at large struggled to determine who would be his successor. No airmen of flag rank wanted the job, leaving the choice between Capt. John Towers, the darling of the aviation community, and Capt. Ernest J. King, who had already been selected for promotion to rear admiral. CNO William V. Pratt advised King to submit a formal request for the post, which he, Pratt, immediately forwarded to the secretary of the navy. King, who had been lobbying on his own behalf for months, must have jumped for joy at the news. Secretary of the Navy Claude A. Swanson had favored the appointment of Towers, but King had an impressive record—along with the seniority that could not be ignored. President Roosevelt concurred, as did the Senate, which had to confirm the appointment of all bureau chiefs. Thus on 3 May 1933, Ernest J. King became second chief of the Bureau of Aeronautics.[2]

King's ascendancy was foreshadowed by another dramatic change in leadership: Roosevelt's inauguration. FDR's accession to the highest post in the land in March 1933 marked a major shift in the navy's fortunes. Unlike Hoover, the new president was a friend of the navy and was soon willing to approve a public works funding program that would bring the fleet up to "Treaty Strength" while simultaneously stimulating the nation's faulty economy.

By the time Roosevelt was inaugurated on 4 March 1933, banks were failing throughout the country and the United States seemed on the verge of economic collapse. Within days the new president called Congress into an extraordinary session to enact emergency legislation designed to alleviate the drastic state of the economy. Establishing a program of public works was one of the prime objectives on Roosevelt's agenda.[3]

From the onset of the Depression the Navy Department had tried to finance the construction and modernization of warships through funding for public works under the persuasive argument that such action would provide jobs and stimulate the economy. Although the navy had received such funds, President Hoover had consistently opposed their use for ship construction. Instead, they had been funneled through the Bureau of Yards and Docks to provide employment at politically sensitive navy yards and shore establishments.

After Roosevelt's election, the navy hierarchy renewed its efforts to obtain public works funds for new construction. Rear Adm. Emory Land, the newly appointed chief of the Bureau of Construction and Repair, was immediately thrown into the political fray surrounding New Deal appropriations for naval construction. Land was no stranger to the workings of Congress, having learned his trade under Moffett's tutelage as assistant chief of BuAer, where he been responsible for preparing the budget data presented to Congress for the "Aviation Navy." Now as chief constructor of the navy, he worked efficaciously to get the words *warships* and *airplanes* included in the definition of public works. Land then became the "point man" for the political campaign waged to obtain Roosevelt's approval for the $253 million expansion program the navy hoped to fund under the provisions of the National Industrial Recovery Act (NIRA).

On the day before the act was to be passed, Land, in company with Admiral Pratt and Rear Adm. Samuel Robinson, flew to President Roosevelt's home in Hyde Park, New York, to present an estimate of the shipbuilding program. Together they drafted an executive order allocating $238 million for the construction of 32 ships (including *Yorktown* and *Enterprise*). Although Roosevelt seemed willing to allot another $9 million to acquire the 290 planes needed to outfit these vessels, he was unwilling to spend more money (close to $6 million was requested) for the 55 patrol planes also wanted by the navy.[4]

During the next few months the navy was continually rebuffed in its efforts to secure further funding for aircraft under the public works provision of the NIRA. In the meantime, Secretary of the Interior Harold Ickes had taken over as federal emergency administrator of public works. Refusing all suggestions for further allocations, he quickly became the navy's chief nemesis in its efforts to secure funds for more aircraft. The difficulties faced by the navy with Ickes in charge is best described by Michael Allen West, whose doctoral thesis on the House Naval Affairs Committee is unmatched for its insights into the political realities of naval funding during the 1930s:

> Relishing his reputation as a curmudgeon and looking upon the Navy requests with a jaundiced eye, Ickes presented a similar problem in the field of public works allocations that the Department experienced with Budget Director Douglas on regular appropriations. Quite simply, when it came to prying dollars out of "Uncle Harold's" hands, the department and its congressional allies had met an adversary worthy of their mettle.[5]

Ickes's objections were overcome on 23 October, when Roosevelt finally relented and approved the allocation of another $15 million in public works funds for aircraft purchases, to be divided equally between the army and the navy.

The first allotment of funds from the Public Works Administration was made on 17 November 1933. The navy's share came to $7.5 million, of which the lion's share (over $6 million) went to buy new planes. The remainder was spent to modernize existing aircraft by installing new navigation instruments and radio sets.[6]

Although the additional funding provided under the Public Works Administration allowed BuAer to acquire a considerable number of new aircraft, it was becoming painfully clear that the 1,000-plane limit was totally unrealistic based on the number of ships that were rapidly being added to the fleet. Since the enactment of the 1926 program, 15 cruisers and an aircraft carrier having a combined aircraft complement of 212 airplanes had joined the fleet. In addition, the navy was building 2 more aircraft carriers and 6 cruisers that would require the addition of another 273 airplanes. The bureau estimated that the number of aircraft required for full efficiency was 2,184 planes. Yet despite the growth of naval aviation, the 1934 budget for the "Aviation Navy" was actually less than the expenditures for 1920![7]

In retrospect, aviation's troubles were entwined with the lack of a clearly defined building policy that affected the entire navy. Funding for both ships and aircraft was still provided in the same manner as public works. First, each program had to be authorized by both houses of Congress, then funding had to be approved on a yearly basis by separate appropriation bills passed by the House of Representatives.

During his tenure as CNO, Admiral Pratt had proposed an eight-year building program that would have rectified this problem. Pratt's goal was to bring the navy up to its authorized treaty limits, obtain airplanes for these warships, and build certain nontreaty auxiliaries that were needed by the fleet.[8] When Adm. William H. Standley succeeded Pratt as CNO on 1 July 1933, he was intent on continuing the efforts of his predecessor to promote the construction of new ships by pushing for "an annual building program which would not only provide for replacement of ships as they become obsolete" but also keep the "Navy modernized and up-to-date."

Under Standley's leadership, the Navy Department began to press Congress to enact legislation to modernize the fleet. In the press and at public appearances, both he and Secretary of the Navy Swanson made a concerted effort to stress the need for a replacement building program to complement the new ships being funded by the Public Works Administration. In late November, Swanson directed Standley to provide estimates of the cost of the program to the judge advocate general for use in drafting a legislative proposal that would be presented to Congress. It is likely that Admiral Land, who would have prepared the figures used by Standley, passed this information to Congressman Carl Vinson, chairman of the Naval Affairs Committee. It appears that Vinson used this information as the basis for the naval construction bill (later named the Vinson Act), which he introduced in the following month.[9]

Despite the longstanding complaints from BuAer, neither document appears to have contained any provision to fund the aircraft that would be needed to outfit the new ships in the program. Seeking to correct this imbalance, BuAer began to prepare a five-year building program for aircraft, which King duly forwarded to the judge advocate general (via the CNO) in mid-December. King, it appears, also had help behind the scenes in the person of Henry L. Roosevelt, the assistant secretary of the navy.[10]

When hearings for the Vinson bill got under way in the latter part of January, Henry Roosevelt was the navy's lead witness. Substituting for the ailing Swanson, the acting secretary raised the aircraft issue during his testimony. Within a week he had written the director of the Bureau of the Budget requesting approval to add 650 planes to the navy list over the next five years, raising the total number to 1,650 airplanes. Though sympathetic to the navy's efforts to increase the authorized limits of usable aircraft, the Bureau of the Budget deemed it foolish to attempt to include the details as to the numbers of planes and the cost per year in the legislative proposal that was now under discussion. Instead, it recommended that a proviso be added to the bill authorizing the president to approve the purchase of additional aircraft not covered by the existing 1,000-plane program.[11]

Admiral Standley and Rear Admiral King appeared before the House Naval Affairs Committee when the hearings continued. Standley began by reciting the steps taken by the navy to secure authorization of additional aircraft and the favorable reply received from the Bureau of the Budget. Standley's testimony was followed by that of King, who described in detail BuAer's policy for purchasing aircraft based on the provisions of the Aircraft Act of 1926 and the statutes covering government procurement. King, who was later recognized for his extensive knowledge on a given subject, must have impressed the congressmen present, for the committee readily approved a motion which would authorize the president to "procure the necessary naval aircraft for vessels and other naval purposes in numbers commensurate with the treaty navy." An amendment to this effect was put forth by Vinson and inserted into the legislation (the Vinson-Trammell Act) enacted 27 March 1934.[12]

Although BuAer got most of what it wanted from the Vinson-Trammell Act in the way of more aircraft, it paid a high price in the form of two highly restrictive clauses which made their way into this piece of legislation. The first of these was introduced by Senator Charles Tobey of New Hampshire, who wanted to limit profiteering by arms makers. There was widespread belief that munitions makers had been responsible for World War I, and the Tobey amendment set 10 percent as the maximum amount of profit that could be made under any contract funded by the act. This provision caused at least one manufacturer (Boeing) to forgo navy work in preference to producing planes for the army which had no restrictions on profits.[13]

The second amendment was potentially far more damaging to BuAer's program. Incensed by the aviation industry's "unholy and unconscionable profits," Senator Homer T. Bone introduced an amendment calling for the construction of 50 percent of the navy's aircraft and engines in government plants. The navy argued, to no avail, that the average profits realized by the aircraft industry engaged in building naval aircraft had been less than 4 percent between 1926 and 1933. To attempt to produce half the aircraft needed in government plants would "helplessly swamp technical facilities already overloaded." Furthermore, the navy only had twenty officers capable of directing and executing new aircraft design. To train new officers for this purpose would take at least seven years. Even if this could be done, the resulting designs wouldn't be as good as those produced by private industry and would probably be more costly to produce. Senator Park Trammell, Vinson's counterpart on the Naval Affairs Committee in the Senate, suggested that 25 percent would be a more reasonable figure, which Bone accepted. As enacted by Congress, a final proviso in the bill gave the president the right to suspend this provision of the Vinson-Trammell Act if he determined that the government's plants were inadequate for the task.[14]

CHAPTER 11

A Prophecy of the Future

Wʜɪʟᴇ Rᴇᴀʀ Aᴅᴍɪʀᴀʟ Kɪɴɢ and other high-ranking officials in the Navy Department were engaged in securing the legislation needed to procure new aircraft, the proliferation of carrier types being developed within the Bureau of Aeronautics was beginning to play havoc with the process of selecting planes for service. By the middle of 1931 BuAer was in the process of developing no less than six different carrier types. In addition to the two-seat BM-1 dive bomber, which had just gone into production, BuAer was working on an improved single-seat fighter, a new two-seat fighter / dive bomber, a single-seat fighter / dive bomber, a new tactical scout, and an improved torpedo plane. The number of types under development was more than could be operated on one aircraft carrier at any given time. The restricted amount of deck space available limited the *Lexington* and *Saratoga* to four eighteen-plane squadrons plus whatever spares could be suspended from the overhead in the hangar deck. The main issue confronting the plans division was which mix of aircraft was best.

The logical solution was to consolidate several functions into one common design. Though this concept had proven unworkable in the Martin three-purpose plane, it began to be viewed with renewed favor within BuAer as the need to produce a new dive bomber emerged in the summer of 1931. Construction of the *Ranger*—the first aircraft carrier in the U.S. Navy to be designed from the keel up—was scheduled to begin shortly. Unlike her larger cousins, however, *Ranger*'s short flight deck would prohibit the use of a fully loaded T4M. Thus, she would not carry any torpedo planes. Instead, her most potent weapon would be the "heavy" dive bomber. The only plane of this type in service was the BM-1, an aircraft whose design was already three years old. By the time *Ranger* was scheduled to join the fleet in 1934, this aircraft would be obsolete. To affect a satisfactory replacement, BuAer needed to start working on a new design.

The material division, headed by Cdr. Ralph D. Weyerbacher, was given the task of formulating the performance characteristics for a new dive bomber. Weyerbacher's department had been evaluating the relative merits of the single-seat versus the two-seat design for several months and had compiled a good bit of information comparing the two.[1] This information was forwarded to Cdr. Richmond Kelly Turner, who was then in charge of the plans division. Turner wanted the dive bombers to double as scouts so that more attack planes could be carried on each carrier. This justified the inclusion of the second seater, who was needed to operate the radio used to receive orders and transmit contact reports.[2]

Turner, another late convert to naval aviation, had taken flight training with Ernie King. He had joined BuAer in 1929 just after Towers had been promoted to assistant chief of the bureau and was appointed head of the plans division with Towers's blessing.[3] Because Turner's knowledge of aviation matters was limited, Marc Mitscher was directed to provide Turner with whatever technical assistance he might require.[4] Though the two men had graduated from Annapolis in the same year, Mitscher, whose academic record placed him near the bottom of the class, lacked the seniority for the billet handed Turner. After more than twenty years in the navy, Mitscher was still a lieutenant commander and was outranked by Turner.

Working for Turner must have been particularly galling to Mitscher, who had won his wings in 1916. Although there is no record of Mitscher's feelings on this matter, it had to be but one of many instances in which the Johnny-Come-Latelys were appointed to positions coveted by the more experienced, though still junior, flyers. Undoubtedly this created resentment and frustration among the more qualified airmen, who viewed the JCLs as interlopers who were using aviation as a stepladder to further their careers.[5]

Which one of the two men came up with the idea for the scout bomber is not known, though a memorandum outlining the performance characteristics for this new type was issued under Turner's signature in August 1931. Turner's memorandum called for an experimental dive bomber that could fly 400 miles with a 1,000-lb. bomb, 750 miles with a 500-lb. bomb, or 1,000 miles when equipped with an external fuel tank in lieu of a bomb.[6] This design concept was discussed at length during a conference held in the assistant chief's office on 24 August 1931.[7]

The plane which emerged from Turner's memorandum and the discussions which followed was the BG-1, the last production airplane built for the navy by the Great Lakes Aircraft Corporation. Although the craft was constructed around a conventional airframe with a fixed undercarriage, it had a number of advanced features which enabled it to outperform its BM-2 predecessor by a considerable margin.[8] It was one of the first carrier planes with a controllable pitch propeller and one of the first equipped with adjustable cowling flaps, a device which solved the inherent cooling problems of the Pratt and Whitney 700-hp, R-1535-82 Twin Wasp engine which powered the new dive bomber (the flaps were opened during takeoff and climb to cool the engine and closed at cruising speed to keep drag low).

Exercises and fleet problems were beginning to demonstrate the offensive power of the carrier-based dive bomber. Only the most modern of battleships was immune from the potentially devastating effects of the relatively large bombs, which could now be delivered with a high degree of accuracy. Aircraft carriers, with their unarmored flight decks, were some of the most vulnerable ships. One or two well-placed 500-lb. bombs could easily curtail all flight operations. Carrier commanders were now convinced that the best way to achieve aerial supremacy was to launch a preemptive air strike on the opposing carrier before it had a chance to get its own planes in the air. Once launched, such an attack would be almost impossible to stop since there was virtually no way of detecting the approaching enemy planes and/or directing defending fighters to an intercept before the attack began.

This concept was firmly established within the aviation community by the fall of 1933 as evidenced by remarks made by Capt. Arthur B. Cook during his Navy Day of speech of 27 October. Cook, then assistant chief of BuAer, told his audience of aviation workers at the Curtiss plant in Buffalo, New York, that "the only effective way to stop the attack of bombing planes is to seek out and destroy the ships on which they are based." This could only be

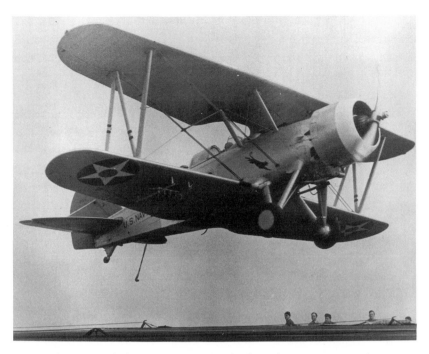

A BG-1 about to catch the arresting gear as it lands on the *Ranger,* 22 March 1938. Note the small flaps on the after edge of the engine cowling and the bomb crutch located under the fuselage. The squadron insignia, a black panther, indicates this to be one of the aircraft assigned to Bombing Squadron Three. *National Archives*

done effectively, he explained, from planes operated from our own carriers. "The airplane," he concluded, "is today one of the most formidable weapons in sea warfare, the aircraft carrier of no less importance than the battleship, cruiser, submarine, and destroyer." As noted in the previous chapter, the navy was actively lobbying to obtain additional public works money for new aircraft and had just won presidential approval to use NIRA funding for this purpose. Cook's remarks were obviously intended to win public approval and political support for the $7.5 million which was about to be earmarked for 130 new airplanes.[9]

Three days before Cook's well-publicized speech, Cdr. Hugh Douglas, the only aviator on the faculty of the Naval War College, gave a routine lecture on air tactics that would prove to be remarkably insightful. Unbeknownst to his audience, Douglas was about to predict the outcome of the most decisive naval battle of the twentieth century—the Battle of Midway some nine years hence. Douglas, who had just completed a two-year tour of duty as *Saratoga's* executive officer, had personally observed the two-day punching match which ensued between the big carriers during Fleet Problem XIII. He must had been on the *Saratoga's* bridge when she was caught flat footed by King's planes on 15 March 1932 and put out of action. This event must have made a deep impression on Commander Douglas, who felt compelled to describe the tactical implications of such an attack to his audience at the Naval War College. "In case an enemy carrier is encountered with planes on deck," he told the assembled officers, "a successful dive bombing attack by even a small number of planes may greatly influence future operations."[10] Little did he know how prophetic this statement would be.

Experience afloat had demonstrated the importance of being the first to locate and strike an opposing carrier. What was needed, according to most naval aviators, was a fast, well-armed scout plane which could attack the enemy's flight deck as soon as it was sighted. Heeding the advice of the fleet, BuAer decided to convert the two-seat dive-bombing fighters then under development into a new class of aircraft, the Scout Bomber, or VSB.[11] Instead of two 100-lb. bombs, the maximum ordnance load was increased to include the capability for dropping the much more powerful 500-lb. weapon.

The first planes to receive the new SB designation were the XSBU-1 and XSBC-1. Both planes evolved out of a BuAer program to develop a replacement for the F8C-4, whose performance had been less than spectacular.

The XF3U-1, had showed considerable promise as a scout when tested at Anacostia. In November 1930, the navy asked Vought to convert the plane

Table 11.1 Striking Power of Aerial Bombs and Shells

	Total Weight (pounds)	Explosive Charge (pounds)
Shells		
8-inch, Mark 6	260	59
14-inch, Mark 15	1,400	470
Bombs		
500-lb., Mark 7	501	392
500-lb., Mark 12 (AP)	516	252
1,000-lb., Mark 5	989	771
1,000-lb., Mark 13 (AP)	102	537

Source: Friedman, *U.S. Naval Weapons*, 276.

Note: The above does not take into account the penetrating power of armor-piercing bombs, the AP type. These were not available in 1934.

The SBU was the first carrier type designed to fulfill the dual tasks of dive bombing and scouting. *National Archives*

into an experimental scout bomber, which it designated as the XSBU-1. Instead of modifying the craft for its new role, Vought removed the engine and as much equipment as possible and used them as the basis for a totally new airplane. The new design had larger wings that were reinforced to survive the stresses of dive bombing, a bigger fuel tank, and provision for a centerline-mounted 500-lb. bomb.[12] The XSBU-1 turned out so well that the navy ordered eighty-four production models.

The new scout was the first VS to exceed the 200-mph speed mark, although it must be noted that this was achieved in a "clean" condition (without a bomb). Deliveries began in late November 1935, with the first planes going to Scouting Squadron Three.

In an effort to increase the striking power of the aircraft carriers then assigned to the Battle Fleet, the navy converted VF-1B—one of two fighting squadrons then assigned to the *Saratoga*—into a light-bombing squadron and renamed it VB-2B. The unit was already flying the first planes to be classified as "Bombing-fighters," a new type inaugurated by BuAer when it changed the designation of the Curtiss Goshawk single-seat fighter from F11C-2 to the BFC-2. The F11C-2s, which were originally procured as single-seat fighters

The BF2C-1 was an unsuccessful attempt to improve the performance of the F11-C (later redesignated BFC-2) by adding the retractable landing gear prominently shown in this photograph. *National Archives*

having a 500-lb. dive-bombing capability, were no match for the new generation of fighters, whose performance was greatly enhanced by the ability to retract their landing gear.

After Curtiss had secured a production contract for the F11C-2, it convinced the navy to issue a change order allowing the company to modify one of the production planes into an experimental prototype to test the new landing gear that Curtiss had come up with. Retracting the wheels was expected to increase the plane's speed by 10 percent so that it would be competitive with the new two-seat fighters the navy was purchasing from Grumman.

While Curtiss completed the rest of the order in the spring of 1933, it proceeded to convert the fifth F11C-2 into the XF11C-3. In addition to the retractable gear, the experimental craft had an upgraded version of the Wright Cyclone engine and a larger fuel tank. Like the retractable landing gear in the Grumman planes, the wheels were retracted into the sides of the fuselage using a hand crank for power, though the actual retracting mechanism was different than that used by Grumman. To accommodate the wheels, which would not fit into the original design, Curtiss had to add faired sections extending down the side of the fuselage.

A section of BF2C-1s in flight, showing the tubular airfoil that was installed below the engine in an unsuccessful effort to solve the vibration problems which plagued this airplane. *U.S. Naval Institute*

When tested at Anacostia in February 1934, the new plane achieved a top speed of 216 mph—an improvement of 11 mph. The XF11C-3 also climbed faster and had a higher service ceiling. The performance figures for the new plane were so impressive that on 26 February 1934 BuAer ordered enough aircraft to outfit an entire eighteen-plane squadron. The new planes were classified as BF2C-1s and were ordered with additional improvements, which included the installation of a controllable pitch propeller, a semi-enclosed cockpit, and the substitution of an all-metal wing structure in place of the wood used on previous models.

The first planes were delivered to VB-5B at Norfolk in November 1934, though carrier operations did not begin until the following March, when the squadron went on board the *Ranger*. Three of the new craft were soon involved in a series of barrier crashes that damaged their gear beyond repair. The cause of these accidents—an unexpected hook bounce—was easily rectified by modifying the design of the tail hook assembly.

This was not the only problem encountered, however. Pilots were soon complaining about the excessive vibration, which was strong enough to loosen the plane's rigging. This was an extremely dangerous situation that could lead to a catastrophic structural failure during pullout. Unfortunately, this conclusion was not reached until after one of the squadron's pilots was killed when his plane disintegrated in midair during a routine dive-bombing exercise. This incident and the subsequent discovery of the airplane's fatal flaw caused the BF2C to be grounded and ultimately withdrawn from service.[13]

CHAPTER 12

The All-Metal Monoplane

B Y THE EARLY 1930s the Bureau of Aeronautics had begun experimenting with a new class of aircraft that had one wing instead of the two that characterized the standard biplane of this era. Although a design based on a single wing offered the advantage of greater speed, it created inherently higher wing loadings, which, all other factors remaining unchanged, diminished maneuverability, lessened rate of climb, reduced maximum ceiling, and lengthened the takeoff run. Worst of all, monoplanes, as the single-winged craft were classified, had higher stalling speeds than their biplane cousins. This was a major problem for BuAer's designers, who wanted to keep the landing speeds of their planes as low as possible. Not only did this make it easier for the pilots to line up on the flight deck, but it reduced the stresses on the plane's undercarriage and the ship's arresting gear. Designing the undercarriage to handle the continual strain of landings was not a trivial matter in the days when every extra pound adversely affected aircraft performance. Operating units about the carriers consistently told BuAer that they were unwilling to raise the landing speeds of carrier planes unless a really striking increase in top speed could be obtained.[1]

Despite these disadvantages, BuAer continued to investigate the potential of the single-wing design and by the beginning of 1934 had three experimental monoplane fighters under development. The most promising was Northrop's XFT-1, whose stalling speed of 63 mph was close to the minimum specified for carrier landings. To achieve this dramatic reduction, the plane's designers had devised an ingenious mechanism for interlocking the flaps and ailerons during landing.

The Northrop Aircraft Company began work on the XFT-1 in May 1933, when it received a contract from the navy to build an experimental fighter based on Northrop's Gamma, the latest in a series of advanced monoplanes designed by the company's founder, Jack K. Northrop. Northrop had pioneered the use of the metal-skinned monocoque fuselage in which the skin of the plane and not the internal structure carried most of the load. Like its civilian cousins, the XFT-1 was a low-wing monoplane that had an enclosed cockpit that was faired into the top of the fuselage. It was powered by a 650-hp engine and had the same deep wheel pants that characterized most of Northrop's early designs.

Test flights conducted at Anacostia after its delivery in February 1934 showed that the experimental craft was capable of achieving a top speed of 235 mph.[2] Although the XFT-1 was the fastest aircraft yet tested by the navy, it lacked the maneuverability of a good fighter. The plane had other deficiencies, including a dangerous tendency to spin and a takeoff run that was much longer than for the typical biplane. The latter was a serious detriment with respect to the needs of flight-deck operations.

The navy returned the prototype to Northrop with a long list of changes needed to remedy the plane's defects. Northrop rebuilt the aircraft in accordance to the modifications suggested by BuAer and delivered the craft, now designated XFT-2, to Anacostia in April 1936 for flight testing. Unfortunately, the design changes did not correct the plane's defects; it still had an unhealthy desire to enter into an uncontrollable spin. It was so unstable that the navy had to ground the plane for fear that it would kill one of the test pilots—a concern which almost came to pass when the plane crashed as it was being returned to the factory.[3] Although the pilot survived the crash, the plane was a total write-off.

While the flight test section was evaluating the performance of the XFT-1 in the spring of 1933, the design section began preparing specifications for the three new prototypes. Contracts for the new planes had to be let in the coming year if production models were to be ready in time to fill the aircraft

The control problems exhibited by the XFT-2 could not be corrected, and the program was terminated when the only prototype crashed while being flown back to the Northrop factory. *National Archives*

complements of the *Yorktown* and *Enterprise*, which were scheduled to enter service in 1937. Admiral King was actively lobbying Congress for more money for aircraft, and it was obvious that he wanted the bureau to be ready to act as soon as the funding was approved.[4]

By March the design section had prepared detailed specifications for the two classes of dive bombers that would be needed to fill out the complements of the new carriers under construction: one to carry 500-lb. bombs (VSB) and one to carry 1,000-lb. bombs (VB). The former was expected to weigh about 5,000 pounds, have a top speed in excess of 215 mph, and have a relatively short takeoff run. The latter would be 1,000 pounds heavier and 10 mph slower. Both planes were to have a stalling speed of 65 mph for landing; had to achieve stable, vertical, "zero-lift" dives using some form of speed-limiting device (e.g., dive brakes) to keep the airspeed under 250 knots; and had to withstand 9-G pullouts with a full bomb load. Specifications for the two types were sent out to the various aircraft manufacturers in mid-March along with a letter soliciting bids for one experimental prototype and twenty-seven production models.[5]

Northrop decided that a single airplane could meet both sets of specifications and submitted a proposal for a low-wing monoplane that would satisfy the requirements for both planes.[6] The proposal was accepted by BuAer, which chose to develop Northrop's plane in the heavy bomber category under the XBT-1 designation.

The most difficult technical problem facing Northrop and the other manufacturers who submitted bids to the navy was how to meet the demanding performance characteristics specified for dive bombing. The navy insisted that the plane's speed in a vertical dive be keep under 250 knots. The diving speed had to be kept low enough so that the G forces and pullout altitudes could be kept within reasonable limits. If this could not be achieved, the altitude of bomb release would have to be increased, resulting in a degradation of bombing accuracy. How to keep the diving speed of a streamlined monoplane below 250 knots was a problem not encountered by the current generation of dive bombers whose terminal velocity was automatically retarded by the high drag-producing effects of their fixed undercarriages and wire bracing.

The best solution was provided by Ed Heinemann, an extremely talented engineer who worked for Northrop. Heinemann concluded that the best approach would be to install split flaps along the trailing edge of the wing to act as dive brakes. He then proceeded to design a control mechanism which permitted both flaps to be extended in a dive, but allowed only the lower flap to be opened during takeoff and landings. Although flaps had been tested in wind tunnel simulations of the XFT-1, there was no guarantee that the concept of split flaps would work.[7] Aeronautical engineering was still pretty much a trial and error process then, and the only way to find out was to build a prototype and test fly it. This, of course, was the whole purpose behind BuAer's extensive program for constructing experimental aircraft.

As was the case with most new designs, the XBT-1 was not without its several flaws. The most serious problem involved the horizontal stabilizer, which, it was soon discovered, had a severe flutter. This defect was noted during the first test dives, which took place shortly after the plane's flight debut in August 1935. When Ed Heinemann viewed motion pictures taken during the dives he was shocked to find the extent of the movement: the stabilizer's wing tips were moving through an excursion of almost two feet. This discovery scared the hell out of the talented designer, who had taken the pictures himself while riding in the plane's rear seat.

Try as they might, Northrop's design team was unable to correct the prob-

The XBT-1 undergoing routine testing at Anacostia. Note the arrangement of the semiretractable landing gear that was typical of the early monoplanes. *U.S. Naval Institute*

lem, until a NACA engineer recommended using perforated flaps to break up wing vortex which appeared to be creating the tail buffeting. He recommended that they try cutting holes in the flaps to reduce the size of the vortices. According to accounts in Heinemann's biography, he had discounted this idea previously, fearing that the holes would increase the stalling speed above the 60-mph limit specified by the navy. Heineman agreed to try it, he explained, because "we didn't have anything else going for us."[8] The entire flap was covered with a series of 3-inch holes which worked like a magic charm, eliminating the flutter even when both flaps were fully extended during the 250-mph terminal velocity dives.

The development of the split-flap dive brake was a milestone in the continuing efforts to improve the aerodynamic performance of the dive bomber —one which was to have a marked effect on the outcome of battle, for it made the SBD, a direct descendant of the BT-1, a superb bombing platform that could be easily controlled in the near-vertical dives preferred by the U.S. Navy. No other dive bomber could match this feat.[9]

It took two years for the Bureau of Aeronautics to design and test a prototype, another year was required for production, and a fourth to evaluate it under actual service conditions. It was not unusual, therefore, for four years to pass before the bureau knew whether a particular design concept had succeeded. By that time the plane might be obsolete and ready for replacement. Under these circumstances it would have been folly for BuAer to commit to any one company, design, or even type of aircraft.

Unwilling to place all of its eggs in one basket, BuAer had issued a separate development contract to the Great Lakes Aircraft Corporation for a second VB prototype. This plane, designated as the XBG2-1, was on a conventional biplane design, a fact, no doubt, that influenced its selection by BuAer.

In the VSB class, BuAer opted to build several scout bombers and issued a number of contracts for a variety of prototypes that included two designs proposed by Chance Vought: the XSB2U-1 low-wing monoplane and XSB3U-1 biplane; a Brewster design for a midwing monoplane, designated as the XSBA-1; as well Grumman's design for the XSBF-1.

The design competition of 1934 also included specifications for a totally new class of torpedo bomber, a plane whose primary mission was to attack heavy surface craft with torpedoes.[10] Since its secondary mission was bombing, the type was classified as a VTB. As in the case of the VS and VSB categories, BuAer elected to build two prototypes: a conventional biplane based on a design submitted by the Great Lakes Aircraft Corporation and an advanced monoplane based on a design proposed by Douglas. The former, designated as the XTBG-1, earned the distinction of being the last biplane torpedo plane purchased by the U.S. Navy. The latter, delivered as the XTBD-1, was destined to become the forerunner of the ill-fated Devastator.

With an eye to the future, the bureau chose to develop at least one monoplane design in each category. The awarding of contracts was shrewdly calculated to provide test data on a variety of new features, such as Northrop's split-flap, offered by various manufacturers to enhance the performance of their model.

Absent from the 1934 design competition were plans for a new fighter. As mentioned earlier, the bureau was still evaluating the capabilities of the three experimental monoplanes which it had ordered the previous year, but the conspicuous absence of further efforts to develop a faster VF in light of the increased speed of the new attack types was indicative of the growing controversy surrounding the desired characteristics of a pure fighter.

For years the bureau had been designing fighter types to double as dive bombers, thereby increasing the striking capability of the limited number of

A pilot of the *Yorktown*'s Bombing Five practicing his dive-bombing technique in the BT-1. Note the telescopic sight projecting through the windscreen and the extended dive flaps. *National Archives*

aircraft carried by the small number of carriers in the U.S. Navy. But in the eyes of many aviators the characteristics needed to make a fighter suitable for dive bombing compromised its performance in air-to-air combat. Though Towers had been successful in eliminating the 500-lb. bomb from the pure VF, they were still required to deliver a 100-lb. bomb in the diving attack.

Table 12.1 Performance Improvements after Removal of Safety Gear

Airplane Performance	F4B-4	BFC-2	F2C-1	BF2C-1
Speed increase (mph)	11.8	9.3	6.7	12.0
Takeoff run, decrease	10%	6%	8%	8%
Service ceiling increase	5,000 ft.	4,100 ft.	1,900 ft.	3,100 ft.

Source: Chief BuAer to Commander, Aircraft Squadrons, Battle Force, 18 June 1934, Bureau of Aeronautics Confidential Correspondence File VF, RG 72, NA.

A few officers within BuAer were even beginning to raise serious doubts about the amount of safety gear that had to be carried in peacetime and its impact on aircraft performance. They persuaded Admiral King, the incumbent chief of BuAer, to issue a memorandum addressed to the senior aviation officer afloat recommending the removal of certain nonessential pieces of equipment from the fighter aircraft at the start of any future hostilities. Included in King's list were:

Flotation Gear

Life raft

Fire extinguisher

Radio, battery, and shielding

Pyrotechnics (pistol, smoke candles, etc.)

First-aid kit

Emergency rations

Starter crank

Landing light

It should be noted that the lightweight biplane was then the mainstay of the fighter force, and the 200 pounds, or thereabouts, of safety gear represented a pretty good proportion of the "useful load" that could be handled by such planes.[11]

After receiving King's memo, Rear Adm. Henry Butler, commander of the Aircraft Squadrons, Battle Force, queried his fighter pilots with regard to King's recommendations. Although some suggestions were made regarding the reduction in the size and weight of the emergency rations and first aid kit, the pilots were not favorably inclined to remove most of the gear included in King's list. Butler's response, reproduced in part below, says much about the navy's philosophy toward its pilots and the wartime provisions for saving their lives after combat or in case of a forced landing at sea:

Flotation gear, such as the inflated bags shown here on an F2B-1, were part of the required equipment the Bureau of Aeronautics insisted be carried by all carrier aircraft operating in the early 1930s. The bags were intended to keep the plane afloat in the event that it was forced to ditch, but the gear associated with these devices added extra weight which hampered an aircraft's performance. *National Archives*

> Morale, being the most important single element of military effectiveness, is greatly enhanced if military personnel are convinced their superiors will make every effort to support them during emergencies, and to save them if disaster overtakes them. . . . Every pilot must know that he is being allowed a reasonable chance for his life, that he has means for saving himself from the normal hazards of over-water flight, and that his superiors will exert every effort to rescue him.[12]

The concern over safety gear triggered a wave of memoranda from a small group of progressive airmen within BuAer concerning fighter tactics and the need to emphasize speed as the primary characteristic for this class of airplane. Spotting continued to be one of the key missions of ship-borne aircraft, and the doctrine of how to protect them in the air was one of the unsettling problems that continued to nag war planners.[13] Protecting large formations of aircraft, including the carrier's strike force, was seen to be one of the primary missions of the fighter, albeit there was still a great deal of uncertainty as to which type of plane would be best suited to accomplish this task.

Many of the squadron commanders in the fleet continued to insist that the two-seater was still the most suitable plane for this purpose. The progressives, which included such future notables as Pat Bellinger, "Wu" Duncan, and Miles Browning, began to push for the development of a high-performance fighter in which speed, and not maneuverability would be the most important flight characteristic. They believed that the primary mission of the fighter was to strike enemy aircraft—not the defensive function suggested by some to justify the "protective" mission envisioned for the two-seater. To these men a true fighter had to be fast enough and have enough firepower to quickly overtake and shoot down an enemy plane. To Browning, who would later be credited with orchestrating the timely launch of the Midway strike, BuAer was overemphasizing maneuverability, climb, and ceiling at the expense of the other characteristics that the "progressives" were pushing for.[14]

Bellinger went so far as to recommend that the flight characteristics of future fighter planes be based on maximum speed, maximum climb, and maximum maneuverability, in the priority listed. Unfortunately for the future fortunes of the navy, Admiral King was not convinced of the order of precedence.[15] Had King been more receptive to the emphasis on speed, it is possible that development of the high-performance monoplane fighter might have been accelerated. Had this been the case, the U.S. Navy could have entered World War II with a better fighter than the overburdened F4F-4, which suffered a degradation in performance when additional ordnance, armor plate, and self-sealing tanks were added to the plane after it had entered production.[16]

CHAPTER 13

End of an Era

Discussions about the theoretical requirements of a high-performance VF and its mission were well intentioned, but they did not address the immediate needs of the fleet, which required a steady stream of replacement aircraft to make up for attrition and obsolescence. The poor shipboard qualities of the first monoplane fighters forced the Bureau of Aeronautics to refocus its efforts on improving the designs of its existing stable of biplane fighters. The fastest of these was Grumman's XF2F-1, which had a top speed of almost 230 mph at altitude. Although the plane had exhibited poor directional stability and had a marked tendency to spin when tested at Anacostia, it was deemed satisfactory for carrier use. The need for additional fighters was so great that a contract for fifty-four production F2F-1s was awarded on 17 March 1934.

Grumman's engineering staff were convinced that they could rectify the negative aspects of the plane's handling characteristics by lengthening the craft's fuselage and increasing its wingspan. This information was passed to BuAer, which agreed to let Grumman incorporate these changes in the last plane of the F2F production run. Since the plane represented a new Grumman design, it would be officially known as the XF3F-1. Papers authorizing the company to proceed with the new design were issued in October 1934.[1]

The F2F-1 entered service in the spring of 1935 with Fighting Two (*Lexington*) and Fighting Three (*Ranger*). The device mounted above the top wing is a gun camera. *National Archives*

What should have been a relatively easy design task for Grumman turned into a nightmare when the prototype crashed during the initial acceptance trials at the company's plant in Farmingdale, New York, on 22 March 1935. The crack-up occurred during the last in a series of test dives designed to verify the plane's ability to withstand a 9-G pullout. As the XF3F-1 streaked downward, the officials and engineers who had gathered to observe the trials suddenly realized that the engine had separated from the rest of the airplane. The test pilot was killed in the resulting crash, which was caused by a structural failure in the airframe.[2]

A second XF3F-1 with a reinforced airframe and strengthened engine mounts was rushed to completion and delivered to Anacostia within a month. As usual, the official trials would be performed by a company pilot. Grumman hired Lee Gelback to conduct the trials, which began on the morning of 17 May 1935. Gelback got into trouble during the ensuing test flight when the plane entered an uncontrollable spin that he was unable to correct, even though he tried standing up in the cockpit—an old test pilot's trick that was supposed to divert the airstream restoring control. Forced to bail out, Gelback watched the plane descend in a flat spin (like a falling leaf) before crashing into the ground. Miraculously, the plane was not a total loss and Grumman managed to salvage enough of the wreckage to rebuild the damaged craft in just twenty-one days. The reconstructed plane was modified once again and

An F3F-1 from Fighting Three landing on the *Ranger* on 22 March 1938. To improve stability the fuselage of the F3F-1 was lengthened by 1½ feet compared to the F2F-1 and had a wingspan that was 3½ feet greater. *National Archives*

returned to Anacostia in June 1935, where it was tested for a third time, passing with flying colors. The difficulties encountered by Grumman while attempting to perfect the XF3F-1 design attests to the uncertain nature of aircraft development process in the mid-1930s and the inherent danger faced by the pilots hired to test the new planes.

It had been essential for Grumman to perfect the XF3F-1's design before the end of the fiscal year as the plane was critical to BuAer's procurement plans. None of the other experimental VFs had proved worthy of production and the fleet was getting desperate to obtain replacements for the fighters which had been lost through the normal rate of attrition. Although the top speed of the XF3F-1 was considerably less than that of the single-wing XFT-2, Grumman's biplane was much more maneuverable and had a significantly shorter takeoff run. The failure to develop a successful monoplane design for carrier use left BuAer with few alternatives when it came time to select which fighter to procure for the fleet. Thus the navy awarded Grumman a contract for fifty-four F3F-1 production aircraft on 24 August 1935.

Delivered in the first eight months of 1936, the new fighters went into service with VF-5B on the *Ranger* and VF-6B on the *Saratoga*. Unfortunately, the F3F-1 was 5 mph slower than its predecessor.[3] This raised the ire of Admirals Butler and Reeves, who were, respectively, the commander, Aircraft, Battle Force and the commander-in-chief of the U.S. Fleet.

Exasperated by the poor performance of the F3F, Butler wrote Reeves to complain about the lack of a suitable VF plane. He wanted an aircraft capable of forcing an engagement with other aircraft, that was heavily armed, and that was designed for the purpose of attacking other aircraft. In Butler's opinion, the basic requirements of the VF were superiority of speed and firepower. Reeves, fully in agreement with Butler's assessment, fired off a letter to the CNO via the chief of BuAer, Rear Admiral King, reiterating the criticisms voiced by his trusted subordinate with the added stipulation that fighters should not be built unless they had "satisfactory radius of action and endurance." Though it had been more than ten years since Reeves had first walked the decks of the *Langley*, the feisty commander-in-chief had lost none of his fervor for carrier aviation! Both men scoffed at the performance of the latest fighters, which had neither the speed nor the armament in their mind "to classify the planes as FIGHTERS."[4]

Reeves's comments implied that BuAer's experimental fighter program had failed to live up to its expectations. This was a slap in the face to King, who had worked hard to promote the continued advance of aviation while head of the Bureau of Aeronautics. King was hoping to be reassigned to the post of commander, Aircraft Squadrons, Battle Force when his two-year tour as bureau chief ended in June. This important command was now a vice admiral's billet, and his appointment to this post would have given King, who we know was extremely ambitious, an early promotion to three-star rank.

The tone of Reeves's letter and the fact that it was addressed to the CNO (via the chief of the Bureau of Aeronautics) suggests that Reeves had more on his mind than fighters. His glowing praise of Butler was an unabashed endorsement of the latter's promotion. Whether or not it was also a direct shot at King is not clear, though some form of political infighting was clearly taking place. There is no record of King's response, if in fact any was recorded, but the timing suggests that it drove King to compile the list of achievements documented in "Bureau of Aeronautics Resume of Progress 1933–1936," which he put together prior to his departure from BuAer.

In all fairness to King, it must be noted that the bureau was already engaged in a program to develop a new carrier fighter. On 1 November 1935 it began evaluating proposals for a new experimental fighter that had been submitted in response to the navy's request for bids. Six manufacturers responded, submitting a number of designs which were appraised by the head of the fighter desk, our friend from earlier chapters, Commander John E. Ostrander Jr. Topping the list was one design submitted by Grumman, followed closely by a design submitted by the Brewster Aeronautical Corporation. Grumman was subsequently awarded a contract for its XF4F-1, a biplane, and a second contract would be awarded to Brewster for its successful monoplane design which would later be purchased in quantity.[5]

No action was taken on Reeves's note until after the midyear rotation of personnel, which took place at the end of June and the beginning of July 1936. By then Cook had taken King's place as chief of BuAer, and Lt. Cdr. Austin K. Doyle had taken over the fighter desk. He was an experienced fighter pilot who had spent the previous year serving as tactical officer on the staff of the commander, Aircraft Squadrons, Battle Fleet. He must have been familiar with, and may even have contributed information used in Butler's memo to Reeves on the value of fighting aircraft to the fleet. Doyle, as one would suspect from his prior association with Butler, recommended that the bureau build an experimental VF equipped with overwhelming fire superiority and as much speed as possible. "It seems logical," he stated, "that we can give them [the fleet] the high speed they want (350?) [sic] at a sacrifice of other characteristics previously considered necessary. Whether such sacrifice is worth while," he continued, "remains to be seen."[6]

The first casualty to emerge from Reeves's memo was Grumman's XF4F-1. Ordered in March 1936, it was a biplane with a projected top speed of 264 mph. While Grumman was working on the mock-up, the navy awarded Brewster a contract for its experimental monoplane fighter that was designed to achieve a top speed of no less than 290 mph! The engineering data included in Brewster's proposal sealed the fate of Grumman's plane, for it proved beyond a shadow of a doubt that the biplane configuration could no longer compete with a successful monoplane design. It seemed pointless for Grumman to continue to work on a design which was not likely to succeed. Bowing to the inevitable, they decided to scrap the XF4F-1 in favor of a new monoplane design in the 290- to 300-mph speed range. The navy accepted Grumman's recommendation to cancel the XF4F-1 contract and allowed them to proceed instead with the new plane, which was ordered on 28 July 1936 as the XF4F-2.[7]

As insurance in case either of the new monoplane fighters failed to live up to expectations, BuAer also proceeded with plans to develop an improved version of the now proven F3F-1. Grumman was also awarded a contract to built an improved version of this design based around the installation of the new 850-hp R-1820 supercharged Wright Cyclone engine. Although the production version of the F3F-2 weighed 500 pounds more than its predecessor, it flew faster (260 versus 230 mph), had a better ceiling, and demonstrated a higher rate of climb when tested at Anacostia in January 1937. Eighty-one of the new planes, designated as F3F-2s, were ordered shortly thereafter.

In the early months of 1937, BuAer, with an eye toward the future, began to formulate plans for the experimental program of 1938. The problematic performance of the current crop of VFs continued to cause considerable concern at the highest levels within the bureau. Under Cook's leadership the staff began to gaze beyond the single-engine designs that had characterized carrier-type aircraft for more than a decade. At the time it appeared that even the newest engines under development would not be capable of furnishing enough power to provide any great increase in VF speed. It looked as if it would be necessary to go into a two-engine design in order to achieve speeds in excess of 300 mph.[8]

Cook wanted the competition to begin as soon as possible even though funding for the new program would not begin until 1 July. At Cook's insistence, specifications for a two-engine, single-seat fighter were quickly prepared and distributed to the aviation industry along with a letter soliciting the submission of competitive designs and proposals.[9] The basic requirements for the new plane reflected a combination of old ideas along with the new. Maneuverability and rate of climb were no longer as important as speed, which was now set at the "maximum obtainable." The standard armament had increased significantly from one .50-inch caliber and one .30-inch caliber machine gun specified a year or two earlier to four .50-inch caliber weapons. But stalling speed was still limited to 65 mph, and the takeoff run was not to exceed 200 feet in a 25-knot wind. BuAer's specification continued to require the craft to be strong enough to withstand a 9-G pullout in terminal velocity dives with two 116-lb. bombs attached to the wings.

Altogether the navy received fourteen designs from six manufacturers. Only one exceeded the 310-mph speed at 10,000 feet. This was a design offered by the Lockheed Aircraft Company. To achieve a projected top speed of 362 mph at 25,000 feet, Lockheed proposed a design using dual turbo-supercharged Allison in-line engines. The size of the plane, it had a gross weight of 10,500 pounds and a wingspan of 54 feet, was far too big for carrier use, so no development contract was issued. None of the other designs was judged to offer sufficient advantage over the single-engine types then in service.[10]

When the VF design competition was renewed in February 1938 the spectacular increase in power from the extremely large displacement engines which had appeared upon the horizon began to affect BuAer's thinking about the next generation of fighters. Wright's new 14-cylinder 1,500-hp R-2600 engine had already been successfully tested, and an even bigger engine, the 18-cylinder 1,800-hp R-2800, was being developed by Pratt and Whitney. The development of these very powerful engines offered the best hope of obtaining the 330–350 mph now deemed necessary to compete with the land planes being developed abroad. Although the previous year's design competition had failed to produce a satisfactory twin-engine design, BuAer wanted to open a new line of development using two engines in case the performance of the single-engine designs fell short of expectations. Thus it issued requests for two designs: one a single-engine type, the other a twin-engine design. BuAer intended to procure an experimental prototype of each in the 1939 fiscal year and sent letters soliciting proposals to all the manufacturers who had previously shown an interest in obtaining contracts from the navy.[11]

The stalling speed for both designs was raised to an unprecedented 70 mph. For the first time, BuAer also added a provision to include wing folding in the specifications, making it mandatory on the twin-engine type, but only a "desirable" feature in the single-engine plane. Wing folding had a marked effect on the number of airplanes that could be spotted. One recent study conducted by BuAer had even shown that 50 percent more planes could be carried if wing folding was incorporated into aircraft's design inboard of the ailerons. It also made deck handling easier, permitted more than one airplane to be handled on an elevator at one time if the plane was small, and allowed much bigger wingspans than would otherwise have been possible due to size restrictions on the elevators.[12]

Of the thirteen proposals subsequently submitted and evaluated by BuAer's material division, the most outstanding in terms of performance was a single-engine design based upon the R-2800 engine submitted by Chance Vought, a division of United Aircraft and a sister company of Pratt and Whitney, manufacturer of the R-2800 engine. Vought, which had incorporated an unusual gull-shaped wing in its B design, had succeeded in obtaining a projected top speed of 351 mph! Only three designs were submitted in the twin-engine

The XF5F-1, shown on 7 September 1940, was an unsuccessful attempt to produce a two-engined carrier fighter. *National Archives*

competition. Of these, the best performer was an alternative design proposed by Grumman using the standard R-1535 engine boosted by two-stage supercharging, a new feature which had been type tested but not proven. Contrary to the original assumptions made by BuAer, the projected speed of Grumman's twin-engine fighter was considerably less (330 mph at 9,500 feet) than the best single-engine designs.[13]

Several individuals within BuAer felt that it would be wise to act on Grumman's proposal for a twin-engine prototype fighter, even though the speed differential gained by the addition of a second engine was disappointing. The plane Grumman proposed building weighed considerably less than the Vought plane, had better visibility for carrier landing, and would have nose-mounted machine guns—a new armament arrangement BuAer was eager to test. Grumman's design was also based on the use of a proven engine, which meant that the plane should be ready for service more quickly than a design such as Vought's, which was based on an engine still in the development stage.[14]

Doyle was particularly concerned about the size, weight, and lead time of the 1,800-hp R-2800 engine, which was considerably larger than any radial engine currently in service aboard the carriers. The propeller alone would weigh in the neighborhood of 600 pounds; maintenance requirements would have to be completely rethought in terms of time and equipment. Whether or not a pilot could handle the huge amount of torque generated by such an engine was another uncertainty. As Doyle aptly pointed out, experience in the past had shown that when an unconventional design was coupled with an untried engine, long delays in procurement would result. Although Vought's design opened up a new field in single-engine design from which it would be possible to proceed to further development as engine power increased, the bureau had to "accept the possibility of long delay, the necessity for slow and careful testing, and greatly increased operating difficulties."

Doyle's boss, Cdr. Arthur C. Davis, expressed similar concerns in a handwritten note to Admiral Cook on 2 May 1938. To Davis, who would later win accolades and the Navy Cross for his exceptional handling of the *Enterprise* during an engagement with Japanese forces in August 1942, it seemed time to decide whether or not they were biting off too much of a gamble in the Vought B because of its unconventional design, great engine torque, and the present development stage of the 2800 engine. "We *must* gamble to make progress," he concluded. "The only question is the *degree* of gamble that is justified when we bear in mind that funds are not limitless and that we must keep on baking bread no matter what we are doing to improve the yeast. . . . Engineering is satisfied that the Vought B would *not* be too much of a gamble and I would defer to their judgment."

Davis concurred with engineering's recommendation to proceed with the single- and two-engine prototypes proposed, respectively, in the Vought B and Grumman alternative designs.[15] Both planes were significantly better on paper than any of the existing types in service. Davis was well aware of the lead time needed before either could be placed into production. In the meantime it would be necessary to continue with the efforts to increase the performance of present designs—to keep on baking bread, so to speak—so that the improved models of existing planes would be available for immediate procurement as needed to meet the fleet's ongoing requirement for replacement aircraft.

By this time the XF2A, Brewster's monoplane entry in the 1936 design competition, had been tested at Anacostia. Although the plane failed to meet the performance criteria for maximum speed, full-scale testing in the NACA Langley wind tunnel showed that plane's speed could be increased by 20 mph if minor streamlining changes were made to the airframe. Although Grumman's entry, the XF4F-2 was faster (it had achieved a top speed of 290 mph), it was plagued by engine problems. This, plus the fact that the XF2A-1 handled better tipped the scales in favor of Brewster's plane when it came to deciding which should be selected for production. A contract for fifty-four F2A-1s was issued on 11 June 1938 making the Buffalo, as the plane was later named, the first monoplane ordered for carrier service by the U.S. Navy.[16]

Though three squadrons of new aircraft were needed in the coming year, BuAer was reluctant to put all of its eggs in one basket. Experience had shown that it would be unwise to rely entirely on an unproven design. Thus Grumman received a consolation prize by way of a production order for twenty-seven F3F-3s. Equipped with up-rated 950-hp Wright Cyclone engines, they were the last biplane fighters to be ordered by the navy. The decision to continue with a known design turned out to be extremely prudent, based on the problems which were subsequently encountered with the F2A-1s after they entered service.

The most serious of these involved the Buffalo's undercarriage, which was never really strong enough to take the punishment experienced during the hard landings which routinely occurred during normal carrier operations. Woefully weak and prone to collapse, the landing gear became the plane's Achilles heel. This serious defect could not be solved without a major redesign and was never corrected.[17]

Of the fifty-four F2A-1s ordered, only eleven were actually delivered to the navy, the rest being released for sale to Finland, which urgently needed new planes to fight the Russians then invading their country. To take their place, the navy ordered forty-three F2A-2s—an improved design that was equipped with more guns and a 1,200-hp engine. Two eighteen-plane squadrons had been delivered by March 1941 and were operational aboard *Saratoga* and *Lexington*. By then the war in Europe had shown the value of armor plate and self-sealing fuel tanks. When these improvements were incorporated in an improved version (designated F2A-3), the added weight was beyond the capabilities of the plane's engine, resulting in a dramatic decrease in the top speed, rate of climb, and ceiling. As the Bureau of Aeronautics was destined to relearn in the years to come, as an aircraft's weight increased, its performance plummeted!

Fortunately a better plane was on the horizon. BuAer's willingness to simultaneously pursue several design approaches at once now paid off handsomely. In the wings waiting to prove its mettle was yet another Grumman prototype: the XF4F-3—progenitor of the famed Wildcat fighter of World War II.

The XF2A-2 was an improved version of the Brewster F2A-1 Buffalo, the first monoplane fighter accepted by the U.S. Navy for carrier use. *U.S. Naval Institute*

In his memorandum of 2 May, Davis had recommended that the bureau undertake additional studies of Grumman's XF4F-2 in order to improve its performance.[18] He felt that the plane's top speed could be significantly increased if it was cleaned up aerodynamically and given a more efficient two-stage supercharged engine. Davis's endorsement caused BuAer to authorize the construction of the XF4F-3, a modified version of the XF4F-2 that was ordered in October 1938. The contract called for the installation of an experimental two-stage, two-speed supercharged 1,200-hp Pratt and Whitney engine.

The plane first flew in February 1939 and was tested at Anacostia that spring. The new engine powered the experimental fighter to a top speed of 335 mph, giving ample evidence of the advantage of the supercharger (or blower as it was commonly called), which compressed the thin air encountered at higher altitudes. This impressive performance and the other improvements led to the plane's immediate acceptance and a production contract for fifty-four aircraft with deliveries of the first aircraft commencing in December 1940.

As for the other experimental fighters ordered in 1938, Grumman's twin-

The XF4U-1 was the first carrier plane to exceed 400 mph. *U.S. Naval Institute*

engine XF5F-1 failed to meet expectations and was never placed in production. Vought's B design, ordered as XF4U-1, was destined to become the most successful naval fighter of World War II—the F4U Corsair.

Doyle was entirely correct in his assumption about the long lead time required to develop the XF4U. Ordered on 30 June 1938, it took two years before the plane was ready to begin preliminary evaluation, its first flight having taken place on 29 May 1941. The effort was well worth the wait, however, as the plane exceeded Vought's original projections by 54 mph, achieving a top speed of 405 mph. When the first service models began rolling of the production line in June 1942 the engine's rated output had been increased to 2,000 hp, enough power to provide a top speed of 392 mph (at 24,000 feet) even though the plane now sported the added weight of six machine guns, 2,400 rounds of .50-inch caliber ammunition, self-sealing fuel tanks, and 150 pounds of cockpit armor. Regrettably, the ship was considered too hot for carrier use (it had a high landing speed, poor forward visibility, and soft oleos, which caused the plane to bounce upon landing) and it was initially assigned to the marines as a land-based fighter. Skepticism concerning the operation of Corsairs aboard ship would not be dispelled until 1944, when modified versions of the aircraft began operating off fleet carriers.

CHAPTER 14

Aviation Doctrine and Carrier Policy
in the Late 1930s

Tहे YEARS FROM 1936 to 1938 marked a period of transition for the navy's air arm. The legislative initiatives passed in 1933 and 1934 set the stage for the largest growth in naval aviation since the end of the First World War. Although aviation doctrine remained unchanged, the procurement of improved aircraft and the deployment of more aircraft carriers began to transform the role of carrier-borne aircraft. Naval aviators were faced with the dual challenge of having to cope with the rapid advancement in aircraft technology while undertaking a 40 percent expansion in the number of squadrons needed to fill out the aircraft complements of the new carriers that were scheduled to be in commission by the end of 1937.

In the ten years since "Bull" Reeves had first posed his "Thousand and One Questions," the eight planes originally assigned to the experimental *Langley* had burgeoned into a formidable fighting force of close to three hundred aircraft distributed among fourteen different squadrons (five VF; four VB; four VS; and one VT). Although there were nine different models in service, they all shared the same basic features: each was a biplane having fabric-covered wings, and they were all powered by air-cooled radial engines in the 600- to 750-hp range. Though most of the fighters now had retractable landing gear, the other types still had fixed undercarriages. Almost half the planes, 47 percent according to BuAer's reckoning (based an average life expectancy of five years), were obsolete, obsolescent, or about to become obsolescent.[1] Not only did the navy need more carrier aircraft, but it needed better planes as well.

The most critical was the need to find a replacement for the underpowered TG-2 ordered in 1930 as an improved version of the Martin T4M-1, a plane whose design was now eleven years old! BuAer had planned to purchase thirteen modern torpedo bombers during the 1936 fiscal year, but neither of the two prototypes was ready in time. The Great Lakes XTBG-1 was rejected outright, while delays in development held up acceptance of the Douglas XTBD-1. Although the navy would have preferred to distribute its production requirements for the large number of torpedo bombers needed —enough to equip four squadrons—among several manufacturers, it was forced to place a single order with the Douglas Aircraft Company for 114 TBD-1s. When the contract was issued on 3 February 1936, it was the largest single airplane order issued by the navy since the end of the First World War.

The all-metal craft was the first monoplane ordered for service aboard the carriers of the U.S. Navy. The TBD-1 (it did not receive the moniker "Devastator" until October 1941) was a very advanced aircraft for its time and had a number of innovative features that would become standard on later carrier types. Foremost of these was the hydraulically operated landing gear, which retracted into the wings, leaving just enough of the wheels exposed to be used for an emergency landing in case the system failed.[2] Operated from the cockpit, the hydraulics also powered the wing-folding system, which permitted the pilot to fold or unfold the wings as needed to facilitate deck spotting and rapid takeoffs. This cut the amount of deck space needed to park the aircraft in half, reducing the normal wingspan from 50 feet to just over 25 feet when folded. Other improvements included an automatic pilot, an intercom system which allowed the three-man crew to talk with one another, and a state of the art radio which permitted voice transmissions and directional finding capabilities as an aide to navigation.

The TBD-1 was a big improvement over what had gone before in the way of torpedo planes. Engine technology had improved appreciably since the introduction of the three-purpose plane and the TBD-1 had a big 14-cylinder air-cooled Pratt and Whitney engine that developed 900 hp at takeoff. At alti-

A formation of TBD-1s from Torpedo Six in prewar markings. *U.S. Naval Institute*

tude the engine delivered 850 hp, giving the unladened plane a top speed of just over 200 mph.

The TBD's range—435 miles with a Mark VII torpedo or 716 miles with a 1,000-lb. bomb load—was acceptable, though not spectacular, for its day. Though provision had been made to launch the new Mark XIII aerial torpedo then under development, no one knew for sure what the new weapon would ultimately weigh.[3] The Bureau of Ordnance estimated that the torpedo would weigh 1,850 pounds, the figure subsequently used in the TBD's design specification.[4] The extra burden placed on the TBD when carrying this weapon— the Mark XIII weighed in at 1,936 pounds when delivered—would have a detrimental effect on the plane's performance. As will be seen in a later chapter, this would not bode well for the TBD pilots charged with conducting the first aerial torpedo attacks of World War II.

The return of the torpedo plane provided the air groups, with the exception of that on board the *Ranger,* with the ability to inflict severe damage on any type of warship.[5] These, and the other new monoplanes being acquired by BuAer, offered the ability to attack targets previously considered more or less inaccessible to the carriers. The performance capabilities brought about by these new planes were not lost on the General Board, which reexamined the role of aircraft in the U.S. Fleet during hearings convened in October 1937 to discuss the aircraft building program for fiscal year 1939.

Although the question of attaching a small carrier to the battle line for air defense was suggested, most participants considered a big carrier to be an important strike force that could be used to inflict maximum damage on enemy surface ships. According to Cook, who testified in his capacity as chief of BuAer, the mission of the carriers was clearly offensive. Though most battleship men believed that carrier planes could cause serious damage to capital ships, few believed that they could sink a battleship. In a fleet action, the role of the carriers would be to slow down the Japanese fleet. As Capt. Royal E. Ingersoll, the director of War Plans explained, the slower U.S. battleships could not engage the faster Japanese battle line unless other units of the navy could reduce the speed of the Imperial fleet. The only means we have of doing this, he insisted, was with bombers or torpedo planes. As one well informed student of naval history has stated, "This idea represented a significant change in the thinking of the Navy's leaders," who now believed that carrier strike planes "could effectively attack enemy capital ships and thereby bring about a decisive fleet action."[6]

In November 1937, Torpedo Squadron Three, attached to the *Saratoga*, began to receive the first TBD-1s delivered for service with the fleet. The new torpedo planes arrived just in time to take part in the fleet exercises of 1938 and would be among the planes that staged a mock attack on Pearl Harbor once again in what was becoming a routine exercise for the airmen. The operational tactics employed by the *Saratoga* during this exercise are particularly noteworthy because of the similarity to those employed by the Imperial Japanese Navy during their surprise raid on Pearl Harbor three years later, on 7 December 1941!

One of the exercises in the fleet problem for 1938 included an assault on the Hawaiian Islands. Its purpose was to test the tactics employed in both occupying an advanced base and defending the Hawaiian area. As in previous years the fleet was divided into two opposing forces. Three carriers (*Saratoga, Lexington,* and *Ranger*) were assigned to the Blue offensive fleet under the command of Adm. Edward C. Kalbus. Kalbus, who knew nothing about aviation, gave Ernie King, his air commander, a free hand in planning the surprise raid designed to cripple Red's defenses.[7]

King, who had taken over command of the Aircraft Squadrons, Battle Fleet in January 1938, was now a vice admiral in what was known throughout the fleet as the "Carrier Command." He intended to divide his command into three task forces to accomplish the mission. *Saratoga* and *Lexington* would operate independently as they launched separate aerial attacks from different locations while *Ranger*'s air group covered a marine assault on French Frigate Shoals. Plans for *Lexington* to attack from the south were scrubbed when an outbreak of tonsillitis among her crew curtailed flight operations. This left only the *Saratoga,* whose air group was comprised of Marine Fighting Squadron Two (VMF-2), flying the Grumman F3F-2 fighter; Scouting Two, flying the Curtiss SBC-3; Bombing Three, flying the Vought SB2U-1; and Torpedo Three, with the Douglas TBD-1. King, who would do everything in his power to ensure success, had temporarily transferred VF-2 to shore duty so that he could replace their F3F-1s with the higher-performing planes of VMF-2.[8]

As the exercise began, King ordered his flagship, *Saratoga,* to approach the islands from a position 800 miles northwest of Oahu, where the carrier and her escorts encountered a weather front which hid the task force during its initial approach to the target. Scheduling her final run-in under cover of darkness, *Saratoga,* then 100 miles north of Oahu, began launching planes at 0450 on the morning of 29 March 1938. Once again the attack group caught the army defenders by surprise, making simulated attacks on the airfields surrounding Pearl Harbor as well as on the radio station at Wailup. *Saratoga* continued toward Oahu until her returning planes could be recovered, all of which landed back aboard at 0835. A second wave launched at 0955 proceeded to Lahaina, where they bombed (simulated) shore defenses in preparation for the marine landings scheduled there the next day.[9]

Saratoga did not go unscathed, however. Twenty minutes after launching the Lahaina assault wave she was sighted and bombed by four patrol planes in the first of three such attacks delivered throughout the late morning and early afternoon. All were vigorously opposed by VF-3's fighters. The *Saratoga*'s damage was assessed at only 8 percent, but she had lost forty-five planes according to the umpires.

A week later, King's carriers teamed up with the planes from Patrol Wing Ten to conduct a coordinated air attack on the fleet. The exercise was designed to test the antiaircraft defenses of the battle force including the disposition of its screen—which was arranged in a circular formation around the capital ships—and the efficacy of the formidable antiaircraft fire which could now be thrown at the attacking planes. The new 5-inch, 38-caliber, dual-purpose gun

with its sophisticated director had now entered the fleet in considerable numbers and was thought an effective means of defending against most forms of
aerial attack.[10]

King was ordered to strike with successive waves of aircraft so that gun
crews could get as much training as possible while providing his squadrons
with practice in coordinating an aerial strike on the enemy's battle line. Had
the effectiveness of the aerial attack been the only objective, then it is likely
that all groups would have attacked simultaneously, but *Enterprise* and *Yorktown* were still on the East Coast and were not available to participate. Thus
the aerial attacks conducted by the carriers were unopposed from the air. This
was unfortunate, as it might have provided valuable lessons on the fighter doctrine needed to escort the strike force and defend the ships below. The lack of
a well worked out fighter doctrine would contribute to the appalling losses in
both planes and carriers experienced during May–June 1942.

The exercises provided the torpedo pilots with a chance to test their new
mounts for the first time. Torpedo Squadrons Two and Three both conducted
simulated torpedo runs on a number of battle wagons. The attacks were preceded by a single "smoker," which laid a smokescreen in front of the approaching torpedo planes to hide them from antiaircraft fire until they were close
enough to drop their "fish." Under actual battle conditions the VTs were
expected to coordinate their attacks with those of the dive-bombing squadrons
and the fighters which were to make strafing and light-bombing runs on the
escorts to suppress antiaircraft fire. The latter were fitted with wing-mounted
bomb racks for 100-lb. bombs.

The only new plane missing from the exercises conducted that year was
the Northrop BT-1. Although the company had completed its first production airplane in November, a strike at the El Segundo, California, plant delayed
delivery of the complete order until August 1938, when the final aircraft,
redesignated the XBT-2, was delivered. The navy had authorized Northrop to
modify this plane so that a new retractable landing gear could be installed
and tested. By the time this particular aircraft was first flown on 22 April
1938, Northrop had sold the El Segundo plant to the Douglas Aircraft Company along with the navy contract for the XBT-2. Following an unfortunate
wheels-up landing accident, Douglas decided, under authority of yet another
change order, to increase the size of the engines, installing a 1,000-hp Wright
engine with a three-blade constant speed propeller in place of the smaller
850-hp Pratt and Whitney engine and two-bladed propeller used on the BT-1.[11]

The finished airplane was flown to Anacostia in August, where it underwent extensive trials, including tests of its dive-bombing characteristics conducted at the Naval Proving Ground in Dahlgren. Following these tests the XBT-2 was delivered to Langley Field for full-scale wind tunnel testing by NACA to investigate further means of increasing the plane's maximum speed and improve its stall characteristics—a problem that surfaced after the BT-1 had entered service.

To solve the stall problem, Douglas added a small spoiler to the leading edge of each wing. This device consisted of a 12-inch rod approximately half-circle in cross section, which was attached to the leading edge of each wing about 3 feet from the fuselage. This and other minor modifications which emerged out of the wind tunnel tests were incorporated in the thirty-six production models ordered on 8 April 1939 under the SBD-1 designation. The number of aircraft on this contract was later increased to provide fifty-seven SDB-1s for the marines and eighty-seven SBD-2s for the navy. The latter had a greater fuel capacity, achieved by removing one of the two cowl-mounted .30-caliber fixed guns on the dash 1 model.[12]

By the time the first SBD-2s—later named Dauntlesses by the navy for morale and publicity purposes—were delivered in December 1940, the war in Europe was well under way and serious efforts had begun to expand the navy in preparation for the conflict to come.

CHAPTER 15

Preparing for War

Wᴴᴇɴ Vɪᴄᴇ Aᴅᴍ. Wɪʟʟɪᴀᴍ F. Hᴀʟsᴇʏ Jʀ. assumed command of the Aircraft Squadrons, Battle Force on 13 June 1940, the U.S. Navy was about to enter the second wave of a massive buildup initiated by Congress two years earlier when it passed the Naval Expansion Act of 1938. The law, the main purpose of which was to provide a 20 percent increase in the ship tonnage authorized for the battle fleet, was intended to counter the growth of the Imperial Japanese Navy, which had begun to expand after Japan's withdrawal from the Washington Treaty in 1936. In addition to increasing the size of the surface navy, the Naval Expansion Act also contained a provision raising the number of aircraft authorized from the 2,050-plane limit set by the Vinson-Trammel Act of 1934 to 3,000.

More legislation enlarging the size of the navy's air arm came in the late spring of 1940. The first increase came on 11 June, when the fiscal budget for 1941 was passed, raising the ceiling on the number of planes from 3,000 to 4,500. An even bigger increase followed several days later when the Third Vinson Act was passed. Included in this act was a provision raising the number of aircraft authorized still further to 10,000. The number of navy aircraft was increased yet again in July, when the Two Ocean Bill was enacted, bringing the number authorized to its ultimate wartime level of 15,000. In just a few months naval aviators found that they were facing a 500 percent increase in the authorized size of naval aviation!

Halsey, who was destined to become the most decorated of all the JCLs, was also one of the last to join this nebulous fraternity. Although Halsey tried to enter naval aviation at the end of his tour as captain of the U.S. Naval Academy station ship *Reina Mercedes* in 1930, his eyesight was not good enough to pass the stringent physical requirements required of all potential pilots. Four years later the door to aviation reopened when Ernie King, then reigning head of the Bureau of Aeronautics, offered Halsey command of the *Saratoga* if he would be willing to take the observers course.[1]

On 1 July 1934, Halsey accepted the offer and arrived at Pensacola. Not content to be a mere observer, the fifty-one-year-old captain wrangled a position in the pilot's course after obtaining a temporary waiver from the Bureau of Aeronautics allowing him to fly while using corrective lenses. As Halsey later explained in his memoirs, "I considered it better to be able to fly the plane myself than just to sit at the mercy of the pilot." After soloing—the last in his class to do so—Halsey went on to complete the second phase of pilot training which included instruction and practice in formation flying, aerobatics, and navigation. He was obliged to shorten the final stage of his training in order to take command of the *Saratoga* in late spring of 1935.[2]

In the months that followed, Halsey, who had been a novice when it came to handling carriers, learned the intricacies of conducting flight operations at sea. His training in carrier doctrine was further enhanced during *Saratoga's* participation in Fleet Problems XVII and XVIII, though the latter exercise was flawed, according to the airmen, who vehemently disagreed with Admiral Claude C. Bloch's orders that the carriers remain tied to the battle line.

During the critique that followed the problem, Halsey's immediate superior, Vice Admiral Frank J. Horne, the senior airman afloat, complained bitterly about the egregious error on the part of the CinCUS. Horne, the fleet's carrier commander, was convinced that tying flattops to the battle line prevented the freedom of movement essential for their own protection. The best way to guard the carriers against air attack was to keep them hidden by evasive movements at high speed. "Once an enemy carrier is within striking distance of our fleet," explained Horne, "no security remains until it—its squadrons—or both, are destroyed, and our carriers, if with the Main Body are at a tremendous disadvantage."[3] This lesson was not lost upon Halsey, who would make use of these tactics in the future. Unfortunately, the actual results of the problem had been inconclusive, and Horne's remarks only served to polarize the differences between the Gun Club and the aviation community.

Halsey's next move was to NAS Pensacola, where he served as commandant while awaiting an opening on the rear admiral's list. He had already been selected for promotion to rear admiral, but the number of admirals was limited by law and he could not be advanced in rank until another rear admiral was promoted, died, or retired. This did not occur until March 1938, when there was a vacancy in the grade. One month later he received orders to take command of Carrier Division Two, comprising the new carriers *Yorktown* and *Enterprise*. Under Halsey's leadership the green crews and their air group were turned into seasoned veterans. After a two-year tour of duty there, he was "fleeted up" to carrier commander, a vice admiral's billet that still retained the official title of commander, Aircraft Squadrons, Battle Force.

As a "type" commander, one of Halsey's main jobs was to make sure that the air force was prepared for combat in the event the United States was drawn into war. Although all pilots assigned to the carriers had completed the advanced training course in carrier aircraft, the eighty-five hours they spent in the air did not qualify them as carrier pilots.[4] This task was left to the individual squadrons which conducted carrier qualifications on a regular basis whenever the squadron went to sea. Pilots and their air crews were also expected to participate in routine gunnery exercises designed to provide practice in the various weapons (guns, bombs, and torpedoes) which they were expected to master. The most basic were the Individual Battle Practices (IBPs) conducted by individual planes shooting at targets laid out on the ground, remote-controlled ships, or target sleeves towed by other aircraft. More advanced exercises known as Intermediate and/or Formation Battle Practices (FBPs) involved one or more sections of aircraft and were used to test and perfect aerial tactics.

The IBPs were tailored to provide practice in the specialized weapons that each unit was expected to employ in order to complete its mission. Bombing and scouting squadrons spent most of their time perfecting their dive-bombing technique, torpedo bombers concentrated on high-level bombing and torpedo attacks, and fighters concentrated on aerial gunnery. Official gunnery exercises were held once a year, with awards given to those pilots and squad-rons which achieved the highest score within a particular category.

There was a great deal of cross-training; fighting squadrons perfected light dive bombing, and all squadrons practiced aerial gunnery (using both fixed and flexible machine guns). The exact nature of the exercise varied with the weapons employed and whether live ammunition, practice bombs, or gun cameras were to be used. The latter were widely employed whenever possible to simulate machine-gun fire, one film frame per shot. Each camera had a built-in clock mechanism which was exposed each time a picture was taken. The resulting image appeared in one corner of the film recording the exact time of the "hit." The clocks on all cameras were synchronized before the start of an exercise so that it was possible to see which plane struck first. This was a critical aspect of air-to-air combat, since it was assumed that the plane that was struck first would have been shot down or disabled before getting off its own shots.

The exercises themselves were usually conducted over a period of several days. This allowed time to indoctrinate inexperienced pilots in the aerial maneuvers needed to employ a given weapon and provided the opportunity for all pilots to hone their flying skills before firing for the record. The results of each pilot's score was recorded on an official form, which became part of the squadron's record and was used to rate the battle efficiency of both the pilot and the squadron.

Dive bombing, considered the carrier's primary strike weapon, was conducted on a regular basis against a fixed target. At least once a year, each squadron "fired" for the record against a moving a maneuvering target. Competition between squadrons was keen, as each tried to win the coveted "E" for excellence awarded to the squadron which achieved the best score in its class—an achievement permitting the winning squadron to embellish their aircraft with the letter *E* throughout the coming year. Each squadron's ranking was based on the average score achieved after the marks of all of its pilots had been totaled. Needless to say, the pilot in each squadron who made the lowest score had to "buy the beer" when the squadron rendezvoused at the officers' club.[5]

By 1940 the record gunnery exercises (RGEs) had become quite sophisticated and were sometimes conducted simultaneously with FBPs of another squadron in order to make the exercise more realistic. The practice fired by Bombing Squadron Six in October of that year was typical of the advanced training which was beginning to emerge. The results of this exercise are remarkably similar to the action which took place eighteen months later at the Battle of the Coral Sea on 8 May 1942, when dive bombers from the *Yorktown* struck the Japanese carrier *Shokaku*.

Bombing Six was still flying the BT-1 when it fired for the record on 23

The BT-1 shown here was similar to those that participated in the gunnery exercise conducted by Bombing Six in October 1940. *National Archives*

October. Prior to the exercise the squadron conducted eight days of intermediate bombing practice during which time they dropped 333 water-filled 100-lb. practice bombs on a target sled towed by the *Boggs,* an old four-stack destroyer that had been converted into a maneuvering target ship. Another day was used to practice squadron approaches to the target. Refresher ground training in camera gunnery was also given to those gunners who showed poor results in the IBP (camera guns) conducted the previous week.[6]

The exercise began with VB-6 approaching the target in a stacked formation at 12,000 feet. The attackers, four F3F-2s from Fighting Squadron Six, sighted the advancing bombers while they were still heading for the target, but were unable to make contact until after the first two divisions were well into their dives. Each of the fighters made one diving attack on the last section of five VBs just as they were deploying into a column before starting their individual dives.

The results of phase one, shown in table 15.1, illustrate the difficulty in trying to stop a dive-bombing attack or even disrupting it once the elements of the attacking force had pushed over. The score achieved by VB-6 while under attack from VF-6 was actually greater in this phase of the exercise than the next, which did not involve any fighter opposition. The reader should take note of the percentage of hits made in both phases (31 percent in A, 25 percent in B), which appears remarkably consistent with the number of hits achieved by the more experienced pilots at the Battle of Midway (see table 19.2).

Table 15.1 Results of FBP Gunnery Practice (Camera)
Fired by VB-6, 23 October 1940

Defending Aircraft			
Plane	Shots	Hits	Time
6-B-4	4	1	No clock
6-B-6	170	0	—
6-B-13	100	6	10 53 06
	—	14	10 53 31
	—	1	No clock
6-B-14	0	0	—
6-B-15	91	2	10 53 04
	—	1	No clock
Total:	365	25	6.85%
VF Attacking Aircraft			
Plane	Shots	Hits	Time
6-F-9	69	0	—
6-F-10	44	4	No clock
6-F-11	42	12	10 53 37
	0	0	—
	0	0	—
Total:	155	16	10.32%

Source: Report of Gunnery Exercise, Bombing Squadron Six, 23 October 1940, File VB-6, Gunnery Year 1940–41, ComAirRonBatFlt, RG 313, National Archives.

In addition to training, gunnery exercises provided valuable information on the potential effectiveness of the weapons employed and often revealed material defects not uncovered during the development process. Such was the case with the Mark XIII-1 torpedo.

Although the performance of the Mark XIII (introduced in 1938), was "excellent when dropped at a speed of 100 knots and an altitude between 40–90 feet," the speed and altitude limits were considered too restrictive for the improved torpedo bomber that was expected to replace the TBD-1.[7] BuAer was developing a three-place torpedo bomber capable of 321 mph at 23,000 feet with a range of 1,000 miles and had already issued contracts to Vought and Grumman to build the XTBU-1 and XTBF-1 prototypes.

Photographs of TBDs dropping a torpedo are rare. Here, a TBD-1 from Torpedo Six launches a Mark XIII torpedo during the gunnery exercise conducted on 20 October 1941. *Naval Historical Center*

In an effort to improve the airborne stability of the weapon during the drop phase, the Bureau of Ordnance modified the tail section, relocating the control surfaces ahead of the propeller and bolting plywood extensions to the horizontal vanes in the hopes that these changes would stabilize the torpedo as it was dropped.[8] Presumably, these changes were made at the urging of BuAer, which recognized the need to improve the aerial performance of the Mark XIII torpedo so that it could be dropped at higher altitudes and faster speeds.

Unfortunately for the pilots who would later have to rely on this weapon in battle, the modified design was plagued by so many defects that one writer has called it "the worst piece of ordnance ever forced upon the Navy." The Mark XIII-1 was so bad that four of ten torpedoes launched during its first operational use in a gunnery exercise sank from sight and were never seen again. Of the remaining six, five experienced erratic runs. Only one of the ten dropped ran hot, straight, and true![9]

In the months that followed, BuOrd discovered that the Mark XIII-1 tended to veer left upon entry into the water and that the wooden tail vanes were likely to break off. No sooner were these problems corrected than chronic depth failures were detected. The propellers were shown to be too weak to stand the shock of high-speed launching and the exploder mechanism needed to be modified to keep it from arming in the air. Even when these defects were eliminated the torpedo could not be made rugged enough to withstand the strain of high-speed drops until the introduction of the drag shroud in 1944. Constructed of plywood and attached to the head of the torpedo, this ringlike device served to reduce the torpedo's airspeed by 40 percent and acted as a shock absorber when it entered the water.[10]

Back in the fleet, Halsey's command began to receive deliveries of both the Douglas SBD-2 dive bombers and Grumman F4F-3s in the spring of 1941. As the fighter and bombing squadrons began to transition into these planes, familiarization and qualification in the new aircraft became top priority.

That summer Fighting Three, commanded by Lt. John S. (Jimmy) Thach, was sent ashore to trade in their Brewster F2A-2s for the new Grummans. Thach, who had been given the moniker "Jimmy" while a midshipman at the Naval Academy, was one of the outstanding pilots in the navy. Assigned to VF-3 as its gunnery officer in June 1939, he quickly won praise for his expertise in aerial gunnery and ability to train other pilots in fighting plane tactics. He was soon promoted to executive officer and then commander in December 1940.

By August 1941 Fighting Three was busy adjusting to their new aircraft and the basic two-plane flying section which had been mandated by the general squadron reorganization ordered by Halsey on 7 July. Under the new doctrine, the six-plane division was broken down into three two-plane sections instead of the two three-plane sections as had been done in the past. The three-plane section had always irked Thach, who felt that a pilot needed to have three eyes when flying in this formation—one to look at the leader, one to look through the gunsights, and one to keep an eye on the other wing man. It was during this period that navy pilots began to receive information about a new, high-speed Japanese fighter plane (the Mitsubishi A6M5 "Zero") that had incredible maneuverability and an exceptional rate of climb.[11]

Thach, the consummate fighter pilot, immediately began thinking of the tactics needed to counter the threat of an aircraft which was potentially faster and more maneuverable than the F4F-3. The solution was a criss-cross maneuver invented by Thach one evening at home using matchsticks on the kitchen table to simulate the aircraft. Thach eagerly presented his ideas to his squad-

Jimmy Thach (*foreground*) and his wingman Butch O'Hare, in their F4F-3 Wildcats. *National Archives*

ron so that it could be tested in the air. He assigned Lt. (jg) Edward H. (Butch) O'Hare's two-plane section the task of playing attacker while his own section acted as defenders. To simulate the Zero's superior performance Thach's pilots would be limited to half throttle. He told O'Hare to attack from any direction he wanted. No matter how the attackers tackled Thach's new formation they couldn't line up for a shot without putting themselves in danger. "Skipper, it really worked, it really works," exclaimed O'Hare excitedly after landing, "I couldn't make any attack without seeing the nose of one of your half-throttle airplanes pointed at me."[12] The Thach Weave, as this tactic would latter be coined, proved to be invaluable in the first months of World War II.

The changes in fighter doctrine which led to Thach's experiment was influenced to a great extent by the aerial battles being fought in Europe and the combat experience of the British, who began sharing information with the United States in the fall of 1940. Well before hostilities began, the question of air defense was being hotly debated at the highest levels of command within the U.S. Navy. As uncertainty over the actual effectiveness of antiaircraft fire

The introduction of folding wings, illustrated here by the F4F-4s on the flight deck of a CVL, c. 1943, allowed more fighters to be handled on the flight deck of the carriers. *U.S. Naval Institute*

began to sink in, the issue of how to defend the fleet against bombing attack became of great concern to the battleship men.

To Admiral Cook, then in command of the Aircraft, Scouting Fleet, it was obvious that the number of fighters on board the carriers was "totally inadequate to furnish fighter protection for the carriers and carrier bombing missions as well as for the ships of the main body."[13] He proposed that Carrier Division Three (composed of *Ranger* and *Wasp* when commissioned) be assigned to the battle line instead of to the scouting force. The duties of these smaller carriers would include distant scouting, antisubmarine patrol, combat air patrol, and defense of battleship spotters. This arrangement would provide the battle line with a strong force of defensive aircraft, leaving the four large carriers free to pursue purely offensive operations. Cook recommended that both carriers embark three eighteen-plane VF squadrons, thus increasing the number of fighters available for fleet air defense from 36 to 108. To pay for the new planes, Cook suggested that the navy take the money appropriated for scout bombers and spend it on fighters.[14]

Although most officers in high command agreed with Cook's proposal regarding the arrangement of the air group on the two small carriers, opinions as to the number of fighters embarked on the large carriers varied greatly. One high-ranking officer recommended that fighter squadrons be eliminated completely from the *Lexington* and *Saratoga* to enhance the number of attack planes. Another admiral advocated that each of the fighter squadrons on board the large carriers be enlarged by nine planes. Although the latter was endorsed by the General Board of the Navy, it could not be implemented until the arrival of the folding wing F4F-4 in the late spring of 1942.[15]

The advent of radar, which began to appear on U.S. ships in mid-1940, changed the dynamics of fleet air defense. The use of radar allowed the combat air patrol to be "vectored" toward the attacking raiders well before the enemy planes came within visual sight. It provided sufficient warning time to launch the additional fighters spotted on the flight deck to support the limited number of aircraft that could be maintained in the air at all times. For command and control the U.S. Navy instituted the practice of assigning a naval aviator as a fighter direction officer (FDO), a concept originated by the British, who claimed that an experienced man could control as many as three fighter groups at one time, vectoring them to interceptions as far as 30 miles from the carrier.[16]

The first time this technique was tried by the U.S. Navy appears to have occurred in March 1941 on board the *Yorktown*, using one of the air-search radar units (the model CXAM) installed by the navy for shipboard use. Although the primitive setup lacked a central display, it was invaluable for directing fighter interceptions and showed the need to assemble a team in a centralized location—later defined as the Combat Information Center (CIC). In July a proposal to equip the *Hornet* with such an installation was approved by the secretary of the navy.[17]

The delivery of the first of the navy's SBDs in the spring of 1941 marked the culmination in BuAer's fourteen-year effort to procure a true multimission aircraft for carrier use. Naval aviators now had an airplane that could perform equally as a heavy dive bomber or carrier scout plane. The craft's large internal fuel capacity made the SBD particularly well suited for long-range scouting. Unlike precious scouts, the SB2Us and SBC-3s for example, it did not require auxiliary fuel tanks to achieve maximum range. Use of these tanks required that they be fitted under the belly of the plane in place of the dive-bombing crutch, which had to be removed. The reverse was required after the planes returned from their scouting mission if they were to be rearmed for attack. This time-consuming procedure was not popular with

The *Saratoga*'s flight deck as she was preparing to launch a deck load of aircraft, taken sometime in 1941. In the foreground is the F4F-3s of Fighting Three, the first to take off. They would be followed by the SBD-2s of Bombing Three, shown warming up their engines. Last off would be the TBD-1s, which can be seen in the background with their wings still folded. *U.S. Naval Institute*

air officers trying to minimize the turnaround time needed to get the returning scouts back in the air. As one veteran pilot explained in correspondence with the author, the airmen wanted to maximize the secondary potential of these planes as attack bombers by arming them to the teeth as soon as possible after the enemy had been located.[18]

Although the SBD had a much greater endurance than either of its predecessors, the problem of trying to navigate over the featureless ocean severely limited the operational search radius of these planes until the new ZB homing receiver could be installed. The need to equip carrier planes with a homing device was demonstrated repeatedly during the many tactical exercises and fleet problems conducted during the interwar period. As Admiral Reeves stated in his comments to CNO Standley in connection with the results of Fleet Problem XVII, "No Fleet commander will abandon his aircraft without making strenuous efforts to get them back to their parent ship." Reeves, who was then serving as commander-in-chief of the fleet, recommended the development of a radio beacon that would provide homing for friendly aircraft without revealing the carrier's position to the enemy.[19]

Unbeknownst to Reeves, the Bureau of Engineering at BuAer's insistence had already begun to develop a secret homing system for aircraft operating from carriers. The task of developing this system was assigned to the Naval Research Laboratory (NRL), which had been working on a rotating beacon device for several years. By the beginning of 1937, the laboratory was investigating no less than four different approaches to the problem and had begun flight testing of individual components. By the summer of 1938, the NRL had completed a full-scale prototype, which was tested in August by the pilots of VF-4 flying off the *Ranger.*[20]

The system, which later became known as the "hayrake" because of the shape of the ship's antenna, consisted of an ultra-high-frequency radio transmitter (later designated as the model YE) on board the carrier and a special receiver (designated ZB) installed on the aircraft. The YE was connected to a special type of rotating antenna which emitted a wedge-shaped radio signal at 15-degree intervals. The signals were coded so that the pilots would know which direction to fly in order to home in on the carrier. To use the system the pilot had to turn on the receiver, tune it to the desired setting, and turn up the volume until he heard the homing signal, which was transmitted as a single letter of Morse code. All the pilot had to do was choose the loudest signal and follow the beam home, which would bring him within 500 yards of the carrier.[21]

By the end of 1940 deliveries of YE transmitters were under way and were in the process of being installed on all of the navy's carriers. Although the first ZB units were to have been received in February 1941, none were available for the extended endurance tests of SBDs conducted aboard the *Enterprise* in the summer of 1941. The long-range scouting flights conducted during this period showed that under normal conditions pilots flying the SBD could expect to accumulate a navigation error of approximately 2 miles for every 100 miles flown. After returning from a 300-mile search the planes would probably miss the carrier by at least 12 miles and perhaps as many as 25 miles. Even under ideal weather conditions an error of this magnitude could place the returning planes beyond visual range of the carrier, forcing them to initiate a standard box search in order to locate their home base. In case of this

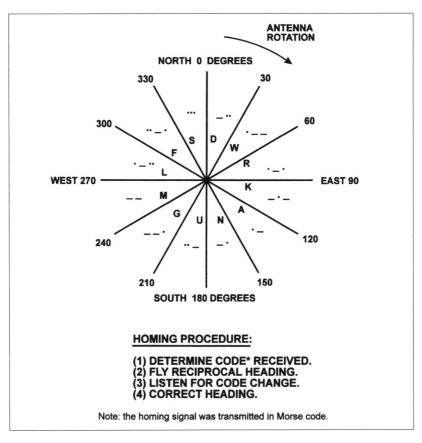

Figure 15.1 Chart showing direction coding used in conjunction with YE-ZB radio homing equipment.

eventuality, scouting doctrine required that the flight plan include a three-hour fuel reserve upon scheduled arrival at point option, the prearranged rendezvous for recovery.[22]

Once the ZB equipment was installed, scouting distances would be limited only to aircraft endurance and the range of the homing device. To the skipper of the *Enterprise* it was essential that this equipment be installed as soon as possible.[23]

CHAPTER 16

Opening Rounds

WHEN THE JAPANESE attacked the American forces stationed at Hawaii on 7 December 1941, the three aircraft carriers then attached to the Pacific Fleet were fortuitously absent from Pearl Harbor. Two of the three, the *Enterprise* and *Yorktown,* were at sea transporting reinforcements to Wake and Midway, while the third, the *Saratoga,* was at San Diego undergoing upkeep and repair. The latter was immediately rushed back to Hawaii and given the job of transporting another squadron of Marine Corps fighters to the beleaguered marine garrison at Wake Island. She was assigned to Task Force 14, under the command of Rear Adm. Frank J. Fletcher, which provided an escort of three heavy cruisers and eight destroyers. Rounding out Fletcher's force was the seaplane tender *Tangier* and the elderly oiler *Neches.* The former was loaded with troops and supplies intended to reinforce the garrison when the task force arrived at Wake on 24 December. The Japanese invaded the island before the relief reached its destination, forcing the cancellation of the mission.[1]

In the meantime, the disastrous effects of the Pearl Harbor raid precipitated a shakeup in the uppermost echelons of the navy, resulting in a number of key personnel changes that affected the command structure of the entire navy. On 17 December Adm. Husband E. Kimmel, commander-in-chief of the naval forces in Hawaii at the time of the Japanese attack, was relieved, and his replacement, Adm. Chester W. Nimitz, designated. Three days later, Adm. Ernest King, who had commanded the Atlantic Fleet since its inception in February 1941 was promoted to commander-in-chief, U.S. Fleet. King soon changed the standard navy abbreviation for this command from CinCUS, with its unsavory connotation (i.e., "sink us"), to the less offensive sounding CominCh.[2]

King immediately dispatched orders to Nimitz, directing him to hold the line from Midway to Samoa, Fiji, and Brisbane "at all costs." The initial mission of the Pacific Fleet was to protect the Midway-Johnson-Hawaii triangle and to maintain the vital communications link between the United States, Australia, and New Zealand.

After reinforcing Samoa, Nimitz began to plan for a series of aggressive hit and run carrier raids on Japanese outposts throughout the Pacific. In late January 1942, he ordered Halsey to attack enemy bases in the Marshall and Gilbert Islands with Task Force 8, built around the *Enterprise* and the *Yorktown,* the latter having been rushed back to the Pacific after the attack on Pearl Harbor to reinforce Nimitz's beleaguered forces. The two carriers sailed from Samoa and proceeded in company until the evening of 31 January, when they separated and headed for their respective targets at high speed in order to be in position to launch early morning air raids on the unsuspecting Japanese bases. The *Yorktown* and her escorts, now designated TF-17 under the command of Rear Adm. Frank J. Fletcher, steamed for Jaluit in the Gilberts while *Enterprise,* screened by three cruisers and six destroyers, headed for a position off Wotje in the Marshall Islands.

Air operations on Halsey's *Enterprise* began before sunrise on the morning of 1 February 1942. First to be launched were the SBDs of Scouting and Bombing Six, which formed the main strike group. Each plane had a full load of fuel and was armed with one 500-lb. and two 100-lb. bombs. After rendezvousing above the carrier, the main attack group headed for a point 15 miles north of the island of Roi, located at the extreme northern end of the Kwajalein Atoll. Next off were nine bomb-laden TBDs of Torpedo Six bound for the naval anchorage at the southern end of the atoll.

Once the primary attack group had cleared the flight deck, six F4F-3s were launched to establish a combat air patrol. They were followed by six more F4F-3s, which took off toward Maloelap Atoll. Armed with two 100-lb. bombs apiece, the fighters were scheduled to attack the airfield at Taroa Island. Last off was another six-plane section of fighters sent to bomb and strafe the island of Wotje.

Halsey, based on the experiences derived from the prewar exercises, expected that the raids would catch the defenders by surprise. The idea was to sneak up on the unsuspecting base under cover of darkness, striking at dawn before the enemy's scouts and/or fighters had a chance to get into the air. It was an ambitious plan that relied on VF-6's fighters to supplement the other attack groups.

While the *Enterprise* was pounding Kwajalein and other targets nearby, *Yorktown* was busy conducting raids on enemy bases in the Marshall and Gilbert Islands. Unfortunately, she encountered bad weather which severely hampered air operations. The actions engaged by both task forces are well documented and need not be repeated here, except, perhaps, for a comment regarding the highly inflated damage reports made by the attacking pilots.

After the war was over, studies of the after-action accounts of both protagonists showed that a large number of the hits claimed by both sides— including those that resulted in sinkings—simply did not happen. Some of these discrepancies can be attributed to errors in judgment made by pilots and air crew, who exaggerated the effects of actual hits observed. In many cases, however, the discrepancies were the result of a compulsion on the part of the pilots to believe that "their attacks, made at high risk and great cost, were personally successful." As one former dive-bomber pilot noted, to a pilot any hit he observed had to have been the result of his effort.[3]

Although the results of these early carrier raids were not very spectacular with regard to the material damage inflicted, they were a great boost to morale. They restored the public's confidence in the navy and showed the Japanese that the U.S. Fleet could still strike back. In retrospect, Halsey's actions were "daring to the point of recklessness."[4] He had attacked six widely separated targets while exposing his dispersed forces to enemy action from as many as four enemy airfields and a number of seaplane bases.

Perhaps the biggest benefit from these attacks was the important lessons learned by the U.S. Navy. The raids revealed several critical flaws in material and the need to improve both the aircraft themselves and the tactics used in their employment. The most blatant defect during the course of the action was the numerous gun failures that occurred in the F4F-3s while they were engaged in dogfights. These failures resulted when ammunition belts shifted in the trays feeding the guns during violent maneuvers. This problem had not surfaced during any of the prewar exercises, when the amount of ammunition carried was never more than seventy rounds per gun.

As for the improvements in aircraft, armor plate and leak-proof gas tanks were a vital necessity for all planes. A nonfogging bombsight was desperately needed by the SBDs, and an identification, friend or foe (IFF) radar transponder was needed so the FDO could sort out the good guys from the bad. More damage, too, would have been inflicted on the enemy's shipping if delayed-action fuses had been fitted to the bombs instead of the instantaneous types used during the attack. The lack of incendiary bullets was also criticized as was the poor performance of the TBDs.[5]

Then, too, there simply were not enough fighters to go around. In addition to providing combat air patrol over the carrier, more fighters were needed as escorts for the bombers and torpedo planes. The commanding officer of *Lexington*'s air group recommended that the number of fighters be increased to twenty-seven, even if this meant reducing the number of scout bombers embarked. He also felt that it was mandatory to provide fighter protection for the torpedo planes, expressing certainty that "their mission would not have been accomplished had they been intercepted by enemy fighters."[6] Although this advice was endorsed by both the captain of the *Enterprise* and Admiral Halsey, it was not heeded in the months ahead.

After Halsey's raid in the Marshalls, Nimitz used whatever carriers were available to conduct additional forays in enemy territory that raised the ire of the Japanese high command. Though these strikes caused relatively little damage, they prompted the Imperial Japanese Navy to rethink its entire Pacific strategy, ultimately leading to the first wartime clash of carriers at the Battle of the Coral Sea.[7]

Toward mid-April Nimitz's intelligence officer, Cdr. Edwin T. Layton, began warning of Japanese intentions to launch an offensive in the New Guinea–Solomon Island area. Port Morseby on the southern coast of New Guinea appeared to be the most likely target. Unknown to Layton, the invasion fleet would be divided into two groups: a main body containing numerous transports with a covering force of heavy cruisers and the light carrier *Shoho*, coded-named the "MO force" by the Japanese; and a carrier strike group composed of the *Shokaku* and *Zuikaku*, which would enter the Coral Sea from the east to destroy any Allied forces that might try to interfere with the operation.

To meet this threat, Nimitz sent *Lexington* with Task Force 11, under the command of Rear Adm. Audrey W. Fitch, to the Coral Sea, where it would join with *Yorktown* and the other ships of Task Force 17 under Rear Adm. Frank J. Fletcher, who would assume tactical command of both task groups. As Layton later described in his memoirs, Nimitz was taking a calculated risk in sending just two carriers to oppose an enemy which Layton estimated might be composed of as many as five carriers. Nimitz had no choice, however, since *Enterprise* and *Hornet* were still enroute to Pearl Harbor after successfully launching the B-25 bombers of Col. James H. Doolittle's Tokyo raid. Layton considered Nimitz's decision "a colossal strategic gamble."[8]

After rendezvousing on 1 May 1942, the task forces separated by a few miles to facilitate refueling operations, a time-consuming process essential to keeping the short-legged destroyers topped up with fuel oil. Fitch's force was still engaged in this operation when Fletcher received word that Japanese warships had been spotted off Tulagi Island in the late afternoon of 3 May. This was just the kind of tempting target that Fletcher had been waiting for. Detaching his oiler and her escort he immediately ordered the rest of his force to steam north at 24 knots in order to be in position for a strike on Tulagi at dawn.

Yorktown's planes hit Tulagi the next morning in a series of air raids conducted by Bombing Squadron Five, Scouting Squadron Five, and Torpedo Squadron Five—without benefit of fighter cover. The *Yorktown* had just eighteen operational fighters aboard, and none could be spared from the essential task of providing a protective umbrella over the carrier.

The results were disappointing to say the least, albeit the poor performance of the SBDs could be attributed to condensation of the bombsights—an old problem encountered once again as the SBDs struck the enemy's ships in Tulagi harbor. The dive bombers started their dives in the cold clear air at 19,000 feet with the intention of dropping their deadly weapons at around 2,500 feet, the normal release altitude. At about 7,000 feet they suddenly hit a layer of warm moist air, which condensed on the cold glass of the windshields and telescopic sights, causing most of the pilots to loss sight of their target just as they were lining up for the release. New sights and coated windshields would eventually solve the problem, but these would not become available until weeks later. The only squadron to find their mark was VB-5, which scored two direct hits and a near miss on three auxiliary minesweepers during their second sortie of the day. The poor accuracy of *Yorktown*'s bombers would later be attributed to a the lack of practice necessitated by their carrier's long sojourn in the South Pacific.[9]

The torpedo planes fared little better. Of the twelve Mark XIII torpedoes launched, only one was successful in striking the destroyer *Kikuzuki*, which had to be beached by her crew and subsequently sank from the damage inflicted.

Although the aerial attacks conducted by *Yorktown*'s planes did enough damage to send the remnants of the Japanese forces steaming hurriedly back to their base in Rabaul, the number of vessels sunk or severely damaged—three small minesweepers, a destroyer, and several landing craft—was scarcely an impressive showing based on the amount of ordnance expended (seventy-six 1,000-lb. bombs and twenty-two torpedoes).

Hitting the small, highly maneuverable, fast-moving vessels encountered at Tulagi proved to be a very difficult task for *Yorktown*'s pilots. Dive-bombing a fast-moving destroyer has been compared to "trying to hit a cockroach racing across a kitchen floor with a small fly swatter."[10] Like any shooting problem involving a moving target, great skill is needed to determine the proper amount of lead, that is, trying to figure out where the target will be when the projectile arrives. Unlike a fighter pilot who could "walk" his tracers into the opposing aircraft, the dive-bomber pilot had only one shot in his gun, thus his aiming point had to be right at the moment of firing to get a hit. This required great judgment and coordination. Hitting a maneuvering ship going at full speed was the mark of a real dive-bomber pilot.

The lead problem was even more acute for the torpedo pilots who were hindered by the low speed and generally poor performance of the Mark XIII torpedo, which was rated at just 33 knots. Hitting a ship making 25–30 knots with such a weapon could only be accomplished if the pilot launched the Mark XIII while maintaining a lead angle to the target of between 60 and 65 degrees (see fig. 16.1). The amount of lead was so great that even the smallest misjudgment in target speed or lead angle would result in a miss, even if the pilot closed to within 800 yards before dropping his "fish." The relative closing speed of the Mark XIII torpedo was so low that the chance of a torpedo hitting a high-speed target was practically nil.[11]

The weaknesses in the Mark XIII torpedo had not been ignored by the senior aviators afloat. For years they had been badgering the Bureau of Ordnance about the need to improve the performance of aerial torpedoes. Few naval aviators were interested in these weapons, and not much money was available to develop these expensive devices, which received little attention from the members of the Gun Club running BuOrd. This situation began to improve somewhat after Rear Adm. William H. P. Blandy became chief of the

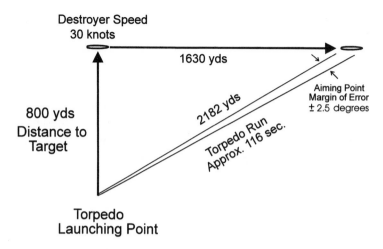

Destroyer Speed
30 knots

1630 yds

800 yds
Distance to
Target

2182 yds

Torpedo Run
Approx. 116 sec.

Aiming Point
Margin of Error
± 2.5 degrees

Torpedo
Launching Point

Figure 16.1 Example illustrating the problem of trying to hit a fast-moving ship with a Mark XIII aerial torpedo. Clearly, the torpedo plane could not approach the target directly abeam and expect to achieve a hit. Evasive maneuvers by the enemy ship added another complication to the fire-control problem, resulting in the high percentage of misses experienced in actual combat.

bureau. While Blandy recognized that the development of aircraft torpedoes had been slow, he didn't think that they were as bad as some of the senior aviators contended. Tragically, in one of the least documented fiascoes of the U.S. Navy in World War II, the torpedo section had grossly overestimated the reliability of this troublesome weapon, claiming that the new Mark XIII-1 would prove to be 80 percent effective when launched from 140 feet.[12]

CHAPTER 17

Scratch One Flattop

AFTER RECOVERING THE LAST of the planes that had attacked Tulagi on 4 May 1942, Fletcher turned south and began steaming toward the pre-arranged meeting point with Fitch's ships. The two forces rendezvoused the next morning, and Fletcher spent the next two days refueling from the *Neosho,* blissfully unaware that they were being stalked by a Japanese carrier force to his north.

On the morning of 6 May, the *Yorktown*'s radar detected a Japanese reconnaissance shadowing the American ships. Although fighters were dispatched to attempt an interception, they were hindered by bad weather, which allowed the four-engine Kawanishi seaplane to elude them. Although Fletcher suspected that he had been sighted by the enemy, he did not think his force was in danger. His ships were well beyond the range of land-based aircraft, and he believed that enemy carriers were still 400 miles to the northwest. Nevertheless, he continued to conduct precautionary air searches in this direction while the task force steamed into the wind toward the southeast in order to make it easier for the destroyers to refuel from *Neosho.*

Late in the day the task force received a radio message from the U.S. Army indicating that one of their search planes had spotted a Japanese convoy steaming toward the Jomard Passage in the Louisiade Islands. The presence of a heavy carrier reported by the army plane reinforced Fletcher's belief that the enemy's main strike force had been located and was heading for Port Moresby. Having drained the *Neosho* of her precious cargo, the nearly empty tanker and her escort were sent south out of harm's way—or so Fletcher thought—while the rest of the task force changed course, at 1930, to the northwest in order to be in position to engage the enemy the next morning.

Unknown to Fletcher, a Japanese carrier force under the command of Vice Adm. Takeo Takagi had steamed around the southern end of the Solomon Islands and had been bearing down on him since midday. Takagi was in the process of refueling when word arrived at 1000 that the American carriers had been sighted. He was forced to dispatch his two carriers—*Shokaku* and *Zuikaku*—south in the hopes that they could catch the American carriers by surprise before nightfall. The two carriers comprised the Fifth Carrier Division, commanded by Rear Adm. Chuichi Hara. Although the Japanese plane was still shadowing Fletcher's carriers, faulty communication procedures prevented the enemy from receiving updated radio reports of the Americans' position, forcing Hara to order a scouting mission to pin down the exact location of the American ships. Shortly after takeoff, Hara's scout planes ran into the same weather front which had earlier saved the Kawanishi seaplane from Fletcher's fighters.[1] Had they been more persistent the Japanese planes would have emerged from the rain squalls to find Fletcher's force refueling at a leisurely pace under clear skies. Unable to find the American ships, Hara was forced to reverse course in order to rejoin Takagi's heavy cruisers, which had completed fueling and were now headed south to provide protective cover.

Neither side realized that their respective forces had passed within 70 miles of each other, close enough for either to have launched a preemptive air strike on the other. But neither did, and by nightfall they were steaming away from each other. At dawn, the opposing carriers began launching air searches trying to locate the other's position.

Fletcher, who had steamed west during the night, launched ten SBDs from *Yorktown* at first light to search to the north-northeast, where he expected to find the Japanese invasion force and the three enemy carriers erroneously reported to be in the area. Hara, having rendezvoused with Takagi's ships, launched his search to the south, not realizing that Fletcher's group had moved off to the west.

At 0722 one of *Shokaku*'s scouts reported that it had sighted an enemy carrier 163 miles to the south.[2] With Takagi's concurrence, Hara ordered a seventy-six-plane strike group into the air headed toward the reported location of the American task force. What the Japanese scout plane had actually spotted was the *Neosho* and her escort.

As the Japanese planes were taking off to sink the unlucky duo, one of *Yorktown*'s SBDs reported sighting two Japanese carriers 175 miles northwest of Fletcher's current position, exactly where the Americans had expected to find them. As Hara had done minutes before, Fletcher too ordered a full deckload of planes to be launched. Both officers knew the importance of getting in the first blow and the value of clearing their respective flight decks of their highly flammable aircraft, yet neither realized that he was about to make a potentially disastrous error. Neither knew the information on the whereabouts of the other's carriers was incorrect![3]

Lexington began to launch aircraft when she had closed to within 160 miles of the target. Getting four squadrons into the air and over the target at the same time was a complicated procedure made more difficult by the difference in cruising speeds of the various types of aircraft and the need to conserve fuel in order to reach the target, which was at the limit of their range. After forming up over the carrier—in itself a procedure which consumed large amounts of fuel—each squadron proceeded independently to the reported location of the enemy ships, where they would rendezvous with the other squadrons for the coordinated attack considered essential to ensure success.

To accommodate the variations in takeoff runs, cruising speed, range, and assembly time, the senior airman on each carrier came up with a departure schedule which was best suited for the particular tactical situation encountered. Cdr. William B. Ault, *Lexington*'s air group commander, opted for a deferred departure. Navy doctrine then in effect specified three types of departures for air strikes: "urgent," which required individual aircraft sections to depart immediately after takeoff without forming up over the carrier (they would try to rendezvous enroute to the target); "normal," in which squadrons rendezvoused over the carrier, but did not wait for the other groups—a procedure which allowed escorting fighters assigned to specific squadrons to join up; and "deferred," involving the attempt to form the whole group into one tactical unit before departing for the target. Though it was more likely to produce a coordinated attack and make better use of the limited fighters available, the deferred departure caused the expenditure of a huge amount of fuel, thus limiting the effective range of the strike group.[4]

Yorktown followed suit eighteen minutes later using a variation of the normal departure that had been worked out by Cdr. Murr Arnold (the air officer) and Lt. Cdr. Oscar Pederson (air group commander). First to take off would be the twenty-five SBDs from Bombing Squadron Five and Scouting Squadron Six. They would orbit the ship until the short-legged fighters of Fighting Squadron Forty-two—the last to take off—had joined up with the dive bombers. In between would be the torpedo bombers of Torpedo Five, which would depart immediately for the target.

With her flight deck clear, *Yorktown* took the opportunity to launch four F4F-3s before recovering the returning SBDs of the early morning scouting mission. When the pilot who had reported the location of the enemy ships landed it was discovered that his radio message had been improperly coded. Instead of "two carriers and two heavy cruisers," the message should have read "two heavy cruisers and two destroyers." Only then did Fletcher learn that his planes were headed for the wrong target. The awful dimension of this mistake reportedly caused Fletcher to lose control, shouting in the presence of officers and enlisted men alike that the young pilot's mistake had "just cost the United States two carriers!"[5] To Fletcher's credit, he quickly realized that the task force had shot its bolt at the wrong target. Aviation knowledge "was absolutely essential for a carrier task force commander," and though Fletcher was a nonaviator, he had learned a lot since early December, when he had first begun working with carriers.[6]

A total fiasco was avoided when a message arrived announcing that an army plane had spotted another group of enemy ships, including a carrier, about 30 miles from those reported by *Yorktown*'s returning scouts. Fletcher and his staff briefly debated whether or not to recall the ninety-three-plane strike group before redirecting them to the new position by radio.

As the air group approached the reported position of the enemy ships, Lt. Cdr. Weldon L. Hamilton, VB-2's commanding officer, began scanning the horizon with a pair of binoculars until he spotted ship wakes far to the north. Turning to the right, the strike group began closing the distance to the enemy ships until they were able to make out the outline of the light carrier *Shoho*. They had found their target!

The battle plan called for the air group to execute a coordinated attack based on the prevailing doctrine of the time. First in would be the three-plane command section of SBDs lead by Cdr. William B. Ault, the air group commander. They would be closely followed by the ten SBDs of VS-2 under the command of Lt. Cdr. Robert E. Dixon. Their job was to disable the flight deck to prevent the enemy from launching his fighters. Each SBD was armed

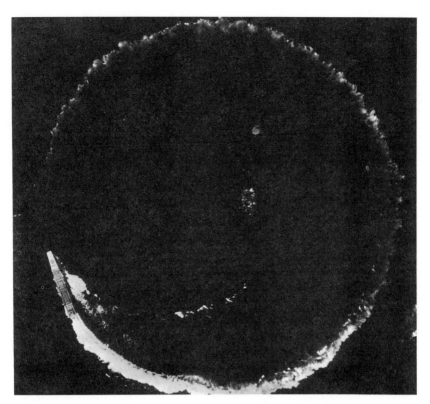

Putting the rudder hard over and continuing to circle was a standard evasive tactic used by Japanese carrier captains to elude aerial attack. If timed properly, such a maneuver made accurate dive bombing more difficult. *National Archives*

with one 500-lb. bomb. In addition to the 500-lb. bomb mounted under the plane's belly, each of the SBDs in Dixon's squadron were also armed with two under-wing 100-lb. fragmentation bombs, which were used to suppress antiaircraft fire. After diving on the enemy carrier to release its 500-lb. bomb, the squadron was to regain height and dive a second time, attacking the screening ships in direct support of the main attack, to be conducted simultaneously by Bombing Two and Torpedo Two.

As Ault's section entered their dives, the enemy carrier began a sharp turn to port, which disrupted their aiming point and caused all three planes to miss the target. Instead of steadying up on a southeasterly course, the carrier continued to swing to port, putting her cross-wind to Dixon's SBDs, which had began to attack from the north. (During Ault's dive, Dixon had swung around to the north to take advantage of the sun and wind direction.) The

The *Shoho*, with smoke billowing from her stern, takes the first of seven torpedoes which would sink the ship in minutes. *National Archives*

unexpected maneuver caught the Americans by surprise; instead of attacking along the length of *Shoho*'s flight deck, the pilots were presented with a much smaller target as the carrier offered her narrow beam to attackers. To Dixon's disgust, none of his planes hit the elusive target.

Hamilton's squadron was forced to wait for Torpedo Two to get into position before starting their coordinated attack. The heavily laden torpedo planes were slowly approaching the target from the southwest and were still some distance away as Scouting Two entered their dives. Struggling to avoid the heavy antiaircraft fire from the two nearest cruisers, they picked their way through the screen, intending to attack the carrier from abeam. While the *Shoho* continued to circle, Lt. Cdr. James H. Brett Jr., VT-2's CO, ordered the squadron to split up for an "anvil" attack against both bows, a tactic which would ensure that at least one division had a perfect "setup."

As VT-2 began to close the target Hamilton's SBDs started down. They began their dives just as the *Shoho* was pointed into the southeasterly wind offering a perfect target to Hamilton, whose 1,000-lb. bomb struck the center of the enemy carrier's flight deck just forward of the after elevator, detonat-

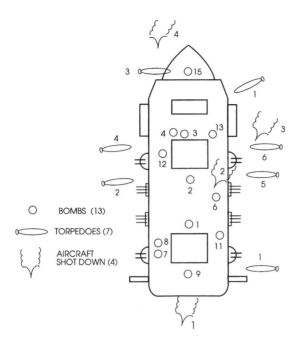

Figure 17.1 Drawing taken from translated Japanese naval documents showing a record of torpedo and bomb hits made on the *Shoho*, 7 May 1942. The number of bombs which hit the flight deck in rapid succession prevented the officials from recording each hit, as indicated by the missing numbers. *Interrogations of Japanese Officials*, 30, U.S. Strategic Bombing Survey

ing with a spectacular explosion—the first of two bull's eyes scored by Bombing Two which caused intense fires to break out below the flight.

Torpedo Two's strike, the first by American torpedo planes against a Japanese carrier, was a textbook example of the anvil attack. As the TBDs drew up to the target, they split up by divisions to simultaneously attack the enemy from port and starboard. They commenced their launching runs moments after the SBDs of VB-2 had entered their dives. The torpedo launched by Lt. Leonard W. Thornhill was the first to find its mark, striking the *Shoho* on her starboard quarter. The blast, which was partially obscured by the billowing smoke raised by VB-2's bomb hits, wrecked the enemy ship's steering gear. Unable to maneuver, *Shoho* continued on a steady course into the wind and was struck in quick succession by four more Mark XIII torpedoes. The devastation wrought by the 320 pounds of TNT attached to these weapons was graphically described by John Lundstrom in *The First Team:* "They tore huge holes in her hull and destroyed both fire and engine rooms. The carrier lost headway rapidly. Water flooded her lower spaces, knocking out power and causing a list. In the decks and topside, fires of great intensity isolated repair parties, while below deck water poured in unchecked."[7]

The *Yorktown's* SBDs now arrived to joined the fray. They dive-bombed the smoking carrier, hitting the stricken vessel at least eleven times with their powerful 1,000-lb. bombs.

The last element to reach the scene were the ten TBDs of Torpedo Five under the command of Lt. Cdr. Joseph Taylor. Obscured by smoke and now dead in the water, and with only two antiaircraft guns still operating, *Shoho* was a sitting duck for the TBDs of Torpedo Five. Although the squadron claimed to have struck the ship with all ten of its torpedoes, postwar analysis of captured Japanese records show that only two additional hits were received. What happened to the other eight missiles is not known. Perhaps they ran too deep, or some might have been detonated by debris or were not recorded by the Japanese authorities, who were unable to keep track of all the ordnance dropped by the attacking aircraft.

In any case the *Shoho* was racked by more violent explosions. With his ship on fire from stem to stern, and holed below the water line, Capt. Izawa Ishinosuke had no other choice than to order all hands to abandon ship. Four minutes later the *Shoho* was gone.

"Scratch One flat top!" signaled Dixon.[8]

CHAPTER 18

The Carrier Battle of the Coral Sea

Although the sinking of the *Shoho* was a tremendous victory for the Americans—she was the first important combatant sunk by the U.S. Navy—it was not the decisive carrier engagement that had been expected. Instead, Fletcher was now faced with the prospect of imminent attack from the same enemy force which had just sunk the *Neosho* and *Sims*. The aerial onslaught on the two American ships had revealed the presence of a powerful enemy carrier force somewhere to his rear.

The *Yorktown*'s radio intelligence unit had monitored the radio transmissions between the enemy carriers and their planes, thus alerting Fletcher to their presence; but Fletcher, tempered by the erroneous position reports received earlier, was reluctant to risk losing his planes until the exact position of the enemy carriers could be identified. He was also concerned about the heavy weather, which would make it difficult for the strike group to find the carrier upon their return, providing that they could locate the enemy in the first place. It would be better to wait until the next morning when the dawn scouting mission could be launched to pinpoint the enemy's position. In the meantime, Task Force 17 would conceal itself under the thick blanket of clouds with "her fighters poised to deal with any strike the enemy might send."[1]

This was exactly what the Japanese commander had in mind, though he had to wait until the carrier bombers which attacked *Neosho* had returned. Twenty-four attack planes (type 97 torpedo bombers) and their fighter escort had already landed, having been recalled when the Japanese realized that no American carriers were with the two ships. The last of the errant bombers was not aboard until 1515.

Although the American carriers were still out of range, Hara ordered the *Shokaku* and *Zuikaku* to send twenty-seven of their best attack pilots aloft for a dusk strike that just might catch the American carriers, which he now believed were steaming in his direction. This ill-conceived gamble turned into disaster when *Lexington*'s radar-directed fighters flew out of the heavy overcast, surprising the unsuspecting Japanese airmen and downing nine of the potential attackers. Hara was fortunate to recover the remnants of the strike group, which struggled to find their way home in the darkness and poor weather.

Round three of this epic engagement, the first in which the enemy ships never sighted each other, began at first light the next morning. Both sides launched air searches and began preparing their respective flight decks to strike the enemy's carriers as soon as they were found.

The *Lexington,* which had the day's search duty (rotated on a daily basis so that the scouting pilots could rest on alternate days) launched a full-circle search of eighteen SBDs. Twelve of the eighteen were assigned to the critical northern sector, where the Japanese were expected to be found. At 0820 one of the American planes spotted the enemy carriers through a brief opening in the overcast. "Below him the Japanese carriers were pointed into the wind, strike groups poised on deck ready for launch, waiting for word from their search planes."[2] They did not have to wait long. Just minutes later one of *Shokaku*'s search planes sighted the American carriers, and the Japanese strike was launched.

Poor atmospheric conditions and initial uncertainty over the exact position of the enemy ships prevented Fletcher from launching his planes until he was sure that they had not made another mistake. He then passed tactical of the task force to Fitch so the latter could have "complete freedom of action for his carriers and air groups."[3]

Like the day before, *Yorktown*'s strike group was divided into two elements which proceeded separately to the target. The dive bombers, twenty-four SBDs (each armed with one 1,000-lb. bomb) under the command of Lt. Cdr.

William O. Burch Jr., formed one element. Their orders were to climb to 17,000 feet and maintain a cruising speed of 130 knots. The second element consisted of VT-5's nine TBDs under the command of Lt. Cdr. Joseph Taylor. Because of their heavy torpedo load, the TBDs were limited to 105 knots cruising speed and flew to the target just above the wave tops. Each element was escorted by a single three-plane section of VFs from Fighting Squadron Two.

As before, *Lexington*'s strike group was divided into three tactical elements: Ault's command section of four SBDs, the eleven SBDs of Bombing Two (six of their number had been assigned to the morning search mission), and the twelve TBDs of Torpedo Two. They were launched using the deferred-departure method, so that all elements would arrive over the target at the same time for the coordinated attack Ault intended to use to strike the enemy carriers.

By 0925 all seventy-five American planes (thirty-nine dive bombers, twenty-one torpedo planes, and fifteen fighters) were headed toward the opposing carriers. Halfway to the target area they glimpsed a number of enemy aircraft headed in the opposite direction. These were some of the sixty-nine planes (thirty-three carrier bombers, eighteen torpedo planes, and eighteen fighters) the Japanese had launched as the Americans were taking to the air. As Burch's group approached the reported position of the enemy carriers, the weather became more and more unsettled, with rain squalls and scattered clouds. At 1032 they sighted the enemy force through a break in the clouds some distance ahead.

The enemy had retained nineteen type 00 (Zero) fighters for Combat Air Patrol (CAP). Three from each carrier were already in the air as Burch's group covered the distance to the Japanese carriers using the clouds for cover. The other thirteen Zeros were warmed up on deck and ready to scramble the moment the American planes were sighted. Without radar, the Japanese had to wait until the American planes came within visual range. This was a tremendous disadvantage in clear weather, let alone on a day when the visibility was severely restricted by the weather.

Undetected by the Japanese fighters, which were patrolling at a lower altitude, Burch's group circled at 17,000 feet, just south of the enemy carriers, while they awaited the arrival of *Yorktown*'s TBDs for a coordinated attack. VT-5 showed up just as lookouts aboard the enemy flattops picked up the American planes. "Burch rolled into his dive so abruptly that his two wing

The *Shokaku* under attack by the dive bombers of Scouting Five. Fogged bomb-sights and evasive maneuvering by the enemy carrier prevented any hits, although the aircrafts' 1,000-lb. bombs threw up great geysers of water, as shown here. *National Archives*

men had to hustle to stay with him."[4] As he began to enter his 70-degree dive, Burch could see the nearest carrier, the *Shokaku,* getting ready to launch more Zeros. As the seven SBDs of VS-5 lined up on the rapidly moving target, they were plagued by a familiar bugaboo: once again their sights and windshields fogged over. Although their 1,000-lb. bombs threw up great geysers of water, none struck the *Shokaku.*

While VS-5 was diving on the *Shokaku,* Lt. Wallace "Wally" C. Short was leading the seventeen SBDs of VB-5 around in a wide circle that would put them into a favorable attack position. While Bombing Five was executing this maneuver the three Zeros which had been scrambled to intercept the American dive bombers had climbed into position and had began to dive on Short's formation just as it pushed over. Although they tried all sorts of fancy tricks to slow themselves down, the Japanese fighter pilots were unable to stay with the SBDs once they "popped" their dive brakes. As the prewar exercises had shown, it was extremely difficult for a fighter to down a dive bomber once it had entered its 70-degree dive, and only one SBD was hit on the way down.

The pilot, Lt. John J. Powers continued his attack even though his plane was engulfed in flames. Powers waited until he was below 1,000 feet to release his bomb, which hit the *Shokaku* on her starboard side abaft the island and exploded as his plane crashed into the sea. Powers's bravery earned him a posthumous Medal of Honor.

As VB-5 regrouped they were delighted to see the results of their handiwork. Despite the evasive maneuvers attempted by *Shokaku*'s captain and their problematic bombsights they still managed to line up on the carrier and score two hits on the big carrier, leaving the flight deck burning furiously. Now it was Torpedo Squadron Five's turn. Dropping to 50 feet and increasing speed to 110 knots, the nine pilots (one TBD dropped out because of engine trouble) fanned out to determine the best position for attack.[5] The intense antiaircraft fire prevented the TBDs from approaching close enough to do any damage with their torpedoes. They were released too far from the *Shokaku* for a reasonable chance of hitting the fast-moving carrier, which was steaming at full speed! None of the six fish that ran true struck the *Shokaku*, though the pilots claimed to have seen three hits. Once again it appears likely that they mistook the near misses of VB-5's 1,000-lb. bombs for hits from their own torpedoes.

Covering Torpedo Five's attack was a section of F4Fs from VF-42 lead by Lt. (jg) Elbert Scott McCuskey. They kept the Japanese fighters off the TBDs, shooting down one of three Zeros which attempted to disrupt the torpedo planes and damaging another before hightailing it for home.

The success of *Yorktown*'s strike group showed what could be achieved by a well-coordinated attack with fighter protection. *Yorktown*'s dive bombers had severely damaged the *Shokaku* for the loss of but two SBDs. More hits would undoubtedly have been made had their bombsights not fogged over, a problem Nimitz later described as "the outstanding material defect" of the action.[6] Had this not occurred, it's probable more hits would have been scored by the dive bombers, quite possibly sinking the big carrier. On the negative side, the failure of VT-5 to score a single hit was an early indication of the folly of trying to attack a well-defended carrier with obsolete torpedo planes and torpedoes such as the Mark XIII, which was so slow that the vessel under attack "could turn and run away from them."[7]

While the *Yorktown* air group was attacking the *Shokaku*, *Lexington*'s planes were struggling to find the target. The air group had become badly separated in the thick cloud cover and had failed to receive the radio report updating the position of the enemy carriers. Four planes (one TBD and three fighters) had already aborted by the time the rest of the strike group reached the end of the navigation leg which was supposed to place them over the enemy. Finding no carriers at this location, Ault ordered the group to swing left, initiating a standard box search. After heading to the north for a short while they spotted enemy ships about 15 miles to the west. Ault ordered the planes in his attack group to circle while he tried to contact Bombing Two, which had become lost in the heavy overcast.[8] In the rush to launch the air strike, *Lexington*'s crew had failed to fully fuel the eleven SBDs of VB-2 which had taken off as part of Ault's attack group. They were running low on fuel and had to abort when they could not find the enemy ships in the intermittent overcast.

Ault had no choice but to attack with the forces at hand. The dive bombers would hit the carrier first to draw any fighters of the enemy's CAP away from the vulnerable torpedo bombers. Because of the low ceiling Ault was forced to made his attack in a shallow glide. Although this added extra exposure to antiaircraft fire, it was a fortuitous choice because the shallow glide placed the SBDs well below the enemy fighters, allowing the four SBDs in Ault's section the luxury of glide bombing the *Shokaku* without interference. Unfortunately, only Ault's projectile hit the enemy vessel. The 1,000-lb. bomb struck the starboard side of the flight deck, inflicting more damage on the smoke-engulfed carrier.[9]

As Ault's command section was commencing its attack, the TBDs of Torpedo Two began to drop down from 6,000 feet. Using a cloud bank to conceal their approach, they descended in a shallow dive which brought them below the cloud level, speeding toward the *Shokaku* at 180 knots.[10] As they broke through the overcast they could see the smoke-enshrouded carrier 2 miles in the distance. The *Shokaku* immediately opened fire and began a radical turn to starboard. This maneuver set up an opportunity for a direct attack against her starboard side. The TBDs fanned out, making individual runs against the *Shokaku*, which outmaneuvered the pitifully slow Mark XIII torpedoes launched much too far from the target to be effective.

While the American strike groups were engaged in attacking the *Shokaku*, their own flattops were busy trying to defend themselves from the sixty-nine Japanese planes sent to eliminate them. Unlike their American counterparts, the Japanese strike group arrived as one unit, emerging from the low-pressure front which shrouded their own carriers to find the U.S. ships in clear skies.

The sixteen F4Fs lofted by TF-17 would be hard pressed to deal with the enemy force, which included an escort of eighteen Zeros.

The assault began at 1118 as the lone squadron of the Japanese torpedo planes split up into three sections to assail the *Lexington* from both sides in an attempt to catch the big carrier in the pincers of a two-horned attack which would prevent the ship from outmaneuvering the "tin fish" launched from both sides. As the enemy planes approached from the starboard bow, *Lexington*'s skipper ordered the rudder full over in an attempt to comb the deadly missiles. As the ship swung to port she was bracketed by three torpedoes which passed ahead and astern. Six more planes suddenly materialized off the port bow (three of the attackers had already been downed by TF-17's CAP). The *Lexington* struggled to turn away. She twisted and wriggled as best she could, but there were just too many torpedoes in the water. The first two plunged deep into the water, failed to adjust to the correct depth setting, and passed harmlessly beneath *Lexington*'s keel. The next two struck her port side, sending shudders throughout the ship as their warheads exploded.

As the *Lexington* tried to outmaneuver the torpedoes launched against her, the Japanese began their dive-bombing attack. The ship was headed away from the enemy planes, forcing the attackers into shallow cross-wind dives that disrupted their bombing runs and exposed them to more antiaircraft fire. Unopposed by any American fighter, they managed only two hits, which struck the flight deck, starting fires and spraying shrapnel among the gun crews, but caused relatively little serious damage.

The loss of eight Mitsubishi B5Ns torpedo planes during the previous evening's abortive strike against the American carriers now came back to haunt the Japanese. The four torpedo planes left to attack *Yorktown* were insufficient for the dreaded anvil technique. One of the four was shot down by antiaircraft fire before it could close near enough to threaten the *Yorktown*, which began to turn away from the attackers at flank speed. The three surviving Mitsubishi torpedo planes closed within 500 yards before releasing their torpedoes which *Yorktown* was able to avoid by skillful maneuvering.[11]

After a five-minute respite, *Yorktown* was assaulted by fourteen enemy dive bombers that were also forced to bomb into a cross wind set up by skillful ship handling on the part of *Yorktown*'s captain. The 15–20 knot wind made accurate bombing extremely difficult for the Japanese pilots, only one of whom managed to hit the carrier. The 550-lb. projectile passed cleanly through the flight deck just forward of the middle elevator, exploding four levels below. Though the bomb killed sixty-four men and started numerous fires below decks, it did little damage to the flight deck, which was quickly repaired.

While both American carriers had been hit, neither appeared to be in serious jeopardy. Although *Lexington* had sustained considerable damage, it appeared after the fighting had ended that her damage-control parties had the situation well in hand. They had put out the fires, pumped out the three flooded boiler rooms, and had corrected the 7-degree list that had resulted from the torpedo damage.

If the results of the battle had been frozen then and there, the U.S. Navy would have returned to port victorious, having severely damaged the *Shokaku* while sinking a light carrier, one destroyer, and several minecraft against the loss of one destroyer and a fleet oiler. But as Samuel E. Morison noted in his classic history of World War II, "The final score of [a] naval battle is not made up until the ships return to port."[12]

At 1247, an hour after the attack had ended, a tremendous explosion shook the *Lexington* from stem to stern. Undetected gasoline vapors leaking from the damaged aircraft fueling system ignited in the first of a series of devastating explosions that turned the gallant "Lady Lex" into an uncontrollable conflagration. By 1600 the doomed ship was dead in the water, drifting helplessly in the gentle swells of the Coral Sea. She continued to burn for nearly four more hours before the destroyer *Phelps* put the old girl out of her misery.

While the loss of the *Lexington* was considered a tactical victory for the Imperial Japanese Navy, the Americans had eliminated the *Shoho,* mauled the Fifth Carrier Division's air group so badly that only 45 planes (out of the original 109) remained operational, and inflicted so much damage on the *Shokaku* that she would be out of action for at least three months. Without air cover, the Imperial Japanese Navy's high command was forced to cancel the Port Moresby invasion. The U.S. Navy's airmen had turned back the enemy, winning the Allies' first strategic victory in the Pacific.

CHAPTER 19

Climax at Midway

W HEN THE BATTERED *Yorktown* returned to Pearl Harbor, she was immediately taken into dry dock and hurriedly repaired for the new threat that had
materialized during her sojourn in the Coral Sea. The loss of the *Lexington*
left Nimitz with just three carriers in the Pacific, and *Yorktown* was urgently
needed to accompany *Enterprise* and *Hornet,* which were about to depart for
Midway Island to intercept the Japanese forces intent on seizing the strategically located island. The story of the navy's cryptologists deciphering the
objectives of the Imperial Japanese Navy have been covered elsewhere and
need not be discussed here.

Nimitz had planned to place Vice Admiral Halsey, the senior carrier commander in the Pacific Fleet, in command of the Midway strike force. But
Halsey had returned from the Doolittle raid suffering from a severe skin ail-
ment which forced him into the hospital immediately after he had debriefed
Nimitz and recommended Rear Adm. Raymond A. Spruance as his replacement. Spruance, a nonaviator, had commanded Halsey's cruisers since the
beginning of the war and was highly regarded by Halsey. Nimitz approved
Halsey's endorsement and ordered Spruance to take command of Task Force
16, which included the aircraft carriers *Enterprise* and *Hornet.*

Task Force 16 departed Pearl Harbor on 28 May 1942, headed for a position to the northeast of Midway. Fletcher in the repaired *Yorktown* followed two days later with Task Force 17. To make up for the losses suffered at the Battle of the Coral Sea, her decimated air group was reconstituted with three of *Saratoga*'s squadrons, which had remained in Hawaii after their ship had returned to the mainland for repairs.[1] Nimitz instructed Fletcher, who as senior officer afloat would assume tactical command of both carrier groups, to stay well beyond the range of enemy scout planes and ordered the two groups to remain at least 10 miles apart to reduce the risk from enemy air attack.[2]

The two task forces rendezvoused late in the afternoon on 2 June 1942 at their assigned position 325 miles northeast of Midway, which Nimitz had optimistically dubbed "Point Luck." A large force of enemy ships was spotted the next morning 700 miles west of Midway by one of the long-range PBYs stationed on the island. Using the latest intelligence reports that he had been receiving from Nimitz's staff at Pearl Harbor, Fletcher correctly deduced that this was the invasion force. He continued to steam in the vicinity of Point Luck until 1950 in the late afternoon of the 3d, when he ordered both task forces to change course to the southwest and head for a position 200 miles north of Midway. From there they could ambush the yet-to-be-detected enemy carrier force that was expected to approach from the northwest. This is exactly where four Japanese carriers (*Akagi, Kaga, Hiryu,* and *Soryu*) under the command of Vice Adm. Chuichi Nagumo were headed, concealed from Midway's search planes by bad weather.[3]

At dawn the next morning Admiral Nagumo launched a 108-plane strike against Midway, unaware that an American carrier group was lying in wait to waylay him. Held back was a second wave of planes armed with demolition bombs in case a follow-up strike was needed. In the meantime, several carrier scouts and float planes from the accompanying cruiser force were dispatched to search for any American forces which might be lurking about. If enemy carriers were detected, Nagumo planned to rearm the planes on deck with torpedoes before sending them off.

Nagumo, like most officers of the Imperial Japanese Navy, was obsessed with the offensive. This resulted in a lack of interest in search and reconnaissance, which resulted in inadequate attention being paid to this critical function of carrier warfare: "In both the training and organization of [Japanese] naval aviators, too much importance and effort were devoted to attack. Reconnaissance was taught only as part of the regular curriculum, and no subsequent special training was given."[4] Unlike the U.S. Navy's Scouting Squadrons, there were no reconnaissance units of any appreciable size in the carrier units of the Japanese navy; thus Nagumo had to rely on float planes launched from his cruiser escort to ensure that no American carriers were nearby.

As Nagumo's carriers were putting the first Midway strike group into the air, the *Yorktown,* which had flight duty that day, was busy launching the combat air patrol which was always sent aloft whenever the task force was in range of enemy aircraft. Following the fighters were ten SBDs sent out as a precautionary measure to search for enemy ships in a 100-mile arc to the northwest.

An hour after *Yorktown* began putting her planes in the air, at 0534, the task force received word via an intercepted radio message from one of Midway's search planes that the enemy carriers had been sighted. No other information was given. Nine minutes later, at 0545, a second dispatch was picked up warning the Midway defenders that many planes were heading their way on a bearing of 320 degrees 150 miles distant.[5] Although this message gave no clue as to the number of carriers or their exact location, it confirmed the presence of aircraft carriers in the vicinity and provided some idea of their location. Armed with this information, Spruance instructed his chief of staff, Capt. Miles S. Browning, to strike the enemy carriers with everything they had at the earliest possible moment.[6] Then came the signal that the task force commanders had been waiting for: Two carriers and battleships bearing 320 degrees, distance 180, course 135 degrees, speed 25. This placed the Japanese carrier about 200 miles west-southwest of Task Force 16.

Fletcher wasted no time in taking action. "We couldn't afford to wait," he later exclaimed. "We had to strike first, strike swiftly, and strike in great force."[7] At 0607, only four minutes after the enemy carriers had been definitely located, he ordered Spruance to "proceed southwesterly and attack enemy carriers when definitely located."[8] He would follow as soon as *Yorktown's* scouts had been recovered.

Within minutes Task Force 16 had changed course and was headed for the enemy at 25 knots in order to close the distance to the enemy carriers. Spruance planned to launch an air strike when his force was within 100 miles of the suspected position of the Japanese carriers (a point they estimated would be reached at about 0900), which was the optimal range for attack. As reports began to filter in from Midway it became clear to Spruance's chief of staff, Capt. Miles Browning, that they could not afford to wait until 0900 to launch their counter strike. He advised Spruance to launch a full deck strike as soon as they could. Browning recommended that they start launching planes at 0700. He estimated that the enemy carriers would be about 155 miles distant, just close enough for the torpedo planes, which were limited to a maximum strike radius of 160 miles, to make it.

Browning, an experienced airman who had earned his wings in 1924, was an outspoken advocate of the need to rid one's deck of strike aircraft at the earliest possible moment.[9] Although it has been said that Browning had a "slide rule brain," there is no evidence to suggest, as postulated by Morison in his famous history of the navy in World War II, that Browning hoped to catch the enemy carriers with their decks full of loaded aircraft.[10] To the contrary, the evidence suggests that all Browning wanted was to hit the enemy carriers with a maximum effort as soon as they were within range—a strategy that was clearly in line with U.S. Navy doctrine (USF-74) and the ideas voiced by Rear Adm. Henry V. Butler, Hugh Douglas, and others during the prewar years.

Spruance ordered his carriers to begin launching aircraft at 0700 as suggested by Browning, using the deferred departure method. Once in the air they were directed to employ the search-attack procedure enroute in order to seek out the enemy whose exact position was still unknown. Lacking in Spruance's dispatch was a definite course for the planes to follow, a grievous oversight which almost led to disastrous consequences. Although the evidence suggests that Spruance and Browning expected the air groups from the two carriers to conduct a coordinated attack, a number of unforeseen circumstances soon precluded any possibility of this occurring as the departing planes soon separated into three distinct formations headed on divergent bearings.

The *Hornet's* air group, led by Cdr. Stanhope C. Ring, was the first to depart. Instead of heading directly for the estimated interception point on a heading of 240 degrees, Ring took them to the west on a course of 265 degrees. The decision to proceed on this bearing appears to have resulted from a last-minute command conference held on *Hornet's* bridge between Ring, his squadron commanders, and the ship's captain, Marc Mitscher, who decided to send the planes farther to the west in the belief that they would encounter the two missing enemy carriers which CinCPAC intelligence had indicated were part of the Japanese force attacking Midway.[11]

Leading the way as they climbed to altitude was Ring's three-plane command section along with the thirty-one other dive bombers from VB-8 and VS-8. Above and behind were the ten F4F-4s from VF-8 which formed the flight's fighter escort. They were followed by fifteen TBDs of VT-8 under the command of Lt. Cdr. John C. Waldron.

Problems on *Enterprise*'s flight deck delayed the launch of her torpedo planes until Spruance, after a ten-minute wait, became impatient and ordered the air group's leader, Lt. Cdr. Clarence Wade McClusky, to proceed without the torpedo planes. McClusky had carefully plotted his own estimate of the enemy's course and position, "computing the likely point of interception by his planes as bearing 231 degrees, distance 142 miles."[12] Now he rounded up the two dive-bombing squadrons that would accompany him and set off toward the new interception point, followed by the fifteen SBDs of Bombing Six under the command of Lt. Richard H. Best and a similar number of planes assigned to Scouting Six, lead by Lt. Wilmer (Earl) E. Gallaher.

Although *Enterprise*'s fighters were already aloft, it took several minutes for them to form up on their leader, Lt. James S. Gray Jr., by which time the SBDs had flown out of sight to the southwest. Gray spotted a torpedo squadron below and joined up, believing them to be from his own ship. In actuality they were chasing VT-8, the last unit of *Hornet*'s strike group on its westerly heading of 265 degrees.

The low-flying TBDs of Torpedo Eight lost sight of Ring's SBDs in the intervening cloud layer, which didn't really matter since Waldron wasn't about to follow the SBDs anyway. Waldron must have disagreed with Mitscher's logic, for at 0825, for reasons that remain unclear, he suddenly decided to make a gradual turn to the left, bringing the planes in his torpedo squadron on a more southwesterly heading. Gray, who was cruising above, assumed that the torpedo planes knew were they were going and continued to follow until he too lost sight of the torpedo bombers when they flew into a low-lying cloud bank.[13]

The last planes to be launched from both carriers were the torpedo bombers of VT-6. They were under the command of Lt. Cdr. Eugene E. Lindsey and departed on the original heading of 240 degrees.

As Spruance made preparations to launch his air strike, Fletcher, having recovered *Yorktown*'s dawn search, set out to catch up with Spruance, ordering his ships to ring up 25 knots on a heading of 240 degrees. Fletcher, whose orders from Nimitz directed him to use Task Force 17 as a strike reserve,

The flight deck crew on board the *Enterprise,* spotting the TBDs of Torpedo Six on the morning of 4 June 1942. Only four of the fourteen planes returned from that day's attack on the Japanese carrier force. *National Archives*

thought it best to wait and see what other enemy carriers Midway's scouts might turn up before he ordered his own planes to attack. As the reader will recall, Fletcher had been misled by the poor contact reports received at the Battle of the Coral Sea and did not want to repeat the mistake he made in committing his entire force against *Shoho*.[14]

As the distance to the enemy closed, however, Fletcher and his air staff began to fret about the possibility of being surprised while *Yorktown's* flight deck was still loaded with aircraft. The sudden appearance of an unidentified intruder on *Yorktown's* radar removed any further doubt as to their next move. Though the exact location of the enemy carriers was still uncertain, Fletcher decided that it would be best to launch at least a portion of *Yorktown's* vulnerable air group as soon as possible.

Plans for the strike were drawn up by Cdr. Murr Arnold and Lt. Cdr. Oscar Pederson, who were, respectively, *Yorktown's* air officer and air group commander. These experienced veterans of the Battle of the Coral Sea extrapolated the enemy's position based on a plot of the sighting reports which had been received earlier and an estimate of the maximum range of the strike aircraft attacking Midway. From this information they calculated that the enemy carriers would be approximately 150 miles distant on a bearing of 240 degrees at 0900. To permit the strike group to attack in concert they came up with a launch plan based on the cruising speed of the aircraft involved, which resulted in a staggered departure similar to that which had been used against *Shoho* in the Coral Sea. The slowest planes, the TBDs, would leave first. They would be followed by the next fastest, the SBDs, and then the speediest, the F4F fighters.

The *Yorktown* launched her air strike shortly after 0830. First off were twelve TBDs of VT-6 under the command of Lt. Cdr. Lance (Lem) E. Massey. Next came seventeen SBDs of VB-3 led by Lt. Cdr. Maxwell F. Leslie. Last off was Lt. Cdr. Jimmy Thach, with a six-plane division of fighter escorts from VF-3. Thach and his pilots were saddled with the overly burdened F4F-4 which was slower and had less range than the earlier F4F-3.[15]

The launch went smoothly, and all planes were in the air by 0906. One hundred and forty-eight American warplanes were now headed toward the enemy (eighty-four SBDs, forty-one TBDs, twenty-six F4Fs), strung out in five widely dispersed elements, each heading in a slightly different direction (see table 19.1).

As *Yorktown*'s strike group climbed for altitude, Nagumo's carriers, which had successfully fought off a series of ineffective attacks from American aircraft based on Midway, was just bringing aboard the last of the first wave of attackers that had been pummeling the island of Midway. Thanks to a report received from one of the *Tone*'s float planes, Nagumo knew that he was now being stalked by an American carrier force. As the last plane was recovered, he changed course to 70 degrees, increased speed to 30 knots, and ordered his four carriers to prepare for an all-out strike against the American flattops.

While this action was taking place aboard the Japanese ships, the leading element of the American planes under Ring's command was approaching the suspected location of Nagumo's carriers. The inexperienced air group commander formed the SBDs into a scouting line abreast—not the wisest choice—which required the pilots to constantly readjust their throttles, causing an unnecessary increase in fuel consumption for themselves as well as for the escorting F4F-Fs, which had to throttle way back to avoid overtaking the dive bombers. The F4Fs were already low on fuel, having used up much of

Table 19.1 American Strike Force, 4 June 1942
(Composition at 0900 Local Time)

	Hornet Air Group Ring's Strike Group Heading: 265 degrees	
Command Section	3 SBDs	Cdr. Stanhope C. Ring
Scouting Eight	15 SBDs	Lt. Cdr. Walter F. Rodee
Bombing Eight	16 SBDs	Lt. Cdr. Robert R. Johnson
Fighting Eight	10 F4Fs	Lt. Cdr. Samuel G. Mitchell
	Waldron's Torpedo Bombers Heading: approx. 215 degrees	
Torpedo Eight	15 TBDs	Lt. Cdr. John C. Waldron
Fighting Six	10 F4Fs	Lt. James S. Gray
	Enterprise Air Group McClusky's Strike Group Heading: 231 degrees	
Command Section	3 SBDs	Lt. Cdr. C. Wade McClusky
Scouting Six	15 SBDs	Lt. W. Earl Gallaher
Bombing Six	15 SBDs	Lt. Richard H. Best
	Lindsey's Torpedo Bombers Heading: 240 degrees	
Torpedo Six	14 TBDs	Lt. Cdr. Eugene E. Lindsey
	Yorktown Air Group Strike Group Heading: 240 degrees	
Torpedo Three	14 TBDs	Lt. Cdr. Lance E. Massey
Bombing Three	17 SBDs	Lt. Cdr. Maxwell F. Leslie
Fighting Three	6 SBDs	Lt. Cdr. John S. Thach

their reserves while they circled over the *Hornet* waiting for the rest of the strike to form up. The fighters were quickly running out of gas and were forced to turn back before the enemy was spotted. All ten ran out of fuel before finding the *Hornet* and were forced to ditch into the sea, a tragic loss which should have been avoided.

Ring had no choice but to continue without his escort. When he arrived at the anticipated point of interception there was no sign of the enemy. Ring, for reasons which have never fully been explained, continued to lead the entire group on the same heading for another 50 miles instead of adopting the standard expanding-box search, which might have located the carriers. Though seventeen planes made it back to *Hornet* and thirteen landed at Midway, Ring's force missed the action.

In the meantime Waldron continued taking his squadron toward the southwest. After flying for another fifty minutes, they spotted two columns of smoke rising over the horizon and were soon able to make out the silhouettes of three carriers. They had found the enemy, but after almost two hours in the air they were dangerously short of fuel and could not wait to join *Hornet*'s dive bombers for the coordinated attack which was supposed to overwhelm the enemy's CAP. Waldron promptly took his fifteen TBDs down to the deck for the low-level attack dictated by the Mark XIII torpedo and they were promptly cut to pieces by the enemy fighters. None of his planes scored a hit and only one plane—that flown by Ensign George H. Gay, the sole survivor of VT-8—got close enough to make a drop. All the rest were shot down during a brief engagement that lasted just six minutes!

Although Gray's fighters had arrived over the Japanese fleet minutes before, they were unaware of Torpedo Eight's plight and began circling at 22,000 feet, waiting for *Yorktown*'s dive bombers to show up, and did not know that McClusky was still searching for the enemy carriers.

McClusky, who had been flying on a southwesterly heading since takeoff, turned to the northwest on the first leg of a large box search at 0935. He planned to fly in this direction, that is, on a reciprocal bearing to that which had originally been reported for the enemy carriers, until 1000, when he would turn to the northeast for the last leg of his search before heading back to the *Yorktown*. With five minutes to go, McClusky spotted the wake of the Japanese destroyer *Arashi* rushing to rejoin Nagumo's fleet after attacking the U.S. submarine *Nautilus*. McClusky decided it must be headed toward the enemy and immediately changed course, following the destroyer's bearing. Within minutes he was able to make out the sight of the enemy task force in his binoculars.

As McClusky was just making his first turn, Lindsey's Torpedo Six, which had been advancing on a more northerly course at a slightly slower speed, began to observe smoke miles to the northwest. They had been flying on a heading of 240 degrees, which was exactly where they would have found Nagumo had he not changed course to the northwest. Lindsey turned right to investigate and soon sighted the enemy ships steaming away at 30 knots.

Veterans of the raids on the Marshalls, Wake, and Marcus, VT-6 was a much more experienced unit than VT-8, and it showed in their attack doctrine. As they approached the nearest enemy carrier (the *Kaga*), Lindsey split the squadron into two divisions, sending Lt. Arthur V. Ely around to the target's port side in an effort to affect the anvil attack. The raiders closed in from both sides and commenced their run a few minutes before 1000. Although five or six of the planes got close enough to launch their torpedoes, none found their mark. Only four out of the fourteen planes which commenced the attack survived. All the rest were shot down while Gray's fighters continued to circle above, oblivious to the ordeal below, waiting for the infamous "Come on down" message that Ely was supposed to transmit if he needed help.[16]

Now it was Massey's turn. VT-3 had been in the air for less than ninety minutes when it too spotted smoke off to the north at 0930. Unlike the other groups, he was still escorted by Thach's fighters, who continued to weave slowly back and forth above the lumbering torpedo bombers in an effort to keep pace with their slower comrades. When Massey changed course toward the smoke, Thach followed.

Leslie's Bombing Three spotted the target at about the same time and made a similar course correction. By 1020 he was over the northeastern portion of the enemy task force and could see three enemy carriers below. Leslie radioed Massey to ask if he was ready to commence the attack. When Massey replied in the affirmative, Leslie began maneuvering his squadron into position to dive on the carrier *Soryu,* which was just beginning to turn into the wind to launch aircraft.

Massey, who was one of the most combat-experienced torpedo pilots in the U.S. Navy, climbed to 2,600 feet in preparation for the high-level torpedo approach that would permit the squadron to dive in and gain speed. As they neared the *Hiryu,* the second division swung out of formation to attack the carrier's port side while Massey's division headed for the starboard side. They were soon besieged by enemy fighters which resulted in Massey's frantic call for VF-3's help, which went unanswered. When the attack began, Thach had taken his planes down to 3,000 feet, hoping to cover the low-flying torpedo planes. His six Wildcats were soon overwhelmed by the enemy Zeros, however, and were now engaged in a fight for their lives.

Massey's lead plane was "flamed" a mile short of the release point; the rest of the division never even made it to the launch point, and none of the torpedoes dropped by the others struck the *Hiryu,* which was able evade the relatively slow American "fish."

When Leslie's planes arrived over the enemy ships they had no idea that they were about to be upstaged by McClusky's dive bombers, who were approaching from the southwest; nor did they realize that Nagumo was about to launch his planned strikes against the American carriers. During their approach to the enemy ships, Best's wing man ran out of oxygen, forcing Best to take his squadron down to 15,000 feet. As Best's group reduced altitude it began to pick up speed, moving them slightly ahead and below the air group commander, who was trailed by the planes from Scouting Six.

Thus, Best was in the lead when they arrived over the enemy task force. Two successive turns to the northeast had disrupted Nagumo's orderly formation, leaving the four carriers widely dispersed. As Best closed the task force he spotted two carriers (*Kaga* and *Akagi*) 5 to 10 miles apart off his port bow, steaming toward the Southwest.[17] Standard dive-bombing doctrine specified that the trailing squadron—which had been Best's until he dropped down, was to take the closest target. Best, thinking that he was still trailing, made for the lead carrier (*Kaga*) and deployed his squadron by divisions into the standard attack formation which would allow each division to dive on the target from a different direction.

Just as he "popped" his dive flaps, McClusky plunged past him headed for the first carrier, followed by the rest of the command section, as well as Gallaher's VS-6. "He had obviously taken that target too," explained Best. "There was nothing to do but pull in my flaps and head for the next carrier in line" (the *Akagi*). Best started rocking his wings to attract the attention of the rest of his squadron, but it was too late; the entire second and third divisions, along with two of his own planes, had followed McClusky and Gallaher down.[18]

When McClusky pushed over at 1022 he caught his wing man, Ensign William R. Pittman, completely by surprise. Pittman's place was immediately taken by Ensign Richard Jaccard, who was also flying in the command section. The rest of the SBDs followed, one by one until all twenty-eight SBD dive bombers were streaking toward the *Akagi* at 260 knots in their 70-degree dives.[19] McClusky and the two other planes in his section missed the target, sending up fountains of water from their two near-misses. Then came Gallaher, whose 500-lb. bomb landed squarely amidst the mass of armed and fueled aircraft spotted aft. The enemy flight deck was immediately engulfed in flames and secondary explosions! At least three more bombs struck the *Akagi*, which became engulfed in flames from stem to stern.

Best saw none of this as he concentrated on setting up on the second carrier. "Don't let this carrier escape," he called over the radio as he pushed over into a near-vertical dive aiming his three-power telescopic sight at a point in the center of the flight deck just ahead of the bridge.[20] Best pulled the release handle, then calmly laid his plane on its right side as he pulled out so he could see the fall of shot. Best claims that he saw his bomb hit by the forward elevator, followed by two hits on the fantail, which blew the carrier's planes into a blazing heap.[21]

As Best headed east to clear the area he saw a squadron of torpedo planes coming toward him. These must have been from Torpedo Three. Since they were heading west, it seems likely that Best had spotted the second division as it was just setting up to attack *Hiryu*. He was about to join up for mutual support when several Zeros flashed by, trying to get ahead of the torpedo planes. Best had second thoughts about this idea and decided to continue east and was treated to the awesome spectacle of the *Soryu* blowing up: "She was a mass of flames from bow to stern, with big explosions springing up every few seconds some where around the deck."[22]

Three direct hits from Leslie's Bombing Three in as many minutes had triggered ferocious deck fires, as bombs, torpedoes, and aircraft gasoline tanks began to detonate. Only nine planes were still armed with their 1,000-lb. bombs when Leslie pushed over at 1025, the rest, including the leader himself, had inadvertently jettisoned their weapons when they triggered their incorrectly installed new electric arming switches. Max Leslie had logged over 4,600 hours as a naval aviator and was not about to watch as the rest of his squadron attacked the *Soryu*. He made one last unsuccessful attempt to contact VT-3 before leading his men down, firing his fixed .50-caliber machine guns at the carrier's bridge until they jammed.

In six minutes the dive bombers from *Yorktown* and *Enterprise* had decimated Nagumo's carrier force, destroying three of his four flight decks with all of their aircraft! The lone survivor, *Hiryu*, quickly mounted a dive-bombing strike against the *Yorktown*, which took three 550-lb. bomb hits that reduced her speed to 19 knots, enough to enable the succeeding wave of torpedo planes to hit the ship again with two torpedoes, which caused her to stop dead in the water (she was sunk two days later by a Japanese submarine while work parties were trying to restore power to the stricken ship).

In the afternoon, the battered remnants of *Enterprise*'s SBDs reinforced with ten refugees from *Yorktown* mounted a counter strike on the *Hiryu*, which was located 110 miles from the task force. In the lead was Earl Gallaher with six planes from VS-6. Completing the strike group were fourteen SBDs from VB-3 under the command of Lt. Dewitt W. Shumway—he had scored the

SBDs of Scouting Six on their way to attack the *Hiryu* during the afternoon of 4 June 1942. *National Archives*

fourth hit on *Kaga*—plus Best's four-plane section from VB-6. All were veterans of the earlier attack that morning.

Gallaher spotted the *Hiryu* and her heavy escort at 1650. He directed Shumway to hit the battleship *Haruna* then nodded down toward the pushover point. As Gallaher's altimeter unwound, *Hiryu* turned hard to starboard according to the standard doctrine. This highly effective evasive maneuver resulted in six misses.

Seeing the near-misses dropped astern, Shumway decided to shift targets. His first section swept past Best's Bombing Six and scored three direct hits, even though it was dogged by Zeros all the way down. For the second time that day another squadron had pushed over and above Best's formation! Undaunted, he pushed over and scored a fourth hit on the now-doomed carrier, which became engulfed in flames. Realizing that the *Hiryu* was finished, the last two pilots in Shumway's squadron switched targets and dived on the battleship *Haruna,* which they straddled with two near-misses.

Although the Battle of Midway would continue for several more days, the

Table 19.2 Air Actions at the Battle of Midway, 3–4 June 1942

Date/ Approximate Attack Time[1]	Squadron	Sorties Launched	Planes Over Target	Hits/ Ordnance Expended	%	Target
3 June/1700	Army B-17s	9 B-17	9	0/36		Transports
4 June/0130	VP-44	4 PBY	3 w/torpedos	1/3		Oiler
4 June/0700	VT-8 (Midway)	6 TBF	6 w/torpedos	0/?		Carrier group
	Army B-26	4 B-26	4 w/torpedos	0/3		Carrier group
4 June/0810	Army B-17s	9 B-17	9	0/72		Carrier group
4 June/0830	VMSB-241	11 SB2U	11	0/11		Carrier group
		18 SBD[2]	16	0/16		Carrier group
4 June/0900	VS-8	17 SBD		Did not engage		Carrier group
4 June/0900	VB-8	14 SBD		Did not engage		Carrier group
4 June/0930	VT-8	15 TBD	15	0/1		Soryu
4 June/1000	VT-6	14 TBD	14	0/?		Kaga
4 June/1025	VT-3	12 TBD	12	0/5		Hiryu
4 June/1022	CEAG[3]	3 SBD	3	0/3		Kaga
	VS-6, Division 1[4]	6 SBD	6	3/6		Kaga
	VS-6, Division 2	5 SBD	5	1/5		Kaga
	VS-6, Division 3	4 SBD	2[5]	0/3		Kaga
	VB-6, Division 2, 3	12 SBD	12	0/12		Kaga
	Total	30 SBD	28	4/28[6]	14%	Kaga
4 June/1025	VS-6 (Best)	3 SBD	3	3/3[7]	100%	Akagi
4 June/1025	VB-3	17 SBD	9	3/9	33%	Soryu
			2	0/2		Isokaze
			2	0/2		Unknown
4 June/1701	VS-6	7 SBD	6[8]	0/7		Hiryu[9]
	VB-3	12 SBD	10[10]	3/10	30%	Hiryu
	VB-6 (Best)	4 SBD	3[10]	1/3	33%	Hiryu
	VB-3	2 SBD	2	0/2		BB
4 June/1730	VB-8; VS-8	16 SBD	16	0/16		Haruna
4 June/1730	6 B-17 (Sweeny)	6 B-17	6	0/?		BBs
4 June/1740	6 B-17 (Blakey)	6 B-17	6	0/?		BBs

[1]Estimated time of push-over or torpedo run-in.

[2]According to Lord, Incredible Victory, 120, sixteen pilots had never flown an SBD until a few days earlier. Henderson decided to glide-bomb instead of dive-bomb because of his pilots' inexperience.

[3]According to Prange, Miracle at Midway, only three planes attacked Akagi; according to Lord, some Division 1 planes attacked Kaga.

[4]As reported by Gallaher in his Report of Action, 4–6 June 1942.

[5]Greene's plane lost while trailing Arashi, Schneider runs out of gas at outer screen; Prange, Miracle at Midway, 260.

[6]VS-6 claimed to have made seven hits, but only four were recorded by Japanese observers.

[7]Whether he attacked with three or five planes is unclear. His radioman says only number two and three followed him down.

[8]One SBD aborted.

[9]Took evasive maneuvers.

[10]Lost to enemy fighters.

outcome was decided when *Hiryu,* the last of Nagumo's carriers, was put out of action (she went under at 0900 the next day). Against the loss of the *Yorktown* and eighty aircraft, Fletcher's carrier force had completely wiped out the Imperial Navy's First Carrier Strike Force, destroying all 4 of its flattops and the 228 operational aircraft embarked on them. Without air support, Adm. Isoroku Yamamoto, the architect of the plan to wrest Midway from the Americans, was forced to call off the invasion and withdraw his forces. As Hugh Douglas had predicted in 1933 (page 128), a few Dauntless dive bombers (see table 19.2) had caught the Japanese carriers at their most vulnerable moment, changing the course of battle and, perhaps, the course of history.

CHAPTER 20

Reassessing Naval Aviation's Contribution to Victory

P RIOR WORKS DISCUSSING the events surrounding the Battle of Midway have largely ignored the importance of the aerial doctrine developed by the navy during the interwar period. With few exceptions, most authors (and perhaps many historians as well) have led the public to believe that the U.S. Navy—outnumbered four carriers to three—was lucky to have won such a decisive victory, given the poor quality of its aircraft relative to that of the enemy. Though the gods of war certainly smiled upon the navy's airmen that day, I feel strongly that the demise of the Japanese strike force was a direct result of the navy's efforts to perfect dive bombing as the central component of its aerial doctrine. The simultaneous arrival of three squadrons of heavily armed dive bombers over Nagumo's ships when they were most vulnerable was certainly fortuitous, but not unpredictable, given the nature of seaborne flight operations and the U.S. Navy's insistence that its own carriers launch their strike groups as soon as possible.

Too much emphasis has been placed on naval aviation's shortcomings in the early months of World War II, particularly with regard to the deficiencies of its torpedo bombers, and not enough on its successes. It is certainly true that the slow, vulnerable TBD-1 Devastator was obsolete, but its successor—

the TBF-1—had already entered the pipeline. A few of the new planes even participated in the Battle of Midway, albeit the TBF-1s deployed from Midway's airstrip fared no better than their elder brethren![1] The real problem with U.S. torpedo doctrine lay in the inherent vulnerability of these planes in the face of large numbers of enemy fighters—a situation which had not been encountered before, and one which could not be avoided given the limited number of VFs available and the need to throw everything we had at the enemy. The extremely poor performance of the their torpedoes—a fault that can be attributed directly to the Bureau of Ordnance—only ensured that no hits would be achieved by the few VTs that did get through.

Likewise, many have touted the performance of the Mitsubishi A6M5 Zero while ignoring the Grumman F4F-4 Wildcat. Although the latter was somewhat slower and less maneuverable than the Zero, the F4F-4 had better armament and could take much more punishment because of the self-sealing tanks and armor—features that enabled Jimmy Thach and his men to give as good as they received.

Not enough credence is given to the Dauntless SBD dive bomber, an exceptional aircraft that was a generation ahead of its famous rival, the Aichi D3A Val. Its ability to remain perfectly stable in a dive contributed to the remarkable accuracy obtained by its pilots on that fateful day. These SBDs were armed with a 1,000-lb. bomb fused to go off a fraction of a second after impact so that it would explode just under the flight deck, causing the maximum amount of damage possible with regard to disabling further flight operations.

No one factor determined the outcome of the battle. The navy's successful effort to break the "Purple Code" of the Imperial Japanese Navy was certainly crucial, as was Nimitz's decision to take a "calculated risk." One must not discount the herculean efforts by the Navy Yard at Pearl Harbor to repair *Yorktown,* either, but only dive bombers and the aerial doctrine under which they were deployed were ultimately responsible for sinking the enemy ships of the Imperial Navy's First Carrier Strike Force.

APPENDIX A: OFFICIAL DESIGNATIONS
FOR U.S. NAVAL AIRCRAFT, 1920–1962

The type designations were established by the secretary of the navy on 17 July 1920, when he isssued a directive which prescribed a standard nomenclature for identifying all ships and aircraft in the navy. In compliance with this directive, all heavier-than-air craft were subsequently designated by the letter V, with the following type letters assigned to designate the various classes:

F   Fighter

O   Observation

S   Scout

P   Patrol

T   Torpedo and Bombing

G   Fleet (Utility)

In March 1922, a change was promulgated which added the identity of the manufacturer and the model number. Initially these preceded the class (mission) designation. Thus the first observation plane built by the Glen L. Martin Company became the MO. Numbers appearing between the letters indicated subsequent designs (except for the first model, where the 1 was omitted). Modifications to the basic design were also identified by number, using a dash to separate the change number from the class letter; for example, the second observation plane designed by Martin would be the M2O-1, with the first modification becoming the M2O-2.

The order of the lettering was reversed a year later (on 10 March 1923), so that the type/class were interchanged with the manufacturer; for example, the sixth fighter built by Curtiss became the F6C-1. The reversal in order was not retroactive and applied to new aircraft only. This system of identifying specific aircraft designs remained in effect until 1962.

APPENDIX B: THE NORDEN BOMBSIGHT AND HORIZONTAL BOMBING

No dissertation on the evolution of carrier aviation in the U.S. Navy would be complete without some mention of the Norden bombsight initiated and developed by the Bureau of Ordnance. Contrary to viewpoint frequently expressed in the public press, the navy's interest and concern for aerial bombardment preceded Billy Mitchell's well choreographed sinking of the *Ostfriersland*. A year and half earlier, on 15 January 1920, the Bureau of Ordnance requested that Carl L. Norden, a leading authority on gyroscopes, develop a stabilized bombsight, which was completed in the spring of 1921 under the designation of the Mark III bombsight. This device could not be used against a moving target, and as Norden was quick to point out, an enemy ship would not be so obliging as to remain still when under attack, leading to a follow-on contract for a more advanced sight, the Mark XI, which took a number of years to develop and perfect.

The acceptance of Norden's second model, the Mark XI bombsight, in 1929 coincided (more or less) with the delivery of the navy's first experimental dive bomber, the XT5M-1. For the next several years the navy pursued the development of dive and horizontal bombing in parallel.

The first gunnery practice involving the Mark XI was conducted by VT-2 in January 1932. The high degree of accuracy obtained during this exercise was facilitated by squadron's commander, Lt. Cdr. John J. Ballentine, who had obtained extensive experience with the new bombsight while working on its development as the officer in charge of the aviation detachment at the Naval Proving Ground, Dahlgren, Virginia.

By January 1933, the navy began testing both methods against a maneuvering target, the radio-controlled ex-battleship *Utah*. Although the results of this practice confirmed the superiority of dive bombing, the horizontal bombers still made a credible showing as indicated by the following data:

	Total Bombs Dropped	Percentage Direct Hits	Percentage Effective Hits
Dive bombers	60	18.2	38.4
Horizontal bombers	71	5.6	23.9

Formation bombing of the *Utah* by both horizontal bombers and dive bombers was subsequently scheduled on a regular basis during the interwar period so that by 1941 the fleet had nine years experience in bombing a maneuvering target.

As can be seen from the Summary of Bombing Exercises shown in table B.1, dive bombing outperformed horizontal bombing by a considerable margin in every case except for the one year (1937–38) when the *Utah* remained on a steady course. As the altitude of the horizontal bombers increased to avoid improvements in anti-aircraft fire (from 8–10,000 feet in 1932–37 to 12,000 feet in 1937–38, and 16,000 feet thereafter), their results got worse, even though they were now using the improved Mark XV bombsight.

Table B.1 Summary of Bombing Exercises, 1932–1941

Gunnery Year	Target Maneuvers		Percentage of Hits by Dive Bombers	Percentage of Hits by Horizontal Bombers
1932–33		Single in line	18.2	5.6
1933–34		More effective	20.0	0.0
1934–35		Effective	13.0	0.0
1935–36		Restricted but effective	17.3	9.4
1936–37		Restricted and effective	23.7	8.3
1937–38	(A)	Steady course	12.7	11.1
	(B)	60-degree changes	11.3	5.6
1938–39	(A)	Steady course	13.9	4.1
	(B)	60-degree changes	14.9	2.4
1939–40	(A)	Antisubmarine zigzagging in formation within fleet disposition	21.8	4.4
	(B)	Unrestricted, but commencing only when attack visually detected	18.1	1.1
1940–41	(A)	Antisubmarine zigzagging in formation within fleet disposition	19.1	1.9
	(B)	Unrestricted, but commencing only when attack visually detected	21.1	1.9

Source: Robert V. Brown, "The Navy's Mark IV (Norden) Bomb Sight: Its Development and Procurement 1920–45" (Washington, D.C.: Department of the Navy, 1946).

Abbreviations

AirRonBatFlt	Aircraft Squadrons, Battle Fleet
AR	Action Reports, Office of the CNO, NA
Ast	Assistant
AVHB-NHC	Aviation History Branch, Naval Historical Center
BatFlt	Battle Fleet, U.S. Fleet
BatFor	Battle Force, U.S. Fleet
BdI&S	Board of Inspection and Survey
BdI&S Trials	Board of Inspection and Survey, Reports of Acceptance Trials of Naval Aircraft, RG 38, NA
BuAer	Bureau of Aeronautics
BuAer CF Files	Bureau of Aeronautics Confidential Correspondence Files, RG 72, NA
BuAer GC Files	Bureau of Aeronautics General Correspondence Files, RG 72, NA
BuAer SC Files	Bureau of Aeronautics Secret Correspondence Files, RG 72, NA
BuAer Trials	Bureau of Aeronautics, Final Reports of Trials and Inspections of Naval Aircraft, 1938–1944, RG 72, NA
BuC&R	Bureau of Construction and Repair
BuEng	Bureau of Engineering
BuEng CF Files	Bureau of Engineering Confidential Files, 1930–1940, RG 19, NA
BuNav	Bureau of Navigation
BuOrd	Bureau of Ordnance
BuShip	Bureau of Ships
CEAG	Commander, *Enterprise* Air Group
Chf	Chief
Chrmn	Chairman

CinCBatFlt	Commander-in-Chief, Battle Fleet
CinCh	Commander-in-Chief, U.S. Fleet (after 1941)
CinCPac	Commander-in-Chief, U.S. Pacific Fleet
CinCUS	Commander-in-Chief, U.S. Fleet
CNO	Chief of Naval Operations
CO	Commanding Officer
ComAirBatFlt	Commander, Aircraft Squadrons, Battle Fleet
ComAirBatFor	Commander, Aircraft Squadrons, Battle Force
ComAirGAF	Commander Aircraft, General Administrative Files
ComAirSctFl	Commander, Aircraft Squadrons, Scouting Fleet
ComBatFlt	Commander, Battle Fleet
ComBatFor	Commander, Battle Force
ComCarDivs	Commander Carrier Divisions
ComDesRon	Commander, Destroyer Squadron
ComSctFlt	Commander, Scouting Fleet
Corr	Correspondence
Conf	Confidential
DirFltTrn	Director, Fleet Training
FTD	Fleet Training Division, Office of CNO
GB File	Files of the General Board of the Navy, SecNav Correspondence Series, RG 80, NA
GBH	Hearings of the General Board, Microfilm Series M14943, NA
GC	General Correspondence
HC-NWC	Historical Collection, Naval War College
HF-NASM	Historical Files, National Air and Space Museum
INA	Inspector, Naval Aircraft
LC	Manuscript Division, Library of Congress
ltr	letter
MC-USMC	Manuscript Collection, USMC History and Museums Division, Washington Navy Yard
M&T	Material and Tactices, relabeled Secret Correspondence, RG 72, NA
NA	National Archives
NIRA	National Industrial Recovery Administration
NHC	Naval Historical Center
NMNA	National Museum of Naval Aviation
NWC	Naval War College
OpA-NHC	Operational Archives Branch, Naval Historical Center
RG	Record Group

RGE	Record of Gunnery Exercise
RFQ	Request for Quotation
RMC	Report of Material Casualty
SC	Secret Correspondence Files
SecNav	Secretary of the Navy
SecNavAir	Secretary of the Navy for Air
SecNav GC File	Secretary of the Navy General Correspondence Files, RG 80, NA
SecNav Reports	*Annual Report of the Secretary of the Navy* (for various fiscal years), Library, Naval Historical Center
SF-USMC	Subject Files, Marine Corps Historical Center, Washington Navy Yard
USBatFlt	Records of the U.S. Battle Fleet, RG 313, NA
USNA	United States Naval Academy
VB	Bombing Squadron

Preface

1. A single torpedo launched from one of four night-flying PBYs struck a tanker attached to the invasion force. Prange, *Miracle at Midway,* 176.

2. Rosenberg, "Realities of Formulating Modern Naval Strategy," 143.

Chapter 1. A Thousand and One Questions

1. Melhorn, *Two-Block Fox,* 112.

2. The *Jupiter* was chosen for conversion in part because of the size of her hold, which would serve as a hangar for the aircraft which her planners thought would be brought up to the flight deck one at a time for launchings and then similarly returned below after recovery. Friedman, *U.S. Aircraft Carriers,* 36.

3. In the previous year he had served as head of the Tactics Department at the Naval War College where his analysis "A Tactical Study Based on the Fundamental Principles of War of the Employment of the Present BLUE Fleet in a Battle Showing the vital Modifications Demanded by Tactics" was a magnum opus on contemporary battleship tactics.

4. Melhorn, *Two-Block Fox,* 112–13.

5. "If war comes it is obvious that we must be prepared to fight and win with another weapon." Quoted by Andrews, "Admiral with Wings," 97.

6. Trimble, *Admiral William A. Moffett,* 183–84.

7. Quotation attributed to Frank D. Wagner. Hayes, "Admiral Joseph Mason Reeves," pt. 1, 52.

8. Section 8, Naval Appropriation Act of 1922.

9. Andrews, "Admiral with Wings," 107.

10. *New York Times*, 4 September 1925.

11. Andrews, "Admiral with Wings," 107–10.

12. Ibid., 109.

13. Ibid.; Reynolds, *Admiral John H. Towers*, 199; Hayes, "Admiral Joseph Mason Reeves," pt. 1, 53.

14. Van Deurs, "Navy Wings," 421.

15. Hone, "Carrier Aviation," 46.

16. Andrews, "Admiral with Wings," 118; ComAirRons to AirRonsBatFlt, 7 April 1926, File UANT 1927–147, NWC.

17. ComAirBatFlt to CNO, 3 February 1927, NWC; Larkins, *U.S. Navy Aircraft 1921–1941*, 48–49.

18. Reynolds, *Admiral John H. Towers*, 204.

19. Swanborough and Bowers, *United States Naval Aircraft*, 124.

20. Reynolds, *Admiral John H. Towers*, 204–5.

21. BuAer Newsletter, 11 September 1926, p. 1; as noted for entry of 9 August 1926, Chronological History File, AVHB-NHC.

22. Andrews, "Admiral with Wings," 105.

Chapter 2. The Diving Attack

1. Frank D. Wagner to Commander Dater, 30 December 1948, NMNA. The exact number and type of planes led by Wagner is also unknown. VF-2 had only six FC6s at the time, and it is highly unlikely that any other types took part leading to skepticism regarding Andrews' exaggerated figure of eighteen.

2. Melhorn, *Two-Block Fox*, 164 n. 50.

3. Ballentine Oral History, 152–53.

4. Rowell, interview on origins of dive bombing, 24 October 1946, transcript; *Fortitude* (Fall 1978); Rowell, "Experiences with the Air Service," 7–9; Turnbull and Lord, *History of United States Naval Aviation*, 217. Rowell originally described the technique as low-altitude bombing, not "dive bombing" as he later referred to it.

5. Rowell interview, 2–3.

6. Turnbull and Lord, *History of United States Naval Aviation*, 218.

7. BuAer to CNO, 25 September 1925, as cited by Pearson in "Dive Bombers."

8. The instructions called for the aircraft to dive from 1,000 to 400 feet at a 45 degree angle. The length and steepness of the dives were based on the structural limitations of the UO-1s.

9. Leighton, "Light Aircraft Carriers," 5.

10. *NAVAIR 00-80P-1*, entry for 13 December 1926. In this account the target was only 100 feet by 45 feet, which might explain the lower percentage of hits (nineteen of forty-five drops) achieved by VF-2.

11. Van Deurs, "Navy Wings," 433. This information appears to have originated

in a letter by Wagner dated 1 January 1927, mentioned in the list of sources contained within the *NAVAIR 00-80P-1,* which has not been located to date.

12. Andrews, "Admiral with Wings," 114.

13. Ibid., 123–24.

14. Hardison ltr, 28 September 1928, Molten Papers, NHC.

15. BuAer News ltr, 18 May 1927, 2, as cited in *NAVAIR 00-80P-1.*

Chapter 3. Policy, Politics, and Procurement

1. Head of Design Section to Chf BuAer, 31 January 1927, 9, GB File 449.

2. CNO to SecNav, Report of Board to Consider and Recommend Upon Present Aeronautical Policy, 7 June 1927, SecNav GC File A1-2.

3. Melhorn, *Two-Block Fox,* 37; see also O.N.I. Monthly Bulletin, 15 May 1919, 65–69.

4. Twinging [CO of *Texas*] to SecNav, 7 April 1919, GBH, p. 926, as cited by Melhorn, *Two-Block Fox.*

5. Whiting testimony, GBH, 1919, p. 1117, as cited by Melhorn, *Two-Block Fox.*

6. Ofstie Memorandum, 26 January 1927, BuAer GC File VF.

7. Handwritten note attached to blue routing sheet preceding Ofstie Memorandum.

8. Sherman to President Naval War College, 26 March 1927, UNC File RG 8, HC-NWC.

9. Trimble, *Admiral William A. Moffett,* 176–78, 199, Melhorn, *Two-Block Fox,* 98.

10. Turnbull and Lord, *History of United States Naval Aviation,* 251, 255.

11. Trimble, *Admiral William A. Moffett,* 177.

12. Warner to Moffett, 4 December 1926, BuAer GC File A1-2(1); "Comments and Recommendations Regarding T3M-2," 13 November 1926, BuAer GC File 00/E.S. Land.

13. Moffet to AstSecNav for Air, 24 January 1927; Warner to Moffett, 3 February 1927, BuAer GC File A1-2 (2).

14. Hone, "Navy Air Leadership," 100, 112.

15. Chf BuAer to SecNav, 21 February 1927, BuAer GC File A1-2 (2).

16. Record of Proceedings of a Board Convened at Navy Department, Washington, D.C., by order of the Secretary of the Navy to Consider and Recommend Upon the Present Naval Aeronautics Policy, 3 May 1927, 1, SecNav SC File A1 (hereafter cited as Second Taylor Board).

17. Trimble, *Admiral William A. Moffett,* 188.

18. Hone, "Navy Air Leadership," 100.

19. Second Taylor Board, 3; Leighton testimony based on typewritten transcript dated Thursday, 5 May 1927, 6, BuAer "Unidentified" SC Files; Moffet to SecNav 14 April 1928, BuAer GC File 00/Leighton (hereafter cited as Leighton testimony); Melhorn, *Two-Block Fox,* 112.

20. Melhorn, *Two-Block Fox,* 107.

21. Leighton testimony, 5.

22. Second Taylor Board, 3.

23. CNO to ComBatFlt via CinCUS, 27 May 1927, as cited by Pearson, "Dive Bombers."

24. Report of Board to Consider and Recommend Upon Present Aeronautic Policy–1st Endorsement, 7 June 1927, 5, SecNav CC File A1-2.

25. On 1 July 1927 an alpha symbol was added to the squadron number to indicate the fleet to which it was assigned; B for battle, S for scouting. This practice continued until 1938, when they were eliminated.

26. CO to Head of Air Department, USS *Lexington,* 28 September 1928, Molten Papers, NHC.

27. ComAirSctFlt to CNO, 15 November 1927, BuAer SC File A5.

28. Dillon to CNO, 1 Dec. 1927, BuAer SC File A5.

29. ComAirSctFlt to CNO via ComSctFlt, 15 Nov. 1927, BuAer SC File A5; see also ComAirSctFlt to CNO, 26 October 1927.

30. Chief Observer to ComAirSctFlt, 11 Nov. 1927, BuAer SC File A5.

31. Ibid.

32. Leighton, "Light Aircraft Carriers," 5.

33. According to the rules then in use at the Naval War College for its board games, two hits with a 520-lb. bomb were enough to put a light cruiser out of commission; it took only one to cripple a destroyer. Leighton felt that four or five 500-lb. bombs "exploded on the deck of a modern light cruiser would completely disable her."

34. ComAirSctFlt to ComSctFlt, 16 Dec. 1927, BuAer SC File A5.

Chapter 4. False Starts: The F8C Helldiver

1. Head Design Section to Chf BuAer, "Design Program," 31 January 1927, 9, GB File 449.

2. Ibid.

3. Bureau of Aeronautics, "Specification for F8C-2 Airplane," 5 May 1927, XF8C-2 File, HF-NASM.

4. Leighton, "Light Aircraft Carriers," 3.

5. Ibid., 4.

6. BuAer GC Contract File C-4251, passim. According to Bowers (*Curtiss Aircraft,* 206), the contract was "for three experimental two-seat fighters." It may be that two separate contracts were issued as a reference to a second contract, No. C-5727, is frequently mentioned in the file.

7. INA to Chf BuAer, 3 September 1927, BuAer Contract File C-4251, NA.

8. BuAer, "Specification for XF8C-2 Airplane," 12 December 1927, XF8C-2 File, HF-NASM.

9. Schlaifer and Heron, *Development of Aircraft Engines,* 193.

10. Memorandum of Bureau Conference on Friday, December 16, 1927, dated 19 December 1927, BuAer Contract File 4251, NA.

11. Ibid.

12. Bowers, *Curtiss Aircraft,* 206; Under-wing bomb racks were added later; see BuAer Contract File C-4251, NA.

13. Pirie, "Early Flight Testing," 57.

14. Chf BuAer to BdI&S, 24 November 1928, Report of Service Trials of Airplane XF8C-2 (A-7673), BdI&S Trials.

15. Tomlinson, *Sky's the Limit,* 202–3.

16. President, BdI&S to Chf BuAer, 7 December 1928, XF8C-2 Trials Report.

17. Memorandum of Conference 14 December 1928, BuAer GC File VF.

18. Contract No. C-4251.

19. XF8C-2 Trials Report, 14; Chf BuAer to Ast SecNavAer, 5 July 1929, BuAer GC File VF.

20. Chf BuAer to President, BdI&S, 21 May 1929, XF8C-2 Trials Report.

21. Memo, Comments Regarding Two-Seater Fighter Initiated by Lt. Cdr. Miles, 10 May 1929; Chf BuAer to AstSecNavAir, 5 July 1929, BuAer GC File VF.

22. Chf BuAer to President, BdI&S, 12 October 1929, XF8C-2 Trials Report.

23. Andrews, "F8C/O2C Helldiver," 18.

24. CO VF-1B to ComCarDivs, 15 January 1931, BuAer GC File VF.

25. ComCarDivs to Chf BuAer, 29 January 1931, BuAer GC File VF.

26. BuAer "Characteristics" (1933); also Matt, *Marine Corps Fighters,* 45.

27. Comments Regarding Two-Seater Fighter, 10 May, BuAer GC File VF.

28. ComCarDivs to ComBatFlt, 29 January 1931 and ComBatFlt to Chf BuAer, 3 Feb. 1931, BuAer VF Files.

29. Andrews, "F8C/O2C Helldiver," 19; CinCUS to Chf BuAer, 1 April 1931, BuAer GC File VF.

30. Rowell interview, 10; Larkins, *Marine Corps Aircraft,* 37.

31. Van Deurs, "Navy Wings."

32. Larkins, *U.S. Marine Corps Aircraft 1914–1959,* 9, 15.

33. *Fortitude* (Fall 1978): 14.

Chapter 5. First Carrier Strikes

1. Reeves to Moffett, 16 February 1928, William A. Moffett Papers, Special Collections, Nimitz Library, USNA.

2. Moffett to Reeves, 23 February 1928, Moffett Papers.

3. Andrews, "Admiral with Wings," 130. How many aircraft were actually spotted is difficult to assess, albeit the exact number is not important. Wilson (*Slipstream,* 122) claims the number was forty-two; Andrews ("Admiral with Wings," 130), quoted here, states that it was thirty-six; a photograph of *Langley* taken *after* she had left San Diego shows thirty-four (see photo on page 53). Note too that

Moffett (to SecNav, via CNO, dated 31 July 1928) claimed that *Langley* operated forty-two planes in the exercise, though I believe this was an exaggeration intended to impress the CNO and the secretary of the navy based on the maximum number of aircraft that could be embarked.

4. Andrews, "Admiral with Wings," 130.

5. Wilson, *Slipstream,* 125.

6. Ibid.

7. Tomlinson, *Sky's the Limit,* 118.

8. Ibid., 119.

9. The forgoing account is based on *Langley*'s logbook entry for 17 May 1928 (RG 24, NA); Andrews, "Admiral with Wings," 131; and Wilson, *Slipstream,* 126. Neither of the latter accounts mention the defender's torpedo attack and both contain significant discrepancies with the information contained in *Langley*'s log.

10. Tomlinson, *Sky's the Limit,* 133.

11. Chf BuAer to CNO, 4 June 1928, Moffett Papers.

12. Wilson, *Slipstream,* 130.

13. O. B. Hardison to Cdr. R. P. Molten Jr., 31 August 1928, Letter-Book, Molten Papers, NHC.

14. CinCBatFlt to BatFlt, "Narrative of Tactical Exercises 5–9 November 1928," BuAer Conf File A6.

15. Senior Member Present to SecNav, 22 December 1928, Folder 1928–29, GB File No. 449.

16. ComAirBatFlt to CNO, 3 February 1927, File UANT 1927-147, HC-NWC.

17. "Aviation in the Fleet Exercises, 1911–1939," Fleet Problem IX, passim.

18. Wilson, *Slipstream,* 135.

19. Ibid., 138.

20. Andrews, "Admiral with Wings," 136–7.

21. Wilson, "Fleet Exercises—Tactics and Strategy," 34.

22. CinCUS to CNO, 18 March 1929, Report of Problem IX, pt. 3, passim; Wilson, *Slipstream,* 144–45.

23. Wilson, *Slipstream,* 148.

24. CinCUS to CNO, 18 March 1929, 30, Fleet Problem IX.

25. Lord, "History of United States Naval Aviation," 1196.

26. CinCUS to CNO, 18 March 1929, 13, Fleet Problem IX.

27. Ibid., 29–30, Fleet Problem IX.

28. Ibid.; Friedman, *U.S. Aircraft Carriers,* 50.

29. CinCUS to CNO, 18 March 1929, 13, Fleet Problem IX.

30. Ibid., 29.

Chapter 6. Perfecting the Dive Bomber

1. Senior Member to SecNav, Building Program of Aircraft for the Navy, 22 December 1928, Folder 1924–39, GB File 449.

2. Moffett to CNO, 4 June 1928, Moffett Papers.

3. Serling, *Legend and Legacy*, 15.

4. Bowers, *Boeing Aircraft*, 162–67.

5. Trial Board, XF4B-1 to ComAirBatFlt, 21 August 1928, BuAer GF File VF4B1/F1-1.

6. Chf BuAer to ComAirBatFlt, 11 September 1928; ComAirBatFlt to Chf BuAer, 21 September, 1928, BuAer GC VF4B-1 File.

7. GBH, 2 October 1928, 247–50.

8. Plans to Material, 24 September 1928; Conference Memorandum of 19 September 1928; Towers, handwritten note, attached to routing slip date stamped October 4, 1928, BuAer GC VF4B-1 File.

9. DirFltTrn to CNO, 24 January 1929, Hearing on the Defense of Ships Against Diving Attack, 6, GBH.

10. Trimble, *Wings for the Navy*, 83; ltr dated 30 June 1928, BuAer GC File C-8778.

11. Trimble, *Wings for the Navy*, 68.

12. Chf BuAer to INA Cleveland, 20 July 1928; Chf BuAer to Glenn L. Martin Co., 20 August 1928, BuAer GC File C-8778.

13. Memorandum: [Visit to Martin plant], 21–22 September 1928, BuAer GC File C-8778.

14. Milburn to INA, 5 Oct. 1928, BuAer GC File C-8778.

15. Towers testimony, 6 February 1929, Defense Against Diving Attack, 18, GBH.

16. Miles, handwritten notes on routing sheet dated 7–8 May 1929, BuAer GC File C-8778.

17. Report of IBP Light Bombing VS-1B 1928–29, BuAer CF File A5-1.

18. Trimble, *Wings for the Navy*, 84.

19. Miles, handwritten notes on routing sheet dated 7–8 May 1929, BuAer GC File C-8778.

20. Chf BuAer to BdI&S, 10 Jan. 30, XT5M-1 Report, 10, BuAer Trials; Milburn to INA, 25 June 1929, BuAer GC File C-8778.

21. Chf BuAer to INA Baltimore, 26 September 1929, BuAer GC File C-8778.

22. Handwritten notes on routing slip, 26 September 1928, BuAer GC File C-8778.

23. Glenn L. Martin Company to INA Baltimore, 10 October 1928, BuAer GC File C-8778; McAvoy to Millburn, 19 October 1929, XT5M-1 Report, BuAer Trials.

24. Turner, Memorandum for Files, 16 October 1929; Miles, Memorandum, 18 October 1929, XT5M-1 Report, BuAer Trials.

25. XT5M-1 Report, 10 January 1930, Recommendations, 13, BuAer Trials.

26. CO NAS Anacostia to Chf BuAer, 26 March 1930, 2, BuAer GC File XT5M-1; Supplementary Report on the XT5M-1, XT5M-1 Report, BuAer Trials.

27. ComAirBatFlt to AirRonsBatFlt, 5 December 1929, BuAer CF File A5-1.

28. Ibid.

29. Ballentine Oral History, 152–53, 155.

30. Pearson, "Dive Bombers," 12.

31. Milburn to INA, 24 July 1928; Chf BuAir to INA, Cleveland, 31 July 1928, BuAer GC File C-8778.

32. See photostat of Martin drawing, BuAer GC File VT5M1/F41.

33. Ballentine Oral History, 166.

34. Inspector of Ordnance, Naval Proving Ground, Dahlgren, to Chf BuOrd, 24 October 1930, BuAer GC VT5M1/F41 File.

35. "How about a D.F.C.," handwritten note on routing slip attached to 2nd Endorsement, Chf BuAer to Chf BuNav, 29 January 1931, XT5M-1 File.

36. Pirie, "Early Flight Testing," 57.

37. Ibid.; Still, *Ride the Wind,* 147.

38. Conference on BM-1 Stability, 17 May 1932, BuAer GC File VBM1/F-1; Swanborough and Bowers, *United States Naval Aircraft,* 294.

Chapter 7. Like Blind Men Armed with Daggers

1. "Aviation in the Fleet Exercises," 62–63; Report of Problem X, Microfilm Series M694, NA (hereafter cited as M694).

2. CinCUS to CNO, Report of Problem XI, passim, M694.

3. ComAirSctFlt to CO Black, Report of Fleet Problem X, 66, M694.

4. GB Hearings on Aircraft Scouting, 3 September 1929, 213, 221–22.

5. Report of Problem XI, 69, M694.

6. Ibid., 68.

7. Turnbull and Lord, *History of United States Naval Aviation,* 273.

8. Hayes, "Admiral Joseph Mason Reeves," pt. 2, 56.

9. *Naval aviator* is the navy's official designation for those qualified as pilots.

10. Buel, *Master of Seapower,* 72–76.

11. Trimble, *Admiral William A. Moffett,* 207, 214; Reynolds, *Admiral John H. Towers,* 222.

12. Clark, *Carrier Admiral,* 31–32; Buel, *Master of Seapower,* 79.

13. Clark, *Carrier Admiral,* 44; Buel, *Master of Seapower,* 83.

14. King and Whitehill, *Fleet Admiral King,* 220–21; Wildenberg, *Gray Steel,* 41, 43.

15. King and Whitehill, *Fleet Admiral King,* 221–22.

16. Remarks of *Lexington* CO [King], 3, Fleet Problem XII, M694.

17. King and Whitehill, *Fleet Admiral King,* 222.

18. Problem XII, "Aviation in the Fleet Exercises," 93.

19. Comments of Admiral Pratt, Problem XII, M694.

20. Hayes, "Admiral Joseph Mason Reeves," pt. 2, 56.

21. Wheeler, *Admiral William Veasie Pratt,* 368.

22. Ibid., 326.

23. "Radio Steers Crewless Ship," *New York Times*, 25 July 1931; Lord, "History of United States Naval Aviation," 1217.

24. Clark, *Carrier Admiral*, 46; Van Deurs, "Navy Wings," 441.

25. Reynolds, *Admiral John H. Towers*, 237–38.

26. Ibid.; Clark, *Carrier Admiral*, 45, 48.

27. Comments of Admiral Schofield, Report of Problem XIII, M694; CO Lexington [King] to CO Black force, 20 March 1932, King Papers.

28. King and Whitehill, *Fleet Admiral King*, 230; Clark, *Carrier Admiral*, 49.

29. CO Lexington [King] to CO Black, 20 March 1932, King Papers.

Chapter 8. Tail Hooks and Tin Fish

1. Trimble, *Admiral William A. Moffett*, 80.

2. Chf BuAer to AstSecNav, 12 January 1931, BuAer GC File VB.

3. The larger engine installed on the TG-2 gave the craft more speed, but added weight that increased the plane's takeoff run, which was already marginal.

4. BuAer "Characteristics" (1933); Report of Problem IX, 30; see also Comments by Admiral Wiley, M694.

5. U.S. Navy Bureau of Ordnance, O.D. [Ordnance Data Sheet] no. 1831, author's collection.

6. Report of Advanced Battle Practice, 22–24 March 1933, 32, BuAer CF File A5-1; Materials to Plans, 27 July 1933, BuAer GC File VT; Ast Chf BuAer to Chf BuAer, 13 July 1933, BuAer GC File VT; "Tests on BB47" 24–25, Binder: Ordnance Allowance, BuAer SC Files.

7. Powel, "Naval Torpedo Station," 98; Van Deurs, "Navy Wings," 304–6.

8. Trimble, *Wings for the Navy*, 43; Van Deurs, "Navy Wings," 302, 306.

9. Powel, "Naval Torpedo Station," 98; ComAirBatFlt to Chf BuAer, 6 April 1929, 2, BuAer M&T Files; Report IBP completed 10 October 1928 and CO VT-9S to CNO, 23 March, 1928, BuAer CF File A5-1.

10. CinCUS to Ch BuAer, 14 August 1929, BuAer M&T Files; Reports of I.P.B.s, passim, BuAer CF File A5-1.

11. CO VT-9S to CNO, 23 March 1928, BuAer CF File A5-1.

12. Powel, "Naval Torpedo Station," 107; CO VT-9S to CNO, 23 March 1928, BuAer CF File A5-1; Jolie, "History of Torpedo Development," 32; Ostrander, Memorandum on Torpedo Development, 31 October 1929, 1–2, BuAer M&T File.

13. Chf BuAer to CinCUS, 29 January 1929; ComAirBatFlt to CinCUS, 6 April 1929, BuAer M&T File.

14. CinCUS to Ch BuAer, 14 April 1929, BuAer M&T File.

15. Powel, "Naval Torpedo Station," 108; Ostrander, Memorandum on Torpedo Development; *Bureau of Ordnance in WWII*, 119–20.

16. CinCUS to Ch BuAer, 14 April 1929, BuAer M&T File; Powel, "Naval Torpedo Station," 109; Memorandum for CNO, 13 August 1934, Operational War Plans File, OpA-NHC.

17. Ast Chf BuAer to Chf BuAer, 13 July 1933, BuAer GC File VT.

18. CO VT-1B to ComAirBatFlt, 10 March 1929, BuAer M&T File.

19. Ast Chf BuAer to Chf BuAer, 13 July 1933, 2; Memorandum on VB-VT Design, attached to endorsement of 27 July 1933, BuAer GC File VT.

20. Ibid.; Powel, "Naval Torpedo Station," 111.

Chapter 9. Advances in Fighter Performance

1. CO VB-1B to Chf BuAer, 3 January 1930, BuAer GC File VFB41/F1-1.

2. Swanborough and Bowers, *United States Naval Aircraft*, 60.

3. Campman to Towers, 28 February 1930, BuAer GC File VF4B1/F1-1.

4. Grumman to BuAer, 1 February 1930, BuAer GC File QM-1983.

5. Thruelsen, *Grumman Story*, 38–39; Grumman to BuAer, 8 February 1930, BuAer GC File QM-1930.

6. A loop, slow roll, fast roll, double roll, Chandelle, Immelman, Split S, wingover, vertical turn, inverted flight, falling leaf, dives in excess of 80 degrees, and spins had to be performed under full-load conditions.

7. Reynolds, *Admiral John H. Towers*, 203–5; Taylor, *Magnificent Mitscher*, 80–82.

8. Plans to Asst Chf BuAer, 11 November 1931, BuAer GC File VF.

9. As cited by Cook, 12 March 1932, BuAer GC File VF4B/F1-1; Material to Asst Chf BuAer, 11 March 1932, BuAer GC File VF.

10. Plans to Chf BuAer, 14 August 1931, BuAer CF File VB.

11. Thruelsen, *Grumman Story*, 61.

12. Wagner, *American Combat Planes*, 381; BuAer "Characteristics" (1933).

13. Shanahan, "Procurement of Naval Aviation," 32–36; Trimble, *Admiral William A. Moffett*, 247; Lord, *History of United States Naval Aviation*, 1288–91.

14. Francillon, *Grumman Aircraft*, 77–78; Thruelsen, *Grumman Story*, 74–75.

15. Class Desk A to Material Division, 10 May 1934, 3, BuAer GC File VF.

Chapter 10. Expansion Begins

1. Lord, "History of United States Naval Aviation," 1301.

2. Reynolds, *Admiral John H. Towers*, 249; Trimble, *Admiral William A. Moffett*, 251–53.

3. West, "Legislative Foundation," 290.

4. Emory Land, "Memoir," as cited in Levine, "Politics of Rearmament," 93; West, "Legislative Foundation," 330.

5. West, "Legislative Foundation," 339.

6. Lord, "History of United States Naval Aviation," 1304.

7. Chf BuAer to JAG via CNO, 12 December 1933, BuAer GC file A18-1; West, "Legislative Foundation," 379; Lord, "History of United States Naval Aviation," 1305.

8. CNO to SecNav, 24 March 1933, SecNav GC File A1-3/QN.

9. Walter, "William Standley," 93; West, "Legislative Foundation," 369.

10. Chf BuAer to JAG, 12 December 1933, BuAer GC File A18-1; Reynolds, *Admiral John H. Towers*, 249–90.

11. West, "Legislative Foundation," 379–80, 394–98.

12. Ibid., 396; Shanahan, "Procurement of Naval Aviation," 85; Albion, *Makers of Naval Policy*, 162.

13. Ibid., 402–3; Turnbull and Lord, *History of United States Naval Aviation*, 285.

14. West, "Legislative Foundation," 420–21, 536.

Chapter 11. A Prophecy of the Future

1. Head of Material Division to Head of Plans Division, 8 August 1931, BuAer GC File VB.

2. Head of Material to Head of Plans, 8 August 1931; Plans to Chf BuAer, 14 August 1931, BuAer CF File VB.

3. Dyer, *Amphibians Came to Conquer*, 107.

4. Reynolds, *Admiral John H. Towers*, 225.

5. A view held by Towers, then the navy's most senior airman. Ibid., 263, 275.

6. Plans to Chf BuAer, 14 August 1931, BuAer CF File VB.

7. Plans to Chf BuAer, 14 August 1931; Cook memorandum for files, 25 August 1931, BuAer CF File VB.

8. Final Report on XBG-1, 22 January 1935, 46, XBG-1 File, BdI&S Trials.

9. Cook, "Naval Aviation and National Security," Speech given at Buffalo 27 October 1927, Van Deurs Subject Files, OpA-NHC; West, "Legislative Foundation," 339–44.

10. Douglas lecture, 23 October 1933, File 1846A, HC-NWC.

11. Pearsons, "Dive Bombers," 13.

12. Moran, *Aeroplanes Vought*, 59; Swanborough and Bowers, *United States Naval Aircraft*, 374.

13. Andrews, "BF2C-1," 17. This was not the first vibration problem to afflict the Goshawks. A previous problem was partially cured by installing a tabular airfoil just ahead of the bomb/fuel tank attachment point (Andrews to the author, 3 March 1996).

Chapter 12. The All-Metal Monoplane

1. Material to Chf BuAer, 23 July 1937, BuAer CF File VF.

2. Wagner, *American Combat Planes*, 386.

3. Jones, *U.S. Naval Fighters*, 137.

4. West, "Legislative Foundation," 398.

5. Airplanes-Request for Information Quotation, 15 March 1934; ditto VSB type, 19 March 1934, BuAer GC File VB; Heinemann, *Combat Aircraft*, 34.

6. Jay [Northrop Gen. Mgr] to Chf BuAer, 22 May 1934, BuAer GC File VB.

7. Heinemann, *Combat Aircraft Designer,* 35; Northrop to Chf BuAer, 25 April 1934, 2, BuAer GC File VB.

8. Heinemann, *Combat Aircraft Designer,* 36.

9. Neither the Ju-87 Stuka, nor the Aichi type 99 (Val) were designed for bombing at extremely high-dive angles.

10. Plans to Ast Chf BuAer, 21 June 1933, BuAer GC File VB.

11. Memorandum by Lt. Cdr. Allen, n.d., BuAer GC File VF, Chf BuAer to ComAirBatFor, 18 June 1934, BuAer CF File VF.

12. ComAirBatFor to Chf BuAer, 29 August 1934, BuAer CF File VF.

13. See Extracts on the Joint Exercises Held off Hampton Roads, August 1934, USF 36, WWII Command File, OpA-NHC.

14. CO VF-5B to Chf BuAer, 22 May 1935, BuAer CF File VF; Duncan memorandum, 12 March 1934 and Browning memorandum, 12 March 1934, both in BuAer GC File VF.

15. Handwritten notation "don't believe I agree—EJK," Bellinger memorandum, 17 March 1934, BuAer GC File VF.

16. For a discussion of the F4F-4 controversy, see Lundstrum, *First Team,* chap. 18.

Chapter 13. End of an Era

1. Jones, *U.S. Naval Fighters,* 125, 140; Francillon, *Grumman Aircraft,* 77.

2. Thruelsen, *Grumman Story,* 85–87; Matt, *United States Navy and Marine Corps Fighters,* 69.

3. BuAer "Characteristics" (1936).

4. ComAirBatFor to CinCUS, 4 April 1936; CinCUS to CNO, 9 May 1936, both in BuAer CF File VF.

5. Class A Desk to Engineering, 11 November 1935, BuAer CF File VF.

6. Doyle, handwritten note dated "7/37/36," BuAer CF File VF.

7. Thruelsen, *Grumman Story,* 92; Swanborough and Bowers, *United States Naval Aircraft,* 204.

8. Cook memorandum on Experimental Program for 1938, 12 February 1937, BuAer CF File VF.

9. Chf BuAer, from ltr, 13 March 1937, BuAer CF File VF.

10. Material Branch to Chf BuAer, 18 June 1937, BuAer CF File VF.

11. Schlaifer and Heron, *Development of Aircraft Engines,* 687; Doyle, typewritten comments on VF competition [May 1938] and BuAer form ltr, 1 February 1938, both in BuAer CF File VF.

12. Memorandum on Carrier Deck Spotting, 27 April 1938, BuAer CF File VF.

13. Material to Chf BuAer, 28 April 1938, BuAer CF File VF.

14. Ibid.; Doyle, typewritten comments on VF competition, 5 May 1938, BuAer CF File VF.

15. Davis, handwritten comments to Chf BuAer, 5 May 1938, BuAer CF File VF.

16. Mizrahi, *Carrier Fighters*, 23; Green and Swanborough, *U.S. Navy and Marine Corps Fighters*, 5; Thruelsen, *Grumman Story*, 102–3.

17. Mizrahi, *Carrier Fighters*, 8.

18. Davis, handwritten comments to Chf BuAer, 5 May 1938, BuAer CF File VF.

Chapter 14. Aviation Doctrine and Carrier Policy in the Late 1930s

1. Utz, "Carrier Aviation Policy," 16.

2. Wagner, *American Combat Planes*, 334.

3. See VB-VT RFQ dated 17 October 1933, BuAer GC File VT.

4. Penciled notation on torpedo ordnance, Plans to Ast Chf BuAer, 21 June 1933, 2, BuAer GC File VB.

5. *Ranger* had a second VSB squadron in lieu of the VTB normally carried aboard big carriers.

6. GBH on aircraft procurement, 5 October 1937, 5; Utz, "Carrier Aviation Policy," 44.

7. Coletta, *Bellinger*, 200; Reynolds, *Admiral John H. Towers*, 276.

8. Ibid.

9. "Aviation in the Fleet Exercises," Fleet Problem XIX; King and Whitehill, *Fleet Admiral King*, 281–82; Reynolds, *Admiral John H. Towers*, 277.

10. ComBatFor comments in "Exercise 74-Air Attack on Fleet," 21 April 1938, 4, Fleet Problem XIX, M694.

11. Francillon, *McDonnell Douglas Aircraft*, 266.

12. Inspector of Ordnance to President of BdI&S, 20 October 1938, XBT-1 Trials; Francillon, *McDonnell Douglas Aircraft*, 267.

Chapter 15. Preparing for War

1. Merrill, *Sailor's Admiral*, 10; Potter, *Bull Halsey*, 27.

2. Ibid., 131.

3. ComAirBatFor to CinCUS, 4 June 1937, Problem XVIII, M694.

4. Lundstrom, *First Team*, 453.

5. Winston, *Dive Bomber*, 142.

6. RGE VB-6, Fired 23 October 1940, ComAir CG File VB-6.

7. Gunnery Officer, VT-3, RGE VT-3, Fired 20 November 1940, ComAir CG File VT-3. Note: ComAirBatFlt attributed the success of the Mark XIII in this exercise to the torpedo maintenance performed by *Saratoga*'s personnel.

8. RGE VT-6, Fired 6 November 1940, RMC sheet 21, ComAir GC File VT-6; *Bureau of Ordnance in WWII*, 120–21.

9. Mizrahi, *U.S. Navy Bombers*, 40; RGE VT-6, Fired 6 November 1940, RMC sheet 21 and 22, ComAir GC File VT-6.

10. *Bureau of Ordnance in WWII,* 120; RGE VT-6, Fired 25 July 1941, Enclosure D, ComAir GC File VT-6.

11. Lundstrom, *First Team,* 478; Thach Oral History, 149.

12. Ibid., 153–54.

13. ComAirSctFlt to CinCUS, 15 July 1939, GB File 420–27.

14. Ibid.; Utz, "Carrier Aviation Policy," 67.

15. Utz, "Carrier Aviation Policy," 66; ComBatFlt to CinCus, 29 August 1939; Chrmn GB to SecNav, 13 June 1940, GB File 420–27; Lundstrom, *First Team,* 301.

16. Friedman, *U.S. Naval Weapons,* 92.

17. Ibid.

18. Rear Adm. F. D. Foley USN(ret.) to author, 22 April 1994.

19. Reeves comments in connection with Fleet Problem XVII, 12 June 1936, BuAer CF File A16; Chf BuAer to Chf BuEng, 9 March 1935, BuAer SC Box F.

20. Chf BuAer to Chf BuEng, 9 March 1935, BuAer SC Files, Box F; BuEng to BuAer, 15 January 1937 and Preliminary Report of VF-4 Tests of XAD Equipment, ComAirBatFor to Chf BuEng, 29 August 1938, both in BuEng CF File F-42-1/69.

21. CO NAS Anacostia to Chf BuEng, 12 August 1937, BuEng CF File F-42-1/69.

22. CO *Lexington* to ComAirBatFor, 3 September 1941, File VSBD-3, Airplane Jackets, RG 313.

23. ComAirBatFor to CinCPacFlt, 16 October 1941, File VSBD-3, Airplane Jackets, RG 313.

Chapter 16. Opening Rounds

1. Lundstrom, "Fletcher Got a Bum Rap," 23–24.

2. Morison, *Two Ocean War,* 103; Morison, *History of USN,* 4: 256–57.

3. Buell, *Dauntless Helldivers,* 69.

4. Ibid., 44.

5. Lundstrom, *First Team,* 76; CEAG to CO *Enterprise,* "Action in the Marshalls," 55–56.

6. Ibid., 56.

7. Layton, *And I was There,* 390–92.

8. Lundstrom, *South Pacific Campaign,* 98–99; Layton, *I was There,* 391.

9. Buell, *Dauntless Helldivers,* 68; Lundstrom, *First Team,* 171, 178.

10. Buell, *Dauntless Helldivers,* 71.

11. Acting CO, VT-6 to CominCh, 21 June 1942, 2, AR Box 535.

12. ComAirBatFor to ChfBuOrd, 21 July 1941, Misc. Corr. 1938–41, ComAir-GAF; Blandy to McCain, 1 March 1941, BuOrd SC File S70-S81.

Chapter 17. Scratch One Flattop

1. Layton, *And I was There*, 398.
2. Lundstrom, *First Team*, 190.
3. Ibid. 190; Morison, *U.S. Naval Operations*, 4:40.
4. Lundstrom, *First Team*, 195.
5. Layton, *And I was There*, 399.
6. Lundstrom, "Fletcher Got a Bum Rap," 25.
7. Lundstrom, *First Team*, 201.
8. ComDesRonOne to CominCh, 22 May 1942, cited by Lundstrom, *First Team*, 510.

Chapter 18. The Carrier Battle of the Coral Sea

1. Layton, *And I Was There*, 401; Lundstrom, *First Team*, 207–8.
2. Lundstrom, *First Team*, 222.
3. Morison, *History of USN*, 4:49.
4. Lundstrom, *First Team*, 230.
5. Aircraft Action Report of Lt. Cdr. Taylor, 8 May 1942, Box 1535, AR.
6. CinCPac to CominCh, 17 June 1942, reprinted in Harms, *Hard Lesson*, 14.
7. Morison, *History of USN*, 4:51.
8. In addition to Ault's command plane, the group was composed of four SBDs of VS-2, six F4Fs of VF-2, and eleven TBDs of VT-2.
9. Lundstrom, *First Team*, 238.
10. CO VT-2 to CO Lexington, 10 May 1942, Box 513, AR.
11. *Yorktown* has a much smaller turning radius than the *Lexington*, and being a smaller ship was more responsive to helm changes.
12. Morison, *History of USN*, 4:56.

Chapter 19. Climax at Midway

1. Prange, *Miracle at Midway*, 81, 82; Spector, *Eagle Against the Sun*, 169.
2. Prange, *Miracle at Midway*, 100–103; Morison, *History of USN*, 4:84; Lundstrom, "Fletcher Got a Bum Rap," 27.
3. Morison, *History of USN*, vol. 4; Prange, *Miracle at Midway*, 104.
4. Fuchida and Okumiya, *Midway*, 181.
5. The reported time of the "many planes warning" differs between sources. The time used here is taken from Morison's original work.
6. Prange, *Miracle at Midway*, 238.
7. Ibid., 239.
8. Morison, *History of USN*, 4:113.
9. See Reynolds, "Truth about Miles Browning," 214–16.

10. Morison, *History of USN,* 4:113.

11. Lundstrom, *First Team,* 333.

12. Ibid., 335.

13. Ibid., 340–41.

14. Lundstrom, "Fletcher Got a Bum Rap," 27; Lundstrom, *First Team,* 332.

15. For details see Lundstrom, *First Team,* 140.

16. Ibid., 342, 346.

17. Ibid., 328.

18. Cagle, "Bombing Five" 57; Prange, *Miracle at Midway,* 261.

19. Thirty-three SBDs left the *Enterprise,* two ran short of gas before McClusky pushed over, less Best's three.

20. Quoted by Lord, *Incredible Victory,* 165.

21. Quoted by Cagle, "Bombing Five," 57.

22. Ibid.

Chapter 20. Reassessing Naval Aviation's Contribution to Victory

1. Ferrier, "Torpedo Squadron Eight," 72–76.

BIBLIOGRAPHY

Archives and Collections Consulted

Marine Corps Museum, Navy Yard, Washington, D.C.

    Aviation Subject Files, Reference Section.

    Rowell File, Manuscript Collection.

National Air and Space Museum, Archives Division, Washington, D.C.

    Aircraft Files, Curtiss-Wright Collection.

    Bruce G. Leighton Subject Files.

National Archives, Washington, D.C./College Park, Md.

    Hearings of the General Board, Records and Transcripts, Microfilm Series M1963, RG 80.

    Records of the Bureau of Aeronautics, RG 72:

        Contract Correspondence, 1926–39

        Confidential Correspondence Files, 1922–44

        Final Reports of Trials and Inspections of Naval Aircraft, 1938–44

        General Correspondence Files, 1925–42

        Secret Correspondence, 1923–38

    Records of the Bureau of Engineering, RG 19:

        Confidential Correspondence, 1930–40

        Secret Correspondence, 1938–41

    Records of the Bureau of Inspection and Survey, Reports of Acceptance Trials of Naval Aircraft, 1919–32, RG 38.

    Records of the Bureau of Ordnance, RG 74:

        Confidential Correspondence, January 1940–April 1942

        General Correspondence, 1924–39

        Secret Correspondence, 1941

    Records of the General Board, Files and Reports, RG 80.

    Records of the Office of the Chief of Naval Operations, Action Reports (WWII), RG 38.

Records of the U.S. Fleet, RG 313:

   Commander Aircraft, Aircraft Jackets

   Commander Aircraft, Subject Files

   General Administrative Files, 1928–42

   Commander Aircraft, Records of the Operations Officer, 1938–41

Records of the U.S. Strategic Bombing Survey, Interrogations of Japanese Leaders, Microfilm Series M1654, RG 54.

Records of the Secretary of the Navy, Confidential Correspondence File, 1927–34, RG 80.

Records Relating to the United States Navy Fleet, Problems I to XXII, 1923–41, Microfilm Series M694, RG 312.

Naval Historical Center, Navy Yard, Washington, D.C.

   Action Reports of the U.S. Fleet in WWII, WWII Command Files, Operational Archives Branch. (Now located in National Archives.)

   NAVAIR 00-80P-1 Reference Files, Aviation History Branch.

Naval War College, Newport, R.I.

   Historical Collection

Nimitz Library, Special Collections, United States Naval Academy, Annapolis, Md.

   Papers of William A. Moffett

   Reeves 1925 Lecture to Army War College

Oral Histories and Personal Papers

Ballentine, John Jennings. Papers. Library of Congress, Washington, D.C.

———. Oral History. Naval History Project, Oral History Research Office, Columbia University (copy in Naval Historical Center, Washington, D.C.).

Bogan, Gerald F. Oral History. Oral History Collection, U.S. Naval Institute, Annapolis, Md.

King, Ernest J. Papers. Library of Congress, Washington, D.C.

Molten, Robert P., Jr. Papers. Operational Archives Branch, Naval Historical Center, Washington, D.C.

Pride, Alfred M. Oral History Collection, U.S. Naval Institute, Annapolis, Md.

Riley, Herbert D. Oral History Collection, U.S. Naval Institute, Annapolis, Md.

Rowell, Ross E. Transcript of Interview on the Origin and Early Use of Dive-Bombing Tactics Held in the Aviation History Unit on 24 October 1946. File: Dive Bombing, Subject Files, USMC History and Museums Division, Washington Navy Yard.

Thach, John S. Oral History Collection, U.S. Naval Institute, Annapolis, Md.

Unpublished Documents and Dissertations

Andrews, Adolphus, Jr. "Admiral with Wings: The Career of Joseph Mason Reeves." Bachelor's thesis, Princeton University, 1943.

Ashbrook, Lincoln. "The United States Navy and Air Power, A History of Naval Aviation 1920–34." Ph.D. diss., University of California at Berkeley, 1946.

Bellinger, Patrick N. "Aviation." Transcript of lecture given at Naval War College 1 August 1924. Naval Historical Collection, Naval War College, Newport, R.I.

Brown, Robert V. "The Navy's Mark IV (Norden) Bomb Sight: Its Development and Procurement 1920–45." Department of the Navy, Washington, D.C., 1946. Microfilm no. NRS II-57, Naval Historical Center.

Bureau of Aeronautics. "Characteristics, Weights and Performance of U.S. Navy Airplanes." 29 September 1933. Department of the Navy, Washington, D.C.

———. "Characteristics, Weights and Performance of U.S. Navy Airplanes." 1 August 1941. Department of the Navy, Washington, D.C.

———. "Characteristics, Weights and Performance of U.S. Navy Airplanes." 1 September 1936. Department of the Navy, Washington, D.C.

———. "Resume of Progress 1933–1936: Confidential Supplement." RG 72, National Archives.

Campbell, Mark A. "The Influence of Air Power Upon the Evolution of Battle Doctrine in the U.S. Navy, 1922–1941." Master's thesis, University of Massachusetts at Boston, 1992.

Hone, Thomas. "The Development of Carrier Aviation." Unpublished manuscript, courtesy Thomas Hone.

Jolie, E. W. "A Brief History of U.S. Navy Torpedo Development." NUSC Technical Document No. 5436, 15 September 1978. Naval Underwater Systems Command, Newport R.I.

Leighton, Bruce G. "Light Aircraft Carriers: A Study of Their Possible Uses in So-called Operations." Unpublished report. Unidentified File, BuAer Sec. Corr. 1925–38, RG 72, National Archives.

———. "The Relation Between Air and Surface Activities in the Navy." Unpublished lecture at Naval War College, 23 March 1928. Naval Historical Collection, Naval War College, Newport, R.I.

Levine, Robert H. "The Politics of American Naval Rearmament, 1930–1938." Ph.D. diss., Harvard University, 1972.

Lord, Clifford L. "History of United States Naval Aviation, 1898–1939." Unpublished manuscript used for basis of book published with Trumball. Lord Folders, World War II Command File, Operational Archives Branch, Naval Historical Center, Washington Navy Yard.

Lundstrom, John B. "In the Beginning: U.S. Navy Fighter Doctrine During the First Six Months of the Pacific War." Manuscript dated 28 January 1974. Lundstrom

Folder, World War II Command File, Operational Archives Branch, Naval Historical Center, Washington Navy Yard.

Lundstrom, John B. "The First South Pacific Campaign: Pacific Fleet Strategy, December 1941–June 1942." Unpublished manuscript. Operational Archives Branch, Naval Historical Center, Washington Navy Yard.

Office of the Deputy Chief of Naval Operations. "Aviation in the Fleet Exercises, 1922–1939." No. 36, United States Administrative Histories of World War II, Operational Archives Division, Naval Historical Center, Washington, D.C.

Pearson, Lee M. "Dive Bombers: The Prewar Years." *Naval Aviation Confidential Bulletin, July, 1946.* Department of the Navy, Washington, D.C., 1946. Aviation History Branch, Naval Historical Center, Washington Navy Yard.

Powel, J. H. "Naval Torpedo Station, Newport, Rhode Island." History No. 130. United States Administrative Histories of World War II, Operational Archives Division, Naval Historical Center, Washington, D.C.

Reeves, James M. "The Battle of Jutland." Lecture delivered at the Army War College in 1925, n.d. Special Collections, Nimitz Library, U.S. Naval Academy, Annapolis, Md.

———. "Thesis on Tactics." Unpublished thesis for Naval War College Class of 1924, 1 May 1924. Naval Historical Collection, Naval War College, Newport, R.I.

Rowell, Ross E. "Experiences with the Air Service in Minor Warfare." Lecture delivered at the Army War College, 12 January 1929. Manuscript Collection, USMC, Division of History and Museums, Washington Navy Yard.

———. "On The Origin and Early Use of Dive-Bombing Tactics." Interview Reportedly Conducted by Admiral F. D. Wagner, Aviation History Unit, Office of the CNO, on March 24, 1946. Aviation Subject Files, Reference Section, USMC, Division of History and Museums, Washington Navy Yard.

Shanahan, William O. "Procurement of Naval Aviation 1907–1939." History No. 37. United States Administrative Histories of World War II, Operational Archives Division, Naval Historical Center, Washington, D.C.

Utz, Curtis A. "Carrier Aviation Policy and Procurement in the U.S. Navy, 1936–1940." Master's thesis, University of Maryland, 1989. Courtesy Curtis A. Utz (copy in Naval Historical Center).

Van Deurs, George. "Navy Wings Between the Wars." Unpublished Manuscript. Microfilm no. NRS 308, Naval Historical Center, Washington, D.C.

Welborn, Mary C. "History of Technical Development of Naval Aircraft" [known as the "Mead Report"]. 13 vols. Aviation History Unit, Office of the CNO. Navy Department, Washington D.C., 1945. Aviation History Branch, Naval Historical Center, Washington, D.C.

West, Michael Allen. "Laying the Legislative Foundation: The House Naval Affairs Committee and the Construction of the Treaty Navy, 1926–1934." Ph.D. diss., Ohio State University, 1980. University Microfilms International.

Xenakes, Peter. "The Battle of the Coral Sea: History's First Carrier Battle." Master's thesis, University of Maryland, 1967.

Books and Articles

Albion, Robert G. *Makers of Naval Policy 1798–1947*. Annapolis, Md.: Naval Institute Press, 1980.

Allison, David K. *New Eye for the Navy: The Origin of Radar at the Naval Research Laboratory*. Washington, D.C.: U.S. Naval Research Laboratory, 1981.

Andrews, Hal. "BF2C-1." *Naval Aviation News* 68, no. 1 (January–February 1986): 16–17.

———. "BT." *Naval Aviation News* 71, no. 6 (September–October 1989): 16–17.

———. "F8C/O2C Helldiver." *Naval Aviation News* 75, no. 1 (November–December 1992): 18–19.

"Annals of Sugar Baker Two Uncle." *Air Enthusiast Eight*. Bromley, Kent: Pilot Press, 1978.

Armstrong, William J. "Dick Richardson—His Life in Aeronautics." *Naval Aviation News* 50, no. 4 (April 1977): 32–37.

Arthur, Charles S. "Flying the Dauntless Dive-Bomber." *Aerospace Historian* (September 1982): 146–53.

Ashbrook, Lincoln. "The United States Navy and the Rise of the Doctrine of Air Power." *Military Affairs* 15, no. 3 (Fall 1951): 145–56.

Barker, A. J. *Stuka Ju-87*. Englewood Cliffs, N.J.: Prentice-Hall, 1983.

Belote, James H., and William M. Belote. *Titans of the Sea*. New York: Harper and Row, 1975.

Blechman, Fred. "Flying the Hayrake." *Foundation* 18, no. 2 (Fall 1997): 80–81.

Brodie, Bernard. *A Guide to Naval Strategy*. 4th (Naval War College) ed. Princeton, N.J.: Princeton University Press, 1957.

Bogan, Gerald F. "The Navy Spreads Its Golden Wings." *U.S. Naval Institute Proceedings* 87, no. 5 (May 1961): 97–119.

Bowers, Peter M. *Boeing Aircraft Since 1916*. Annapolis, Md.: Naval Institute Press, 1989.

———. *Curtiss Aircraft, 1907–1947*. London: Putnam, 1979.

———. "Recollections of a Boeing F4B-4." *American Association of Aviation Historical Society Journal* 38, no. 2 (Summer 1993): 138–44.

Buel, Harold L. "Coral Sea Remembered." *Foundation* 13, no. 1 (Spring 1992): 50–55.

———. *Dauntless Helldivers: A Dive-Bombers Pilot's Story of the Carrier Battles*. New York: Dell Publishing, 1992.

———. *Master of Seapower: A Biography of Fleet Admiral Ernest J. King.* Boston: Little, Brown, 1980.

Cagle, Maury W. "Bombing Five at Midway: The Battle and Its Aftermath." *Foundation* 9, no. 1 (Spring 1988): 55–60.

———. "One Man's Path to Midway." *Foundation* 8, no. 2 (Fall 1987): 27–37.

Clark, Joseph J. *Carrier Admiral.* New York: David Mckay, 1967.

Coletta, Paulo E. *Patrick N. L. Bellinger and U.S. Naval Aviation.* Lanham, Md.: University Press of America, 1987.

"Curtiss Command Helldiver." *U.S. Naval Institute Proceedings* 57, no. 2 (February 1931): 266–67.

Daniels, James G. "The Tragedy of VF-6 at Pearl Harbor." *Foundation* 7, no. 2 (Fall 1986): 80–86.

Dickerson, Clarence E. *The Flying Guns.* New York: Scribner, 1942.

Doll, Tom. *SB2U Vindicator in Action.* Carrollton, Tex.: Squadron/Signal Publications, 1992.

Douhet, Giulio. *The Command of the Air.* Reprint. New York: Coward-McCann, 1942.

Dyer, George C. *The Amphibians Came to Conquer: The Story of Admiral Richmond Kelly Turner.* Washington, D.C.: GPO, 1972.

Elliot, Charles F. "The Genesis of the Modern U.S. Navy." *U.S. Naval Institute Proceedings* 92, no. 3 (March 1966): 62–66.

Ernest, Albert K., and Harry Ferrier. "Avengers at Midway." *Foundation* 17, no. 2 (Spring 1996): 47–53.

Ferrier, Harold H. "Torpedo Squadron Eight: The Other Chapter." *U.S. Naval Institute Proceedings,* October 1964, 72–76.

Folley, Francis D. "Every Good Ship Has a Heart." *Naval History* 6, no. 4 (Winter 1992): 23–26.

Francillon, René T. *Grumman Aircraft Since 1929.* Annapolis, Md.: Naval Institute Press, 1989.

———. *McDonnell Douglas Aircraft Since 1920,* vol 1. Annapolis, Md.: Naval Institute Press, 1988.

Friedman, Norman. *Carrier Air Power.* New York: Rutledge Press, 1981.

———. *Naval Radar.* Annapolis, Md.: Naval Institute Press, 1981.

———. *U.S. Aircraft Carriers: An Illustrated Design History.* Annapolis, Md.: Naval Institute Press, 1983.

———. *U.S. Naval Weapons.* Annapolis, Md.: Naval Institute Press, 1982.

Fuchida, Mitsuo, and Masatake Okumiya. *Midway: The Battle that Doomed Japan.* Annapolis, Md.: Naval Institute Press, 1955.

———. "Prelude to Midway." *U.S. Naval Institute Proceedings* 81, no. 5 (May 1955): 505–13.

Gay, George H. *Sole Survivor.* Naples, Fla.: Midway, 1980.

———. "The TBD-1 Devastator at the Battle of Midway." *Foundation* 9, no. 1 (Fall 1987): 9–11.

Grant, V. F. *Naval Aviation.* Annapolis, Md.: United States Naval Institute, 1929.

Gravatt, Brent L. "On the Back of the Fleet." *Naval History* 4, no. 2 (Spring 1990): 14–18.

Gray, George W. *Frontiers of Flight: The Story of NACA Research.* New York: Knopf, 1948.

Green, William, and Gordon Swanborough. *U.S. Navy and Marine Corps Fighters.* New York: Arco, 1977.

Gunshol, Lawrence. "December 7, 1941: Search and Attack!" *American Aviation Historical Society Journal* (Summer 1993): 108–13.

Guyton, Boone T. *Air Base.* New York: Whittlesey House, 1991.

———. "Flying the Boeing F4B." In *Carrier Fighters,* by J. V. Mizrahi. Northridge, Calif.: Sentry Book, 1969.

———. "Flying the Vought SB2." In *U.S. Navy Dive & Torpedo Bombers,* by J. V. Mizrahi. Northridge, Calif.: Sentry Book, 1967.

———. "The Making of a Pilot." *New York Times,* 12 June 1941, 6:3.

———. *Whistling Death.* New York: Orion Books, 1990.

Halsey, William F., and J. Bryan III. *Admiral Halsey's Story.* New York: McGraw-Hill, 1947.

Hanson, James R. *Engineer in Charge.* Washington, D.C.: National Aeronautics and Space Administration, 1987.

Harms, Norman E. *Hard Lessons,* vol. 1. Fullerton, Calif.: Scale Specialties, 1987.

Hayes, John D. "Admiral Joseph Mason Reeves, USN, Part One—to 1931." *U.S. Naval Institute Proceedings* 24, no. 11 (November 1970): 48–57.

———. "Admiral Joseph Mason Reeves, USN, Part Two—1931 to 1948." *U.S. Naval Institute Proceedings* 26, no. 1 (January 1972): 50–64.

Heinemann, Edward H. *Ed Heinemann, Combat Aircraft Designer.* Annapolis, Md.: Naval Institute Press, 1980.

Holley, I. B., Jr. *Ideas and Weapons.* Reprint. Washington, D.C.: Office of Air Force History, 1983.

Hone, Thomas C. "Managerial Sytle in the Interwar Navy: A Reappraisal." *Naval War College Review* 28, no. 4 (September–October 1980): 89–101.

———. "Navy Air Leadership: Rear Admiral William A. Moffett as Chief of the Bureau of Aeronautics." In *Air Leadership: Proceedings of a Conference at Bolling Air Force Base,* edited by Wayne Thompson, 83–117. Washington, D.C.: Office of Air Force History, 1986.

Hoyt, Edwin P. *Blue Skies and Blook.* New York: Paul S. Ericksson, 1975.

Hughes, Wayne P. *Fleet Tactics Theory and Practice.* Annapolis, Md.: Naval Institute Press, 1986.

———. Capt. USN (Ret.). "Naval Tactics and Their Influence on Strategy." *Naval War College Review* 34, no. 1 (January–February 1986): 5–15.

Johnson, Edward C. *Marine Corps Aviation: The Early Years 1912–1940.* Washington, D.C.: United States Marine Corps, History and Museum Division, 1977.

Jones, Lloyd S. *U.S. Naval Fighters.* Fallbrook, Calif.: Aero Publishers, 1977.

King, Ernest J. and Walker Whitehill. *Fleet Admiral King, A Naval Record.* New York: W. W. Norton, 1952.

Lacouture, John E. "The Gallant Sea Hawk, VADM Bill Davis." *Foundation* 14, no. 2 (Fall 1993): 56–62.

Larkins, William T. *U.S. Marine Corps Aircraft 1914–1959.* New York: Orion Books, 1988.

———. *U.S. Navy Aircraft 1921–1941.* New York: Orion Books, 1988.

Laub, Robert E. "The American Torpedo Attacks at Midway." *Foundation* 9, no. 1 (Fall 1987): 44–46.

Lautenschlager, Karl. "Technology and the Evolution of Naval Warfare." *International Security* (Fall 1983): 3–51.

Layton, Edwin T. *And I Was There.* New York: William Morrow, 1985.

Leighton, B. G. "Airplanes and Guns: The Promise of Military Aviation." *Atlantic Monthly,* April 1928, 530–39.

———. "The Relation of Aircraft to Sea-Power." *U.S. Naval Institute Proceedings* 54, no. 9 (September 1928): 731–44.

Ley, Willy, and Herbert Schaefer. "How About Penetration Bombs?" *U.S. Naval Institute Proceedings* 67, no. 12 (December 1941): 1712–16.

Lord, Walter. *Incredible Victory.* New York: Harper and Row, 1967.

Lundstrom, John B. *The First Team: Pacific Naval Air Combat from Pearl Harbor to Midway.* Annapolis, Md.: Naval Institute Press, 1984.

———. "Frank Jack Fletcher Got a Bum Rap." *Naval History* 6, no. 2 (Summer 1992): 22–27; and 6, no. 3 (Fall 1992): 22–28.

Martin, Harold M. "Service Aircraft." *U.S. Naval Institute Proceedings* 57, no. 8 (August 1931): 1039–42.

Matt, Paul R. *United States Navy and Marine Corps Fighters, 1918–1962.* Fallbrook, Calif.: Aero Publishers, 1962.

McCarthy, Charles J. "Naval Aircraft Design in the Mid-1930's." *Technology and Culture* 3, no. 2 (Spring 1963): 165–75.

McEniry, John H., Jr. *A Marine Dive-bomber Pilot at Guadalcanal.* Tuscaloosa: University of Alabama Press, 1987.

McFarland, Stephen L. *America's Pursuit of Precision Bombing, 1910–1945.* Washington, D.C.: Smithsonian Institution Press, 1995.

Melhorn, Charles M. *Two-Block Fox.* Annapolis, Md.: Naval Institute Press, 1974.

Merrill, James M. *A Sailor's Admiral: A Biography of William F. Halsey.* New York: Thomas Y. Crowell, 1976.

Mersky, Peter B. *U.S. Marine Corps Aviation 1912 to the Present.* Baltimore, Md.: Nautical and Aviation Publishing, 1983.

Miller, Edward S. *War Plan Orange: The U.S. Strategy to Defeat Japan, 1897–1945.* Annapolis, Md.: Naval Institute Press, 1991.

Mizrahi, J. V. *Carrier Fighters,* vol. 2. Northridge, Calif.: Sentry Books, 1969.

———. *U.S. Navy Dive & Torpedo Bombers.* Northridge, Calif.: Sentry Books, 1967.

Moore, Tom. "I Dive-Bombed a Jap Carrier." *Colliers,* 10 April 1943.

Moran, Gerard P. *Aeroplanes Vought 1917–1977.* Temple City, Calif.: Historical Aviation Album, 1978.

Morison, Samuel Eliot. *History of United States Naval Operations in World War II.* 15 vols. Boston: Little, Brown, 1958.

———. "Six Minutes that Changed the World." Reprinted in *Foundation* 9, no. 1 (Fall 1987): 3–8.

———. *The Two-Ocean War.* Boston: Little Brown, 1963.

Morrison, Wilbur H. *Above and Beyond 1941–1945.* New York: St. Martin's Press, 1983.

———. *Wings over the Sea.* New York: A. S. Barnes, 1975.

Murphy, Edward R. *Heroes of World War II.* Novato, Calif.: Presidio, 1990.

Musciano, Walter A. "Rex Beisel and His Bent-Wing Bird." *Foundation* 14, no. 2 (Fall 1993): 72–79.

Naval Aviation 1934: A Textbook for Midshipman. Annapolis, Md.: Naval Institute Press, 1933.

Okumiya, Masake, and Jiro Horikoshi with Martin Caiden. *Zero.* New York: Dutton, 1956.

Olds, Robert. *Helldiver Squadron.* New York: Dodd Mead, 1945.

Palmer, Carlton D. "The Pioneer Days of Naval Aviation." *Foundation* 6, no. 2 (Fall 1985): 29–36, 40.

Parker, Ralph C. "An Analysis of the Air Menace." *U.S. Naval Institute Proceedings* 58, no. 5 (May 1932): 649–62.

Pinkowski, Edward. "Admiral of the Air." *Our Navy,* 1 July 1945, 12–14.

Pirie, Robert B. "The Development and Impact of Early Flight Testing." *Foundation* 4, no. 2 (Fall 1983): 16–22, 56–60.

Potter, E. B. *Bull Halsey.* Annapolis, Md.: Naval Institute Press, 1985.

Prange, Gordon W. *At Dawn We Slept.* New York: McGraw-Hill, 1981.

———. *Miracle at Midway.* New York: McGraw-Hill, 1982.

Pratt and Whitney Division, United Aircraft. *Pratt & Whitney Aircraft Story.* Hartford, Conn.: United Aircraft, 1950.

Reeves, James M. "Aviation in the Fleet." *U.S. Naval Institute Proceedings* 55, no. 10 (October 1929): 867–70.

Reynolds, Clark G. *Admiral John H. Towers: The Struggle for Naval Air Supremacy.* Annapolis, Md.: Naval Institute Press, 1991.

———. *The Fast Carriers: The Forging of an Air Navy.* New York: McGraw-Hill, 1968.

———. "The Truth about Miles Browning." In *A Glorious Page in Our History.* Missoula, Mont.: Pictorial History, 1990.

Richardson, Charles J., Jr. "The Strike." *Foundation* 13, no. 1 (Spring 1992): 72–81.

Riley William A. "The Navy's Light Bombing Wing." *American Aviation Historical Society Journal* 3 (July–September 1958): 148–51.

Roland, Alex. *Model Research: The National Advisory Committee for Aeronautics 1915–1958.* 2 vols. Washington, D.C.: National Aeronautics and Space Administration, 1985.

Roemer, Charles, E. "SBC-4—Navy's Last Combat Biplane." *Foundation* 5, no. 2 (Fall 1984): 42–45.

Rosenberg, David A. "The Realities of Formulating Modern Naval Strategy." In *Mahan is Not Enough: The Proceedings of a Conference on the Works of Sir Julian Corbett and Admiral Sir Herbert Richard,* edited by James Goldrick and John B. Hattendorf. Newport, R.I.: Naval War College Press, 1993.

Rowell, Ross E. "Annual Report of Aircraft Squadrons, Second Brigade, U.S. Marine Corps, July 1, 1927 to June 20, 1928." *Marine Corps Gazette* 13, no. 4 (December 1928): 248–65.

———. "The Air Service in Minor Warfare." *U.S. Naval Institute Proceedings* 55, no. 10 (October 1929): 871–75.

Sanders, Richard Allen. *The Northrop Story.* New York: Orion, 1990.

Schlaifer, Roberts, and S. D. Heron. *Development of Aircraft Engines and Fuels.* Boston: Harvard University, 1950.

Schmidt, Hego. "Aircraft Engine Relations to the Needs of Naval Aviation." *Society of Automotive Engineers Journal* 28, no. 5 (May 1926): 509–13.

Serling, Robert J. *Legend and Legacy: The Story of Boeing and Its People.* New York: St. Martins Press, 1992.

Sherman, Frederick C. *Combat Command.* New York: Dutton, 1950.

Sibila, Alfred I. "Designing the Bent-Wing Bird." *Naval History* 9, no. 1 (February 1995): 48–51.

Skiera, Joseph A., ed. *Aircraft Carriers in Peace and War.* New York: Franklin Watts, 1965.

Smith, Myron J., Jr. *The American Navy, 1918–1941: A Bibliography.* Metuchen, N.J.: Scarecrow Press, 1974.

Smith, Peter. *Dive Bomber.* Annapolis, Md.: Naval Institute Press, 1982.

Smith, Robert C. *Close Air Support.* New York: Orion, 1990.

———. *History of Dive Bombing*. New York: Nautical and Aviation, 1981.

Spector, Ronald. *Eagle Against the Sun*. New York: Free Press, 1985.

———. *Professors of War*. Newport, R.I.: Naval War College Press, 1977.

Stafford, Edward P. *The Big E*. New York: Ballantine Books, 1974.

Stern, Robert. *SB2C Helldiver in Action*. Carrollton, Tex.: Squadron/Signal Publications, 1982.

Still, Henry. *Ride the Wind*. New York: Julian Messener, 1964.

Strean, B. M. "Lessons Learned Are Forever." *Naval Aviation News* 68, no. 1 (January–February 1986): 26.

Sudsbury, Elretta. *Jackrabbits to Jets: The History of NAS North Island, San Diego*. 2nd ed. San Diego: San Diego Publishing, 1992.

Swanborough, Gordon, and Peter M. Bowers. *United States Military Aircraft Since 1909*. Washington, D.C.: Smithsonian Institution Press, 1989.

———. *United States Naval Aircraft Since 1911*. 2nd ed. Annapolis, Md.: Naval Institute Press, 1976.

Tate, Jackson R. "We Rode the Covered Wagon." *U.S. Naval Institute Proceedings* 104, no. 10 (October 1978): 62–69.

Taylor, Theodore. *The Magnificent Mitscher*. New York: Norton, 1954.

Taylor, Theodore C. "Tactical Concentration and Surprise—in Theory." *Naval War College Review* 38, no. 4 (July–August 1985): 41–49.

Thruelsen, Richard. *The Grumman Story*. New York: Praeger, 1976.

Tillman, Barrett. *The Dauntless Dive Bomber of World War II*. Annapolis, Md.: Naval Institute Press, 1976.

———. "Winged Excaliber." *Wings* 7, no. 2 (April 1977): 20–41.

Tomlinson, Daniel W. *The Sky's the Limit*. Philadelphia: Macrae Smith, 1930.

Trimble, William F. *Admiral William A. Moffett*. Washington, D.C.: Smithsonian Institution Press, 1994.

———. *Wings for the Navy*. Annapolis, Md.: Naval Institute Press, 1990.

Turnbull, Archibald D., and Clifford L. Lord. *History of United States Naval Aviation*. New Haven, Conn.: Yale University Press, 1949.

Tuleja, Thaddeus V. *Climax at Midway*. New York: Norton, 1960.

U.S. Congress. *Pearl Harbor Attack: Hearings Before the Committee on the Investigation of the Pearl Harbor Attack, Congress of the United States, Seventy-ninth Congress, First Session, Pursuant to S. Con. Res. 27., A Concurrent Resolution Authorizing an Investigation of the Attack on December 7, 1941, and Events and Circumstances Relating Thereto*. Washington, D.C.: GPO, 1946.

U.S. Navy, Bureau of Ordnance. *U.S. Navy Bureau of Ordnance in World War II*. Washington, D.C.: GPO, 1953.

———, Naval Air Systems Command. *United States Naval Aviation 1910–1980, NAVAIR 00-80P-1*. Washington, D.C.: GPO, 1981.

U.S. Strategic Bombing Survey. *Interrogations of Japanese Officials*. Washington, D.C.: GPO, 1946.

Van Deurs, George. *Wings for the Fleet*. Annapolis, Md.: Naval Institute Press, 1966.

Van Fleet, Clarke. "Early Raiders." *Naval Aviation News* 61, no. 2 (February 1979): 30–39.

Vlahos, Michael. *The Blue Sword*. Newport, R.I.: Naval War College Press, 1980.

———. "Wargaming, an Enforcer of Strategic Realism: 1919–1942." *Naval War College Review* 39, no. 21 (March–April 1926): 7–22.

Wagner, Ray. *American Combat Planes*. Garden City, N.Y.: Hanover House, 1960.

Walter, John C. "William Harrison Standley, 1 July 1933–1 January 1937." In *The Chiefs of Naval Operations,* edited by Robert Love Jr. Annapolis, Md.: Naval Institute Press, 1980.

Wead, F. W. "Naval Fighting Planes." *U.S. Naval Institute Proceedings* 57, no. 8 (August 1931): 1089–91.

Wheeler, Gerald E. *Admiral William Veazie Pratt: A Sailor's Life*. Washington, D.C.: Department of the Navy, 1974.

Wildenberg, Thomas. *Gray Steel and Black Oil*. Annapolis, Md.: Naval Institute Press, 1996.

Wilson, Eugene E. *Air Power for Peace*. New York: McGraw Hill, 1945.

———. "Air Tactics and Aircraft Design." *U.S. Naval Institute Proceedings* 61, no. 12 (December 1935): 1767–71.

———. "Fleet Exercises—Tactics and Strategy." In *Aircraft Carrier in Peace and War,* edited by Joseph A. Skiera. New York: Franklin Watts, 1965.

———. "Naval Air Tactics & Aircraft Design." *Society of Automotive Engineers Journal* 23, no. 4 (October 1928): 353–59.

———. "The Navy's First Carrier Task Force." *U.S. Naval Institute Proceedings* 76, no. 2 (February 1950): 158.

———. *Slipstream: The Autobiography of an Air Craftsman*. New York: McGraw-Hill, 1950.

Winston, Robert W. *Dive Bomber*. New York: Holiday House, 1939.

Wooldridge, E. T., ed. *Carrier Warfare in the Pacific*. Washington, D.C.: Smithsonian Institution Press, 1993.

Zogbaum, Rufus F. *From Sail to Saratoga: A Naval Autobiography*. Rome: Tipografia Italo-Orientale, 1961.

Note: Page numbers in italics denote photographs.

Thomas Wildenberg, a resident of Silver Spring, Maryland, is a writer and naval historian whose special interest is the U.S. Navy between the world wars. He is a frequent contributor to the Naval Aviation Museum's *Foundation*, has written a number of articles on the development of the interwar navy, and is the author of *Gray Steel and Black Oil: Fast Tankers and Replenishment at Sea in the U.S. Navy, 1912–1992*.

Mr. Wildenberg was recently appointed the National Air and Space Museum's Ramsey Fellow for naval aviation and is currently at work on a biography of Joseph Mason Reeves.

The Naval Institute Press is the book-publishing arm of the U.S. Naval Institute, a private, nonprofit, membership society for sea service professionals and others who share an interest in naval and maritime affairs. Established in 1873 at the U.S. Naval Academy in Annapolis, Maryland, where its offices remain today, the Naval Institute has members worldwide.

Members of the Naval Institute support the education programs of the society and receive the influential monthly magazine *Proceedings* and discounts on fine nautical prints and on ship and aircraft photos. They also have access to the transcripts of the Institute's Oral History Program and get discounted admission to any of the Institute-sponsored seminars offered around the country.

The Naval Institute also publishes *Naval History* magazine. This colorful bimonthly is filled with entertaining and thought-provoking articles, first-person reminiscences, and dramatic art and photography. Members receive a discount on *Naval History* subscriptions.

The Naval Institute's book-publishing program, begun in 1898 with basic guides to naval practices, has broadened its scope in recent years to include books of more general interest. Now the Naval Institute Press publishes about 100 titles each year, ranging from how-to books on boating and navigation to battle histories, biographies, ship and aircraft guides, and novels. Institute members receive discounts of 20 to 50 percent on the Press's nearly 600 books in print.

Full-time students are eligible for special half-price membership rates. Life memberships are also available.

For a free catalog describing Naval Institute Press books currently available, and for further information about subscribing to *Naval History* magazine or about joining the U.S. Naval Institute, please write to:

Membership Department
U.S. Naval Institute
118 Maryland Avenue
Annapolis, MD 21402-5035
Telephone: (800) 233-8764
Fax: (410) 269-7940
Web address: www.usni.org